HOW TO
MAKE A BUCK
AND STILL BE
A DECENT
HUMAN BEING

HOW TO MAKE A BUCK AND STILL BE A DECENT HUMAN BEING

A Week with Rick Rose at Dataflex

Richard C. Rose and
Echo Montgomery Garrett

 HarperBusiness
A Division of HarperCollins*Publishers*

FIRST EDITION

Designed by Irving Perkins Associates

Library of Congress Cataloging-in-Publication Data

Rose. Richard C.
    How to make a buck and still be a decent human being : a week with
  Rick Rose at Dataflex / Richard C. Rose, Echo Montgomery Garrett.—
  1st ed.
      p. cm.
    ISBN 0–88730–584–9 (cloth)
    1. Dataflex Corporation. 2. Computer industry—United States.
  3. Used computers. I. Garrett, Echo Montgomery. II. Title.
  HD9696.C64D377   1992
  380.1'4500416—dc20   92–52611

---

92 93 94 95 96 CC/RRD 10 9 8 7 6 5 4 3 2 1

Dedicated to the associates, customers,
and suppliers of Dataflex Corporation

Contents

Preface

I first came in contact with Dataflex Corporation and Rick Rose in January 1991 while on assignment for a magazine called *Success*. I attended one of the company's morning sales meetings and spent a few hours afterward interviewing Rose. What had sparked my interest in the story was that the salespeople who had been with the company a year or more routinely sold ten times the average amount of computer equipment and services in Dataflex's industry. Nonetheless, when I initially learned that the sales meetings were two hours long and held almost daily, my eyes glazed over. I couldn't imagine what could possibly take so long or merit such frequent discussions. However, I emerged from my first two-hour session hungry to hear more and thoroughly convinced that Rose had plenty to say that the business world needed to hear.

So much ink has been devoted to big business and its ups-and-downs, yet, according to Dun and Bradstreet, small businesses are producing the lion's share of new jobs in our economy and account for 50 percent of our nation's gross private product, which excludes governmental expenditures. The 1980s were declared the decade of the entrepreneur, but relatively few books have offered insights into the thousands of entrepreneurial companies that sprang up across the country. For one thing, leaders at the helm of small companies are too busy running their businesses to take the time to write about them. Second, having the ability to build a business is one thing, being able to teach others how to do it is another skill altogether. Rose is a wonderful storyteller, though, and totally immerses himself in teaching people who work with him to learn from others' experiences, including his own. I approached Rose about collaborating on this project, explaining what I saw as a tremendous void in the business literature. I wanted this insider's view of a company to allow readers to get to know the people in it. Too often we're told how spectacular a company is, but rarely do we hear from anyone beyond the highest-level executives. Rose gave me free reign and ready access to everyone at the company.

In recent years, Dataflex, which has 185 employees, has been included in lists of the best-managed small companies in the United States compiled by *Forbes* (Dataflex appeared on its list in 1989 and 1991), *Business Week* (the company has been listed for three years in a row), and *Fortune*. In 1991, *Financial World* named it number 78 among America's 500 Fastest Growing Companies. Dataflex's annualized five-year sales growth was 66 percent, and its return on equity was 20 percent with no debt on the books. Such publications as *Inc., Forbes,* and *Success* have chronicled Rose's management techniques, while the financial press, such as *Barron's* and *Investor's Business Daily,* have hailed Dataflex as a bright spot in the computer reselling industry.

During my seven-year career as a business journalist, I have encountered hundreds of business people, including such enigmatic entrepreneurs as Virgin Atlantic Airways' Richard Branson, who recently sold Virgin Records to Thorn EMI for a record $1 billion; Finis Conner, founder of Conner Peripherals, arguably the most spectacular quick start-up of the 1980s; and Donald Burr, founder of People Express Airlines, one of that decade's biggest flops. In reporting on business owners and managers, I found that although many espouse the management philosophies that are in vogue and some follow through on those philosophies, most take what could be described as a flavor-of-the-month approach to running their businesses, which results in an often-disastrous lack of consistency. Rarely have I met someone in the business world as dedicated as Rick Rose is to ferreting out the best business advice available and applying it consistently to help those around him.

Dataflex was not a 1980s high flyer, leveraged to the hilt. The company has no debt on the books and plenty of cash in the bank. Although its story includes a rescue from the brink of bankruptcy, no fancy deals were cut, and no junk-bond kings were lurking in the wings. Dataflex's turnaround and subsequent success came the old-fashioned way: through hard work and the passion of a caring management.

During the year and a half that I spent researching the company, Rose was continually taking new risks, as were his associates. This book allows you to experience an action-packed week at Dataflex and to track Rick Rose as he leads the sales meetings, troubleshoots problems, encourages visions of greatness, wrestles with ethical dilemmas, and celebrates the successes of his associates. These pages chronicle an outstanding achievement in business: the creation of a workplace where people are given the freedom and the inspiration to be the best that they can be.

—Echo Montgomery Garrett

Introduction

The young man comes tearing into the parking lot, scrambles out of his dad's 1981 Ford Escort, and races to the employees' entrance on the side of the two-story building. He strides past his new boss's office and turns the corner leading to the conference room just in time to see Rick Rose, the newly promoted president and chief executive officer of Dataflex Corporation, with his hand on the doorknob. He quickens his pace, catching the door as it is about to close, and slips inside the room. It is 7:00 A.M., and the door clicks shut behind him. Rose doesn't look at him.

Mentally, the newcomer does a quick head count. Seven people are at the sales meeting this morning.

The banter around the conference table is fast and furious. Far from being above the fray, Rose tosses out more than his share of jokes and barbs. The young man chooses a seat, not close to the head of the table where he knows Rose will sit, but not on the outskirts either. Placing a legal pad in front of him on the table, he shifts uneasily in his chair, relieved that he made the meeting on time. Rose made it clear during the interviewing process that he is a stickler about punctuality. Then, almost as if on cue, the room falls silent.

Rose, whose build and carriage instantly telegraph both his days spent on a football field and his military background, stands up and gestures toward the young man. "I'd like to introduce all of you to Lance P. C. Manion," he says. "Lance is joining our sales force." Everyone in the room shifts toward the young man, whose frown melts into a broad smile that makes his dark eyes crinkle. He relaxes a little under the chorus of welcomes.

Manion's nervousness is apparent, but understandable in light of his circumstance: His real name is Ken Constantino, and it isn't his first day with the New Jersey-based computer reselling firm. Lance P. C. Manion—an alias, without the initials, of course, used by Sam Malone on the television show "Cheers"—is the new identity Constantino has adopted. He has actually been a salesperson with the company for six months.

The affable, six foot tall twenty-three year old achieved success early on, scoring a $100,000 contract for computers and services with Barclay's Bank in New York only a month after he had joined Dataflex in February 1987. But it was all downhill from that point.

Instead of scrambling for new business, Constantino spent most of his days baby-sitting Barclay's, fretting over the prospect of losing the business. By April, one rookie who had joined the five-person sales team at the same time as Constantino decided he couldn't take the heat and quit. From that day on, Constantino had felt the pit in his stomach grow as small failure piled upon small failure, ultimately convincing him that he didn't have what it takes to make it as a salesperson at Dataflex. Finally, that pit turned into a yawning canyon. Gone was the fire in his belly that sparked when he first realized Rose believed in him. Rose had helped Constantino become a believer also—a believer that Rose could transform a college graduate, whose only previous sales experience was selling potable water to the U.S. Navy, into a professional salesperson.

The fear that he didn't have a knack for selling was what had propelled him into Rose's office, late on the previous Friday afternoon. After the weekly "pond-scum" meeting—at which sales neophytes air their concerns and seek advice from the sales veterans—Constantino appeared in the doorway of Rose's office, resignation in hand. He haltingly explained why he couldn't hack the high-pressure world of computer sales any longer. "I wish it could be like the first day again, Rick," he sighed, his forehead wrinkled with worry.

Rose listened politely. Then he leaned forward and made a proposal that caused Constantino to suck in his breath sharply. "As of today, you are terminated, but on Monday I want you back in the office, and I want you to start all over as a salesperson," Rose said, quietly yet firmly. "I would be doing you and this company a disservice if I let you quit now. On Monday I'd start the search for someone exactly like you. You are exactly what we're looking for, and we're exactly what you want."

Constantino was normally quick with an answer. His response when the company's chief financial officer, Gordon J. McLenithan, had posed the standard interview question, "What is your greatest weakness?" during the interview process was already company legend. A quick wit, Constantino had retorted cooly, "Chocolate pudding."

But on that fateful Friday, Rose's offer left him momentarily speechless. It took him a few minutes to grasp that Rose was offering exactly what he had wished for: a second chance. Finally, Constantino broke into a broad grin and said, "So I'll see you on Monday, Rick."

When Monday finally rolled around after what seemed an interminable weekend, Constantino, a.k.a. Manion, felt the same jittery excitement that had surged through his body the first time he had attended one of the morning sales meetings.

Rose went all out to make his reentry into Dataflex a fresh start. Constantino wore a name tag that read Lance P. C. Manion while the human resources manager introduced him to everyone in the company. Constantino got plenty of quizzical looks because only the sales staff had been informed of the unusual agreement between him and Rose. Later in the day, Rose himself conducted the orientation session, making it clear that he was taking this exercise seriously. Although Rose is widely known as a prankster, Constantino's rebirth was no joke.

Rose's faith in Constantino did not go unrewarded. The following year, the 1988 Sales Recognition Event—an event Rose had initiated for the sales staff two years before—was held in Boca Raton, Florida. On a yacht cruising down the intercoastal waterway, Constantino was awarded the honor of Rookie of the Year. Constantino ambled up to the podium and accepted the award as Lance P. C. Manion. Back in the office the following Monday, Manion died a quiet, unmourned death, and Constantino, his confidence restored, was hard at work in the cubicle his alter ego had occupied for so many months.

RICK ROSE: Being the best that we can be is a journey that is without destination. And to be the best, we have to step out on the wing and take chances. That's what life at Dataflex is all about. It is not about limiting failures; it's about magnifying successes. It is not about comparing ourselves to other people or even to our own past experiences. It is about taking the time to look at a challenge from a different angle, giving people the freedom to come up with an original solution.

One of the biggest problems in American business today is that we strangle new ideas before they can get out of people's mouths. We're too busy saying, "This is the way we've always done it." At Dataflex we try to get people to speak up within their first few days at the company. Otherwise, that window of opportunity to tap into fresh ideas before a person is influenced by the culture here is slammed shut. We do everything we can to encourage people to stick up for themselves and contribute their opinions. If you don't participate in a meeting, you are thrown out. I don't care if it's your first day. I want to hear what you have to say.

Dataflex is participating in one of the most competitive markets in the world: selling computers to companies in the New York area. Our business is constantly in a state of flux, and that requires nimble thinking. If you aren't changing, you are dying, and I believe that's true of any business.

Giving Ken Constantino a second chance was risky, and I wonder how many other presidents out there would have allowed themselves the flexibility to make such an offer. I am far from perfect, and I am not claiming to have all the answers. However, at Dataflex I've finally gotten the chance to try the theories I've developed during my twenty-year career in the computer industry, and, for the most part, they have proved to be a potent remedy for the malaise that was afflicting this company.

Perhaps the most important lesson I've learned is that the bar of excellence is an individual one. We want people to be able to look in the mirror and give an affirmative answer to the question, "Am I doing all I can to be the best that I can be?" And we want them to answer that question with integrity. We're not looking for compliance. We're looking for commitment. You never gain empowerment if you settle for compliance because as soon as you turn your back, that uncommitted associate is going to stop complying.

Scores of people at Dataflex have thrown caution to the wind and have experienced the thrill of wing walking. I hope what you learn in this book will nudge you out on the wing, too.

On the surface, Dataflex appears to be an unlikely birthplace for dreams. It doesn't manufacture anything. The people who work there are, for the most part, young—average age twenty-eight—and unexceptional. The industry the company is in—selling personal computers to corporations—could fairly be categorized as troubled. Indeed, the woes of many of its better-known competitors—like ComputerLand Corporation, the Oakland, California-based franchisor of personal computer stores, and Businessland, Inc., which teetered on the edge of bankruptcy before being acquired by JWP, Inc., of Purchase, New York, in August 1991—have routinely made headlines. Nynex and Inacomp merged, and CompuCom Systems, Inc., the nation's seventh-largest computer reseller, based in Dallas, recently abandoned the retail business by selling or closing its Computer Factory outlets.

Even the building that houses Dataflex fails to command attention. The company moved into the low-slung gray building with tidy burgundy trim and an American flag displayed out front in April 1990. The only thing outstanding about the 65,000 square-foot building is its surprising location. You might expect to find it in some industrial park or perched on a hillside clearly visible from the New Jersey Turnpike. Something, anything, to get the name out, since the company targets blue-chip clients like Bristol Meyers–Squibb, Merck, Prudential Insurance, and scores of others that themselves bear household names. Instead, it is tucked away in a quiet residential neighborhood, one of half a dozen commercial buildings in the midst of several middle-class homes lining Park Avenue in Edison, New Jersey. At first glance, you would probably mistake it for a small, private elementary school.

In a way, you'd be right. Indeed, it is Rose's commitment to teaching his associates (he refuses to use the word *employees* because he thinks the word has taken on a negative connotation) what he believes are the elemental truths of business that have fueled the fortunes of this small, publicly held company. "I'm a frustrated schoolteacher," shrugs Rose, who holds a degree in mathematics from the University of Miami. "But after a few months as a graduate student teacher, I realized I could never make the money in academia that I would need to support the family I hoped to have one day."

The rough-and-tumble business of reselling desktop computer equipment from major manufacturers, including IBM, Hewlett-Packard, Compaq, and Apple as well as competing for the right to service the equipment, has afforded Rose more opportunities to teach than he would have had in a classroom on some college campus. It has also made him and many others at the company wealthy.

Rick Rose and Gordon McLenithan were hired by the company's founder, Jeffrey A. Lamm, in 1984 when the personal computer industry was still in its infancy. Their mission was to get Dataflex back on track. Rose was brought aboard for his sales savvy, McLenithan for his financial expertise.

Those were heady days when fortunes were being made in unlikely quarters. And Dataflex, which Lamm had launched with $500 from his dining room table in 1976, looked on the surface to be on the ground floor of something good. Yet, within weeks of coming on board at Dataflex, the duo realized that the company was not only suffering an identity crisis, but that its financial picture was bleak as well.

"When I first got interested in the company, I was asked to take a look at the financial statements," says McLenithan. "They seemed to be in pretty good shape. But once I got on board and started to dig underneath them, it really got scary.

"We had no cash flow. I discovered that we were on credit hold with every one of our vendors. I had to get cash to our vendors, so we could get off credit hold, so I said, 'Let me take a look at the inventory.' Half the stuff in the inventory was out of date. Half of our receivables was old money that would never be collected. We had a lease base where we were depreciating product over seven years, but because technology was changing so rapidly, it would be obsolete after three. Nobody wanted it.

"It took me a year to build the confidence of our vendors to the point where they extended full credit to us."

Further complicating matters was the fact that Rose and McLenithan could not have been more different, and Lamm, being a typical entrepreneur, wasn't quite sure how to direct the two new managers. So he fell to pitting them against each other, assuming that the victor probably had the right answer. McLenithan says, "Jeff would ask one of us one thing and then say the other had said the opposite. One time he got caught in the same room with us after he'd started an argument between us, and I think he was terrified at what he had done. We were screaming so loud that they could hear us all over the building."

Worse, McLenithan, who was reserved and cautious, looked at Rose as a loose cannon. For his part, Rose still recalls the first presentation he saw McLenithan make. "It was on why the company didn't need a sales force," recalls Rose, who had been hired as a vice president of sales.

Says McLenithan wryly, "About the only thing we had in common was that we both hated debt."

Rose was born on November 30, 1947, in Boston, Massachusetts, and five years later his family moved to a small town called Cutler Ridge in south Florida. His grandfather was a bookie and ran a crap game on the train from Boston to New York. His father, Elliot Rose, was on his way to becoming a juvenile delinquent when a judge gave him a choice: jail or military school. Elliot's mother, a prudent woman, packed her only child off to military school in Kentucky.

The streetwise kid from Boston made a turnaround, eventually serving in World War II, and graduating with the class of 1947 at the U.S. Naval Academy. While he was overseas fighting in Korea, his partners bankrupted a housewares mail-order business. Next he tried his hand at sales, finally winding up selling insurance pension plans. His easy charm often won him customers.

Rick Rose remembers his late father as a happy-go-lucky fellow, always chasing the big score. "He was one of the best salesmen I've ever known, but my mother never knew whether we would be eating steak or beans from one night to the next," says Rose, who has a sister, three years younger, and a brother eleven years younger.

Security became important to Rose, and he saw a chance of that in the discipline of the military. He won an appointment to the U.S. Naval Academy and played football as a defensive halfback. "Only

8 percent of the people who apply get appointments," Rose says proudly. He spent three years at the academy before a devastating knee injury during football practice landed him in the hospital for three months and ended his playing days.

Says Rose, "I caught an interception during practice and got creamed. They operated on my knee, but that only made it worse."

The year was 1968. The Vietnam War was escalating. But Rose knew that the nature of his injury would preclude him from pursuing his dream of becoming a pilot in the marines. The superintendent called the twenty year old into his office and gave him a choice: He could either continue his military career with limited duty and a minimum of five years' service, or take disability and allow the government to pay for the remainder of his education under the G.I. Rehabilitation Bill. Rose chose to return to Florida and complete his education at the University of Miami, where he graduated in 1970.

Shortly after graduation, at age twenty-three, he married his college sweetheart, Robin, and following in his father's footsteps, settled on sales. He started selling insurance policies for a Prudential Insurance office in Coral Gables, Florida. He sold more than $1 million worth of policies his first year, garnering The Rookie of the Year Award at a time when the company had more than 35,000 sales agents. His secret was paying one dollar per name to a fellow who had the scoop on young men in the south Florida area who had recently been discharged from the armed forces. Rose knew that these young men would no longer be covered by military insurance, so they would likely be in the market to convert their military coverage.

Every Friday all forty agents in the office would gather for coffee and doughnuts. "Mr. Gaynor, a thirty-year veteran with the company, would ask, 'Who sold five new policies this week?' " Rose recalls. "If you raised your hand, he flipped you a five cent cigar. I didn't even smoke, but I wanted that cigar." Rose was taking home $135 a week.

In 1971 Rose was hired by Applied Digital Data Systems (ADDS) in Happauge, New York, as its first outside salesperson. He worked from an office in Miami and won the High Sales Volume award his first three years with the company. In 1972 his son Scott was born. Rose, who had always dreamed of having a large family, was ecstatic. The following year he was promoted to southern regional manager.

At the end of his fifth year with ADDS, the company owed him $250,000 based on the commissions he'd been promised. "I was called into the office of the vice president of sales and marketing and told, 'There is no way we can pay you all that money. We never asked you to sell that much. Here's what we're going to do. We'll give you this bonus and some stock options, and if that isn't good enough, we'll fire you,'" recalls Rose, looking grim at the memory. "I couldn't believe it. I had sold twenty times the amount they had expected me to sell. I called my dad and told him what had happened. And he said, 'Son, here's the Golden Rule in business: You've got to circle the wagons and shoot them before they shoot you.'

"I felt sick. Here was my hero in business telling me that it was basically a dirty world. I spent the weekend thinking about what he said and decided I couldn't conduct myself that way. I decided I'd rather treat people decently and take a few lumps from the people who are out to get you than miss out on all the good that I believed had to be out there."

Shortly thereafter Rose landed the position of national sales manager of the computer terminal division at Hazeltine Corporation, a New York–based government contractor. During his tenure there, the division surpassed its quota for the first time since it was established in 1969. Rose oversaw a staff of sixty people, including twenty-five sales representatives in ten offices in the United States.

In early 1979 Rose made the jump to David Jamison Carlyle Corporation (DJC), a California-based computer peripherals company, as vice president of sales. But it was not an easy time for Rose. His marriage to Robin broke up over what Rose calls a "basic philosophical difference": She had decided she didn't want any more children, and his heart's desire was a house full of them. His frequent trips away from home on sales calls hadn't helped matters either.

But while his personal life was suffering, Rose's career star continued to rise. DJC's revenues were at about $5 million in sales when he started with the California-based company. By 1982 DJC had nine sales offices, nineteen sales people, and more than $50 million in annual revenues. Rose had opened the East Coast office in New Jersey and spent most of his time there, which brought him into Jeff Lamm's sphere.

Rose himself is quick to admit—almost proud of the fact—that he was a thorn in the flesh of management at his previous employers. "Invariably the powers that be would call me in and ask, 'How are you doing it?' " says Rose. "Then I'd tell them, and by the end of the conversation they'd be backpedaling, saying, 'Well, we're glad it works for you.' "

Six feet tall and boyish looking, with straight, thick black hair and brown eyes, Rose loves everything about sales—except the stereotypical "back-slapping, expense-accounting goon" image that diminishes the profession. To this day, his determination to separate himself from that hand-pumping buffoon manifests itself in his reluctance to shake hands in a business setting. He will shake hands, but only when pressed. Although he'll wear a suit when necessary, he looks far more at home in nondescript jeans and a Polo shirt. Exuberant, impetuous, and quick with one-liners and practical jokes, Rose had dreamed of fashioning a sales force—long before he came to Dataflex—that would be far removed from the image he detested.

Gordon McLenithan was on a different path. A conservative numbers man through and through, he had spent the first 10 years of his career at Price Waterhouse. At the accounting firm, he primarily audited small companies, which were in dire need of help from their auditors. "I loved dealing with entrepreneurs," says McLenithan, "because I'd give them advice, and they'd implement it immediately." That early experience gave him firsthand experience of the day-to-day challenge of running a small business.

He left Price Waterhouse and spent three more years at Amerada Hess, heading the oil exploration and refining the company's audit operations. However, over the years, McLenithan, who became a certified public accountant in 1970, the same year Rose graduated from college, chafed at the lag time it took to get decisions made. As he puts it, "It was a company that was run more on loyalty to the chairman than on a person's technical capabilities. Management consisted of yes-men. Worse, it seemed like there was a sign posted that said, 'Don't smile.' " When he realized he couldn't influence any change there, he resigned.

In 1980 he became the executive vice president of a $20 million, construction-equipment distributor called Jesco, Inc. Two years later he became vice president of finance at Eutectic Corporation, a $60 million manufacturer of consumable welding equipment and supplies. At both companies, he was able to apply some of the skills he had learned dealing with entrepreneurs during his Price Water-house years.

Eutectic was a U.S. division of a privately held, "ultrasecretive" Swiss-based company. McLenithan was disconcerted by the cloak of secrecy even before a longtime executive confided that before executives were hired, their horoscopes were done by an astrologer in Paris. "That was the clincher for me. It gave me a eerie feeling," says McLenithan, who was also putting up with a killer commute. He became increasingly restless and began dreaming of going into business for himself doing business consulting and taxes.

That's how he first came in contact with Dataflex. He gave the company's general manager some tax advice. The man was impressed and started courting McLenithan, offering him the reigns over finance. After consulting his wife Doris, a native of Germany, and their two teenage daughters, McLenithan still took five months to consider the move. He finally accepted an offer of a good salary and stock options. Within two weeks of arriving on the premises of the forty-employee company, McLenithan realized that the financial records were a quagmire. Some days he wondered if he shouldn't dust off his résumé and walk away from the whole mess.

Then, as if McLenithan didn't already have enough trouble on his hands, Rose arrived on the scene. "Rick was brash and aggressive and wanted to do things his own way," says McLenithan, aged fifty-two, who still has a penchant for the dark blue suits that company executives favor when they are wooing Wall Street during dog-and-pony shows. Rose used to tease him about wearing three-piece pajamas to bed.

McLenithan's office is immaculate and sparsely but tastefully decorated. The carpet is ice blue, giving it a placid feel that suits McLenithan's demeanor. The only photos on the wall are the corporate shots of himself, Rose, and Lamm taken year after year for the annual report. A Scotch-Irishman, McLenithan suddenly adds, his pale green eyes glinting mischievously, "Rick thought accountants were out to stop him."

After a particularly loud shouting match in the warehouse, McLenithan finally confided in Rose one afternoon that he estimated the company could limp along for only a few more months before declaring bankruptcy. That is, unless some miracle should occur. After bandying about whether there was anything about the company worth saving, Rose and McLenithan ultimately decided it was time to work some miracles.

HOW TO
MAKE A BUCK
AND STILL BE
A DECENT
HUMAN BEING

1

Measurements

If you are an expected guest at Dataflex, before you reach the doors of the lobby, you notice your name and a "Welcome" on a small board. The lobby itself isn't anything special. No ostentatious displays of original art à la the infamous and now failed Centrust Savings and Loan Association in Miami. No bubbling fountains. A stockholder who stopped by would probably walk away with an impression of neatness and efficiency.

Maria Infusino, the receptionist, greets you warmly, in between answering the phone by the second ring. Then you start reading what is displayed: framed letters hung on the mauve walls. There are dozens of them in the lobby and more lining the walls leading to the conference room. Each one is from a client or a supplier praising the individuals who make up Dataflex.

You see the articles from *Forbes, Barron's,* and *Business Week* preserved and displayed as well. Perhaps there is something special here, you think. On the other hand, maybe it's hype. After all, scores of companies have gotten the press excited at one time or another. But like a high school romance, the ardor quickly cools when some blemish—real or imagined—appears.

And Dataflex is in a tough business. Price wars have ravaged profit margins in personal computer sales. Even International Business Machines Corp. (IBM), with which Dataflex spent much of the mid-1980s forging strong ties, has not been immune to the eco-

1

nomic crunch of the late 1980s and early 1990s. However, Rick Rose neatly sidestepped many of the problems experienced by other computer resellers.

Rose eschewed trying to be all things to all PC buyers, but instead targeted the high end of the business. The company's customer base is strictly large corporations in the New York, New Jersey, and Connecticut area, which Rose says have about 20 percent or $5 billion worth of the industry's potential. He wanted to keep the lines of distribution short, so he and McLenithan could visit any customer within a day.

Rose spends much of his energy training his salespeople to meet the needs of their customers and to be prepared for the sudden twists and turns in the marketplace. Finally, rather than expanding by scattering retail outlets in pricey business districts—the strategy of Businessland and ComputerLand—Dataflex's sales and ware-house operate from the same location. Rose also carefully selected the computer brands that the company would concentrate its efforts on selling, rather than carrying clones and brands of every kind of personal computer.

The question of expanding came up at a board meeting a few years ago. Others were enthusiastically talking about the idea of strategically putting Dataflex operations in different regions across the country. Rose grew quieter and quieter. Finally, he nixed the idea. One, he believed he had spent more than enough of his life on a plane, and he wanted to stay close to home so he could spend more time with his second wife Linda, whom he met at DJC and married soon after his arrival at Dataflex, and his three sons (when he turned fourteen, Scott, his son from his first marriage, chose to live with his father). Two, he correctly predicted that strategy would prove costly and risky. Witness the problems of Computerland and Businessland.

Rose's single-minded drive to take Dataflex to great heights has paid off handsomely. Dataflex salespeople who have been with the company more than a year sell ten times the average in their indus-try. Indeed, when Rose came on board in 1984, fifteen salespeople were bringing in $5 million in sales, and 70 percent of that business came from one account, which Jeffrey Lamm himself serviced. In 1991, twelve salespeople were within a whisper of a total of $100 million in sales with net profits of $4.5 million.

* * *

When you enter the conference room around the corner from the lobby, a few salespeople are already seated, munching on bagels or muffins and swapping pleasantries about the weekend. The conference table is long and has seating for forty people. Like the lobby, the room is tastefully done in cool gray, mauve, and blue. There are few distractions: The Dataflex wheel—a design device the company uses in explaining its services—is the only wall adornment, and miniblinds cover the windows, blocking any temptation to gaze outside. A colorful doll bearing the moniker King Customer perches on a table at the front of the room.

With five minutes until the door closes, the rest of the troops, including Rose, come pouring in. Rose, wearing a white button-down shirt monogrammed with his initials, a tie, and light gray slacks, puts down his personalized Dataflex coffee mug and turns to shut the door. Everyone is still laughing and joking while he walks over to the white board in three steps and scratches out a single word. For a split second, you have a flash of a high school football coach in a locker room, mapping out strategies to defeat the team's arch rivals.

Rose's voice, devoid of regionalisms and pleasant yet commanding, snaps you back to the present.

"The word of the day is *analogous,*" Rose announces with a flourish, underlining the word for emphasis. "Can anybody tell me what it means and use it in a sentence, relating it to our business?" Rose always begins the sales meeting with this exercise. The importance of a good vocabulary was impressed on him during the year he spent in prep school before his acceptance to the U.S. Naval Academy. Rose had done poorly in English until that year. "I was lucky enough to get a teacher like Robin Williams' character in *The Dead Poets' Society,*" Rose recalls. "He infused his class with excitement and inspired me to love the power of words. He also taught me that you could change people's attitudes through motivation." And since the whole purpose of these meetings is to improve communication skills, the exercise fits Rose's agenda.

Alan Fendrick practically leaps out of his chair with an answer: "One of the purposes of this class is to be able to communicate that the services we offer are not analogous to those that our competitors offer. The point being that everyone in our business says the same words: 'We do service. We do software support. We are the best.' The key is learning what's unique about Dataflex."

Tall and gangly with brown hair that is only controllable through frequent haircuts, Fendrick's entire face and his arms get in on the action when he talks. His words fly out at a machine-gun pace. He was a twenty-two-year-old stand-up comedian and magician whose biggest claim to fame was an appearance in the "stupid human tricks" segment of "The David Letterman Show" (his talent was juggling fire, eating an apple, and jumping on a pogo stick simultaneously) before Rose hired him as a salesperson. After six years at Dataflex, he has captured the top sales spot. The year 1991 was a big one for Fendrick: His first child, Joshua, was born, and he sold almost $30 million worth of computers and services.

A few other people use the word in sentences. Rose then gives an example.

Next he unveils the company's new mission statement: *Our vision is to be the provider of quality desktop computing solutions to corporations, which will maximize customer satisfaction while maintaining our profitability.*

"Arrogant? You bet," says Rose, standing pitched forward with both hands on the conference table. "I don't want people pigeonholing us as a rack 'em, stack 'em hardware mover."

Then Rose poses a question. "What could happen that would mean that we don't sell hardware anymore?" His goal goes beyond the surface question: Rose is constantly striving to motivate people to think about the business in a new light. On this particular morning nobody delivers a scintillating answer, but Rose listens patiently, once again seated at the head of the table, before revealing his own views on the subject.

He moves on to talk about a few of the high points from *Customers for Life,* the best-selling customer-service book written by Carl Sewell, owner of Cadillac's number one dealership, and Paul Brown, a business journalist. The book reaffirms some of the steps Rose and his troops have already taken, and he uses it to strengthen their convictions that the Dataflex way works.

"Fire the consumer relations department," reads Rose, then adds, "Customer service is too important. *Everybody* should be in the customer service business and have the authority to solve problems that arise. If you don't make the customer happy, you are history. It doesn't matter what else you do."

Other gems he proffers from the book for the group: "The easiest way to fail is to try to please everybody." "We should thank our competitors for giving terrible service, because they're the ones that make it possible to succeed." "If you would do it for a friend, do it for a customer."

"That is so true," says Rose. "Always remember our customers are our friends, so treat them that way. And be willing to admit it when you make a mistake. When we do make a mistake, every manager who had an opportunity to correct it and didn't should call the customer to apologize."

Finally, he reads: "If you take too long to come to an answer, you can lose a customer. The difference between success and failure can be 30 seconds."

Rose camps out on that last point for a few minutes. "I disagree with that," he says, standing up and pulling off his jacket. "It's fifteen seconds in our business. You can't always afford the luxury of formulating the absolute best possible answer. It's often more important to come up with a good answer quickly." He stops pacing, jabbing his finger in the air to emphasize his last words, then pauses, searching the faces of the eight men and four women around the table.

"Why do we do this day after day? Why do we read these books aloud? They often just repeat what we already know, so why do we do it?" he asks, waving the book above the heads of his listeners. "We are communicating how to sell, so you don't have to bump into the barbed-wire fence of experience for the next twenty years on your way to becoming a professional salesperson. We are condensing a twenty-year process into one or two years." And in fact, that is his entire purpose in these drill sessions.

Rose turns the focus back to customer service. "Who's more important? Your customers or your associates?" he asks. The question sparks something like the old debate about the chicken or the egg.

Rose leans back in his chair and puts his hands behind his head, eyes sparkling with amusement. Finally, he asks, "How can we expect our associates to treat customers well if our associates aren't treated well? Our technicians didn't feel at home here, for example, because they didn't have any space they could call their own. Now you could argue that they are only in the office for the first half hour every morning. But we gave them their own cubicles because we've got to create a family atmosphere. People aren't going to be committed to you unless they know that you are committed to them.

"These are the basics."

He lunges for the black marker and scribbles "18 percent" on the white board. "For example, we have to sell our equipment at an 18 percent gross margin. It takes a very disciplined person not to take business below that margin. Our overhead is 10 percent, which leaves 8 percent; 3 percent goes to taxes, which leaves a 5 percent net profit. Lucky for us, several of our competitors aren't able to do the simple math I've just done on this board.

"We run our business as if every day is a recession. Why would I allow 'fat' in the company just because times are good? We will do anything for the customer, but it must make business sense for us. Our competitors are caught in the trap of trying to make the sale at all cost without looking at the bottom line. Don't make the same mistake."

That is just the first hour.

The second half of the meeting is devoted to "self-actualization." That means improving your self-esteem by decreasing the difference between your self-image (who you think you are) and your self-ideal (who you'd like to be).

In the past few weeks, each salesperson has made a list of strengths and a list of weaknesses. Then during the class each person is called upon individually to stand in front of the board and write down the strengths and weaknesses that the class attributes to him or her.

Rose starts this session by saying, "We have spent three weeks discussing self-actualization because your self-esteem is critical to this company. You are the people who are going to take us to $200 million in sales. All I have to do is smooth the pathway for you."

The subject of today's scrutiny is a relative newcomer who has been with the company almost six months. His peers' comments come rapid fire and are brutally honest. When there is finally a lull in the remarks, he has written the following on the board:

Strengths	Weaknesses
Dedication	Meek/not aggressive
Participation	Doesn't work smart/wastes time on onion accounts
Experimental	Lacks emotion

In a soft voice, he reveals his own summation of how he perceives himself, which dovetails with the group's perception. The strongest criticism delivered by his peers is that he doesn't "work smart." One salesman who works in a cubicle next to the young man tells him that he spends far too much time on accounts that aren't worth chasing. Such accounts are called "onion" accounts in Dataflex lingo.

Rose says, "You have the skills, but we don't have time for waltzing around with people. I think you need to push yourself up the scale of confidence. Your excitement about this company is muted by your tentativeness." He pauses, focusing his piercing stare on the salesman standing at the board. "You do like working here, don't you?"

"Yes," says the man, his voice low.

Rose says, "Well, then you have to be able to transmit that."

The salesman, who worked at Computer Factory before coming to Dataflex, says, "I guess I'm just used to doing things another way. The culture feels foreign to me here."

Rose answers, "So how long are you going to trot around in the mud here? We are giving you every chance to succeed."

Turning to address the group, the president says, "We have to have lethal weapons. We often only get one shot, and when we execute, that shot must be dead on. That's why we work so hard in this room on improving your aim."

The salespeople spontaneously burst into an emotional debate about whether the atmosphere is too intense for new people to handle. "After all, we go through about fifteen new salespeople per year before one finally sticks," notes Ken Constantino, who has felt the heat himself.

Top saleswoman Diane Katz retorts, "But if a person makes it through that first year, they stay. We haven't had anyone leave after that. There are only a limited number of spots in this room, and I want to make sure we have the right people in those spots."

Says Maurice Scaglione, "I think we're missing a few by not being more supportive."

Fendrick chimes in, "Adversity builds character. Those who you lose, you probably would have lost anyway."

Elaine Mosher suggests alleviating some of the pressure by not posting rookies' sales numbers on the board that hangs in the sales department.

When one salesman complains that he doesn't get enough help from the veterans on the sales team, Rose explodes out of his chair. "Are you chained to your desk? Are you held down with duct tape? How many times have you gone to someone, asked for help, and been told, 'No'? In most organizations you couldn't get two sentences from the top salespeople. What do you think we do every day in here for two hours?"

That tirade effectively puts a punctuation point on the discussion for a moment. Then Fendrick extends an offer to make himself available to help the man who complained. Rose collects himself and calmly concedes that the company has been built by four sales superstars. He agrees that it's time to develop some good, solid salespeople who may not achieve that superstar level but will nonetheless be good producers.

"I can't motivate anybody," says Rose. "I can only create a climate that allows people to risk and grow." He asks the group to consider how it can be more nurturing of new people and to come to next Monday's meeting with ideas.

Sweat beading on his forehead, Rose concludes, "What got us here today is not necessarily going to get us where we want to go. We must take chances and change." At exactly 9 a.m. he opens the door and another day begins at Dataflex.

How to Conduct a Meeting that No One Wants to Leave

The secret to much of our success is starting the day off with a sales meeting that gets everybody headed in the right direction. We hold those meetings every day except Thursday. Besides the sales meetings, I also conduct a meeting for the entire company at 11:45 a.m. on Fridays and another on Friday afternoon called the pond-scum meeting. (*Pond-scum* is an affectionate term for first-year salespeople.) This book will chronicle a few of these meetings to give you examples and will explain how meetings can boost your productivity.

When most people think of a sales meeting, they tend to think of a bunch of people getting together on Friday afternoon to eat doughnuts, drink coffee, and shoot the breeze. It's a social gathering with very little meat. No wonder business books are filled with advice about how to cut down on meetings or skip them altogether.

I learned the value of meetings when I was living in Atlanta, working as southern regional sales manager for Hazeltine Corporation. Two days a week I conducted a meeting for the six salespeople. I started noticing that more business was written on those two days. In one year, our region went from being the worst region to number one with the exact same personnel. And I think it was due to the camaraderie that developed as a result of those meetings.

Meetings can also be a terrific problem-solving tool. If an issue comes up during the course of the two hours that involves a manager or another associate, I'll stop the action and get the person on the phone right then. I'll ask them to come into the meeting as soon as they can. That way we are able to resolve issues on the spot because we have the decision makers in the room together. Small companies don't always take advantage of their flexibility like we do.

Meetings at Dataflex are serious, planned, frequent, and inspiring associations of people who work within a particular process.

The sales meetings are:

1. held every day except Thursday,

2. conducted according to a schedule published thirty days in advance,

3. started promptly at 7:30 A.M. (We recently made the morning meeting a little later because some people have hour-long commutes.) Any latecomers know better than to knock on the door once it is closed. If somebody can't commit to being here on time, how on earth can I trust them to keep their commitments to their customers? Being hard line about punctuality within the company drives home its importance before tardiness costs our salespeople some big account.

4. the speaker's responsibility. If the speaker loses the interest of the listeners, he or she will quickly know it. If somebody's thinking, "I'd

rather be somewhere else" during a meeting, he or she has permission to get up and leave at any time, no matter who is speaking. This approach makes boring, unproductive meetings a thing of the past.

I also tell any outside speakers to be prepared. I don't care who is leading the meeting. If it's boring, leave.

It goes back to what I said about wanting people to treat you like you would treat them. As a salesperson, time is my most precious commodity, so if I ask someone to sit in a meeting, I'd better make it worthwhile. Because I would want the same for myself if the situation were reversed.

There are no penalties for not attending these meetings. First-year salespeople are the only ones required to attend. In fact, one salesman a few years ago didn't like a personal evaluation given to him by the group. He stopped coming to the meetings for six weeks. Then one day he showed up. There were no reprisals, and he rejoined the group without comment from me or anyone else. You can't say you're giving people freedom of choice and then send out conflicting messages.

5. participatory. You get thrown out of the meeting if you don't participate. No leeches allowed. It's not fair to suck up the creative juices flowing in that room unless you are willing to give blood in return.

At any time during the two-hour period, an associate can stop the meeting and challenge someone who has been sitting there like a bump on a log. If the group agrees that the person isn't contributing, that person is asked to leave. We've had people quit the company after being thrown out of a meeting. But that's OK. They simply didn't grasp what we are trying to do here. Our goal is to help people realize that they are in a supportive environment where they can say anything— except nothing. As a result of these rules, our meetings are more dynamic and interesting.

Sales is like medicine: It's not an exact science, and it's always changing. These meetings help us keep up with that change.

Rick Rose bolts out of the conference room like a shot. He strides quickly down the hallway leading to his office. His head is slightly ahead of his body as he walks, his jaw jutting forward. He rolls up on the balls of his feet and bounces slightly—a study of motion and purpose.

Rose pokes his head into Tim Mannix's office. Mannix, fifty-two, the senior vice president, is sitting at his desk, his back to the door. Above his head is a lovely print of Connemara in western Ireland, a fetching green landscape divided by a web of stone walls. It is the most remote part of the country. "Connemara is where the Irish Catholics were driven," he explains. "It's rocky soil and hard to farm. Oliver Cromwell wanted to make sure that no one Irish family could ever gain power, so he decreed that land had to be divided up among all the children in a family, rather than be passed down to the eldest son. The land was divided into so many parcels that people could barely survive on it. Thus began the great immigration of Irish sons." Mannix and his wife Cathy, who is also of Irish descent, visited the area on their twenty-fifth anniversary. A leprechaun grins from his spot on the wall below the print.

To Mannix's right, an IBM PC glows. A small round table, well suited for private chats, is perfectly centered in the gray-carpeted room. On the well-polished cherry table sits a candy dish that Mannix keeps stocked with lemon drops, as well as a small calendar, which provides any visitors with a thought for the day. Today's wisdom comes from Winston Churchill: "Never, never ever quit."

Rose says, "Tim, I got a call from a customer yesterday. He casually mentioned that the phone rang more than four times in tech support. What's going on?"

Mannix turns around in his chair and, in a magnificent, deep voice like that of James Earl Jones, replies, "We're so critical of ourselves. But we are removing the defects. I'll check with Ken this morning to see if they're having scheduling problems again. I'd be willing to bet the call came in at lunchtime."

Mannix spent twenty-two years at IBM before taking early retirement to start his own consulting firm in Boca Raton, Florida. He worked with Dataflex for two years as a consultant before Rose convinced him to join Dataflex in January 1991 as the third partner. "I consider the fact that Tim Mannix is here a credit to my ability as a salesman," says Rose. "IBM valued him so much it offered to send him anywhere in the world, but he didn't want to leave Boca Raton. Two years later, I convinced him to leave the warmth of Florida for Edison, New Jersey."

Mannix laughs and concedes that Rose's powers of persuasion prevailed. "I had to be comfortable on four points," says the senior vice president, whose full beard and towering 6 feet 4 inch frame make him look more like a lumberjack than a former IBMer. "First, my bride had to approve the move. She agreed that it was a wonderful opportunity. Second, I had to be certain my partner, Nick Nicholson, wouldn't be left in the lurch with our consulting business. My solution to that was to give him all the assets of the business and be certain he had the resources to run the business for a full year.

"Third, I had to be certain of spiritual support. Every morning for sixteen years I'd met with a group of five men at Denny's in Boca Raton for a prayer group and afterwards we'd go to mass together. Those men had been there for me through good times and bad. They're the kind of friends you can call on day or night. They reassured me that we would still continue our friendship. Finally, I had to find a parish that was active and where I could use my talents. One of my loves is singing, and I didn't want to give that up." To choose where to live, he drew a circle around the area that was within thirty miles of Dataflex. Then he started visiting parishes in the surrounding towns until he found one he liked.

"Of all the things I miss," says Mannix, "I miss my prayer group the most. I haven't found that here yet."

Once he'd overcome his personal concerns, Mannix drew up a list of pros and cons about accepting a partnership with Rose and McLenithan. Mannix was most concerned about whether Rose would be able to cede control of the areas for which Mannix would be assuming responsibility. "My decision to come on board came down to my belief that I could trust both Rick and Gordon," he says. "I truly believed that they would treat me as a partner, and they have."

Mannix, whose last position at IBM was as director for worldwide manufacturing plants and controls, has the mission at Dataflex to smooth operations. "I enjoy figuring out how to make things operate right." He also brings a different selling style to the company. While Rose's strength is selling based on enthusiasm and people skills, Mannix relies on numbers and facts. And the latter has become increasingly important at Dataflex with the new concentration on selling services: Customers want quantifiable measurements like productivity gains and reductions in cost when they're purchasing service contracts.

Mannix, McLenithan, and Rose refer to themselves as the three amigos. Even though they couldn't be more different from each other, they have forged an easy friendship and genuinely respect each other's area of expertise. Rose used to wear a large, black sombrero embellished with green sequins during their executive meetings, but the weight of it gave him a headache.

Gordon McLenithan's office, which is slightly larger than Mannix's and five feet longer than Rose's, is next on the right. But Rose doesn't slow down again until he reaches the open door of his office. Hanging on the door of his small conference room to the left of his office is a sign that proclaims: "In God we trust. . . . All others must have data." The sign was a gift from Mannix.

Rose's face, tanned from a week-long salmon-fishing trip in Canada, bears an expression of extreme concentration. You can almost see the wheels turning as he walks behind his desk and punches an automatic dialer. He paces the mauve carpet while a pleasant female voice announces the price of Dataflex's stock. It's up a point, probably the result of Rose and McLenithan's most recent round of visits with groups of investors and the article in last week's *Fortune* citing the company as one of America's fastest growing 100 companies. (Dataflex took the seventy-fifth spot.)

Next he punches in a request for IBM's stock price. The news isn't good. He takes the pulse of Compaq Computer Corporation. Founder and Chief Executive Officer Rod Canion's sudden ouster from the company hasn't had much of an impact on the stock, even though the event took most analysts by surprise. Finally, he checks the price of Merisel, Inc., a local distributor that sells to resellers. Rose bought its stock at four dollars. Today it's at twelve dollars a share.

Without fail, Rose starts his day this way. The habit is ironic, since he doesn't particularly like the stock market. Indeed, Jeffrey Lamm practically forced him to take stock in Dataflex. In 1984 the two men were meeting in Lamm's living room, hammering out the details of Rose's employment. It was the culmination of a three-year courtship, during which Lamm had tried numerous times to woo Rose from his job as vice president and director of sales at DJC. But when a British company bought out DJC and demanded that Rose hire several more salespeople because "sales were too dependent on a few," Rose decided it was time to move on. "I didn't want to put a bunch of warm bodies in the sales department, just because some guy in London wasn't confident that I could trust the salespeople I already had."

The discussion with Lamm, lanky and bald, had hit the money stage. "Jeffrey said, 'Rick, I want to give you stock options for 200,000 shares,' which at the time was 10 percent of all the outstanding shares associated with the company," says Rose. "I told him I didn't want the shares."

Peering from behind his wire-rimmed glasses, Lamm replied, "Rick, today our stock is at $1.50 a share. With what you're capable of doing here, those shares will be worth millions of dollars someday."

Still smarting from encounters with stock options in other companies, Rose turned down Lamm's offer cold. But Lamm persisted, saying, "I'm going to make you take the shares. I don't care whether you want them or not. They are not in lieu of any compensation. I know you don't understand this, but I'll give you the money you want *and* the shares.

"Look, it's not my fault that three other guys treated you unfairly. All I can do is let you know that I intend to treat you as a partner. Whatever I would do for myself, I will do for you."

Rose finally shrugged his agreement. The two sat and talked about the day when the stock would be worth more than $6 a share and the company would book more than $25,000 worth of business a day. Says Rose, "If we don't do $350,000 a day now, we're disappointed."

A classic entrepreneur, Lamm was a rarity in his recognition that it was time to pass the baton to someone else and in his willingness to do so. Although he shared Rose's dedication to training, Lamm didn't finish high school. The Brighton Beach, New York, native dropped out to join the air force. He became a radar specialist, repairing equipment on Strategic Air Command bombers in the 1960s before launching his career in the nascent computer industry in 1969 at Data Products Corporation. His last job before starting Dataflex was as a regional sales manager at Infoton, Inc., based in Burlington, Massachusetts, for which he sold computer screens to New York-area businesses.

Lamm knew Dataflex needed a person with the leadership skills to take the company to the next level. As soon as he was certain

Rose and McLenithan had a firm grip on Dataflex, he stopped being involved with the company on a daily basis. During 1990 and 1991 he sold 738,700 shares of Dataflex stock for a total of $7.565 million and moved to Florida. Today Lamm, aged forty-eight, remains on the board but owns virtually no stock in the company he founded. He spends his time golfing and fishing in Florida, where he now makes his home.

Reflecting on that original agreement discussion, Rose admits, "I was somewhat skeptical. But I wanted to believe him, and he turned out to be a man of his word. I can't think of a higher compliment."

Lamm's insistence that Rose take the options, as well as a good salary, was part of what convinced Rose to place another bet on someone else's pony, rather than strike out on his own.

Rose's daily routine reveals his grudging respect for the power the gyrations of the market have over the company's fortunes and his. Despite the fact that the stock market has made him a wealthy man—Dataflex's stock increased from a low of seventy-four cents a share in 1984 to a high of seventeen dollars a share in 1991—Rose remains disenchanted with the whole process. A mathematician with a keen mind for forecasting, he likes to be in control of the numbers that relate to his company and, thus, his performance.

Rose is fond of telling his associates: "Winners love to be measured. Only losers hate numbers. They don't want to be held accountable for their actions."

Rose certainly doesn't mind being held accountable. Indeed, Dataflex is known among analysts who follow the company for hitting its forecasts on the nose. The balance sheet shows no debt. In its August 6, 1991, issue, *Financial World* named Dataflex number one on its list of emerging stars among small-growth companies in the United States. Its annualized five-year sales growth was 66 percent, and its return on equity for the past five years averaged 20 percent. The company had the lowest SG & A (sales, general and administrative expenses) in the industry, at 8.6 percent for the year that ended March 31, 1991. It turned inventory at a rate of 8.3 times a year compared to the 6.2 industry average.

And, to hear Rose tell it, he has tried to be agreeable to Wall Street's demands. When analysts and institutional investors told Rose and McLenithan—during one of the four to five road trips they embark on each year—that the stock was low because Dataflex didn't have enough sales, the duo concentrated on increasing revenues. Sales shot up by more than 50 percent a year for three years in a row after the two men asked the sales staff to concentrate on selling hardware. Next the partners were told that profits weren't growing fast enough. So, again the executives asked the salespeople to shift their energies to selling services, which are three times more profitable than are hardware sales. For the next three years, profits increased more than 60 percent each year. Then the criticism was that the company's float was too thin, so Dataflex did a secondary offering in April 1990 to increase liquidity.

In 1991, Rose says he was told, "You are doing great, but your industry isn't doing well.' I thought, 'Wonderful. Not only do I have to make sure my company is doing well, they're telling me that I have to make sure my competitors do well, too.' That was too much." He laughs and shakes his head.

Like that of most small companies, Dataflex's stock performance remains a wild card, and its president chafes a bit about that fact. When he admitted his innate distrust of the market and his original disinterest in the options Lamm offered, Rose looked vaguely sheepish but somewhat defiant all at once. Not many presidents of publicly held companies readily declare their distaste for the action on the exchanges.

Even Dataflex's annual report reflects Rose's no-nonsense approach to the public markets. You won't find any bells and whistles in its pages. (Unless you count 1987, when its annual report was printed so that you had to turn it sideways compared to the traditional format.) Year after year, there are no fancy words from the management team. No pages of glitzy photos and fancy artwork. Just the facts, ma'am, in a plain vanilla package. And neat graphs that spike consistently upward in every category.

Except for the untamable beast that is the stock market, Rose has a love affair with numbers. When you walk through the different departments at Dataflex, you'll notice nifty computer-generated charts and graphs, replete with full-color graphics. Everything is measured, the performances both of departments as a whole and of individuals. The sales department is dominated by a 20 foot-by-8-foot board that shows the daily sales of all the salespeople with weekly and monthly totals.

The wall to the left of this board is covered with plaques that honor the top salespeople by month and by year. At the corner of that wall, just outside Rose's office, hangs a large, brass bell.

Rose has barely settled in his chair when the bell erupts with a sharp clanging. He jumps up and darts out the door to hear the latest success story. Stacie Bender, the sales assistant on Alan Fendrick's team, finishes ringing the bell and tells Rose that Fendrick has completed the $300,000 sale to New York Telephone. Fendrick never touches the bell pull himself, preferring to let one of his team members do the honors.

For the past few years, Fendrick and Diane Katz have been jockeying for the number one sales spot. Like Fendrick, Katz may seem an unlikely pick to be one of the star performers at a high-flying company. A forty-year-old New Jersey native, Katz spent many of her working years toiling for two physicians as a medical secretary earning $15,000 a year. In 1983 she answered a three-line ad in her local paper for an "inside sales position." Katz wasn't even sure what that meant, but she knew she "had the gift for gab." Although at that time an inside sales person at Dataflex essentially did all the legwork for the salespeople without the benefit of a commission check, she accepted the job. It meant a $3,000 raise, and in those days, $3,000 was a lot of money to Katz.

A blonde with brilliant blue eyes who resembles the actress Joan Van Ark, star of the television show "Knot's Landing," Katz is fast talking and demanding. As an inside sales person, she knew her job was to push orders through the process. But in 1983 Dataflex was anything but efficient, and Katz was viewed as a troublemaker. Workers in the warehouse would groan when they'd see her descending upon them, gum popping, jaw flapping, and well-manicured finger wagging.

"The warehouse manager wouldn't answer her questions when she'd come in the warehouse," recalls Rich Dressler, vice president of materials management and a former UPS shipping clerk who joined the company around the same time Katz did. "I couldn't believe the way he treated her. I'd go over and try to help her. Nobody would even talk to Diane at the company Christmas parties, except me. She'd sit alone with her boyfriend in a corner."

But when Rose came on board, he saw in Katz the kind of die-hard enthusiasm and determination he knew it would take to turn the company around. He also believed that she was a tremendously talented go-getter whose talents had gone untapped partially because she was a woman. "There she was running around doing the jobs of these guys who spent most of their days out playing golf and wining and dining the clients," Rose recalls. "The fact that women still don't get paid the same amount as men for the same work proves that something in the thinking of corporate America is seriously out of whack.

"In a way I'm prejudiced because I think women often do a better job than men do. They are willing to work harder when they perceive an opportunity because they have been so stifled in business. And they don't believe anybody owes them anything. They are willing to work for whatever they get."

As an example of what he was looking for in a salesperson, Rose hired his wife, Linda, now forty-five, who has a master's degree in psychology and had been one of the top salespeople at DJC where she and Rose met. When he hired Linda to work at Dataflex, shortly after he had arrived at the company, she was pregnant with their first child, but Rose felt he needed her influence even if it would be for a limited period. Linda Rose's desk was right beside Diane Katz's, and the two became fast friends.

A few weeks after Linda Rose was hired, the sales staff complained to Rick Rose in a morning sales meeting that he was giving her preferential treatment. "You're right. I do favor her, but you're mistaken if you think it's because she's my wife," Rose replied testily. "Take a look at the numbers, and you'll see that I treat her differently because she's the number one salesperson here. Rank has its privileges. I can't promise I'll marry you if you become the number one salesperson, but there will be perks."

Within ninety days of his arrival, Rose sacked all twelve salespeople. Among the supporting staff for the sales department, there were only two survivors. One was Tom Beer, whom Rose transferred to a sales spot from his position as the PC technical support person. Beer's résumé included time as a prison guard and a short stint in sales with a competitor. The other was Katz, who was one of only twelve of the original forty employees remaining after McLenithan and Rose finished purging the ranks.

With Linda and Rick Rose selling and Beer promoted, that put the sales team up to a whopping three members. The fourth spot on the new sales team was offered to Katz. She jumped at the chance, and for the next six years, Katz won the honor of Salesperson of the Year.

Rose admits that he was somewhat taken aback by Katz's smashing success. Katz tells customers everything about herself from day one, believing that it helps her "bond quickly" to them. She also makes no bones about the fact that she is completely nontechnical and has no interest in becoming a techie. He says, "I don't always understand or agree with Diane's technique, but that doesn't make it wrong." Nonetheless, sparks often fly between her and Rose in the morning sales meetings when Katz puts forth an opinion. Conflict is the hallmark of her relationship with Rose.

Rose launches into one of the stories that has become part of the folklore of Dataflex. Katz came into his office one day and asked how much she would have to sell to get a car like his. Rose plucked what he thought was an impossible number out of the air.

"If you sell $600,000 worth of equipment per month for six months in a row, I'll give you my car," he promised. At that time the record per month for any salesperson stood at $300,000.

A year later, Katz danced into his office and asked for the keys to his Mercedes 300SD. She had met his condition. "When I have a burning desire to succeed, I am absolutely obsessed," says Katz, who is known for antics like singing to customers. "I made cold calls all day long. I left my chair only to go to the bathroom. I ate lunch at my desk every day for months."

As Katz started to walk out with his keys, Rose offered to buy her a brand-new Mercedes, and Katz, of course, agreed. She picked out a sportier model: a navy blue Mercedes 560SL.

Fendrick, who is twenty-nine years old, has tried to remake himself in Rose's image. He adopted Rose's habit of arriving at the office early. He built his client base by making 150 calls a day. He is the person you are most likely to find in the president's office at any given time. He peppers Rose with questions about everything from selling to the meaning of life. Practically any time Rose tosses out a question to a group, you can bet Fendrick will respond. Since his first week of work when he got locked out of a sales meeting at 7:31 A.M. and found a dinner invitation at the boss's house retracted when he arrived thirty minutes late, Fendrick has scarcely missed an opportunity to be in Rose's presence.

And lately, Fendrick has had the upper hand in the competition between him and Katz. With blue-chip clients like New York Telephone, Chase Manhattan, and Citibank, the bell rings frequently for Fendrick and his crew. Rose, who is wearing a pin that declares, "Katz'll Klobber 'Em," meaning that he's betting on Katz to come out on top in the current quarter, applauds Fendrick's sale gleefully. He strides over to Fendrick's cubicle, twenty feet from the bell. Fendrick is on the phone with a client. Rose gives him the thumbs up, then goes back into his office.

At Dataflex, competition is viewed as healthy and is heartily cheered. Yet Rose has managed to instill in the associates an overriding concern for the health of Dataflex as a whole. The prominently displayed graphs measuring individuals' performances reflect the meshing of the company good with the struggle for excellence on a personal level.

RICK ROSE: We train people at Dataflex to have the work-with attitude. People work with each other, and that interdependence is critical to our success.

Most people start out dependent, then they become independent and finally interdependent. They come into a new situation, insecure and dependent on their co-workers' advice and assistance.

Alan Fendrick joined this company seven years ago as a twenty-two-year-old stand-up comedian. He didn't know anything about personal computers. And he certainly didn't know anything about selling—although he was brash enough to have told you differently at the time. He was in a position of total dependence. He was like a baby who had to be taught to crawl, walk, talk, and feed himself.

Alan, however, was a quick study and absorbed the daily lessons well. Independence reared its head once he had tucked a few private victories under his belt. He'd learned how the system worked, how to marshal the resources of Dataflex, and how to fight for change. His confidence veered to the edge of cockiness.

The cultures of many companies force people into this stage of growth and freeze-dry them there. Rampant independence pits people against each other, and you wind up with warring competitive forces in the office. Achieving harmony in a company filled with people in the independent mode is impossible. You are too busy trying to avoid chaos to aspire to the harmony that the next level of growth would bring forth.

At Dataflex we fast-forward through the independent stage by rewarding those who master interdependence.

About six months after Alan came on board, he volunteered to teach a sales training class on creativity using his experience writing stand-up comedy routines. When he stood in front of the class teaching his peers word-association exercises and techniques to come up with outrageous one-liners and then listened as they applied the concepts to business, he grasped, in that instant, the notion of interdependence. He told me later that seeing me as a participant willing to learn from him taught him that it was all about sharing and helping each other. Even though he was feeling extremely defensive, he also asked for and got constructive criticism after he finished the class. From that day forward, Alan demonstrated his acceptance of the notion of interdependence through his commitment to helping those around him succeed. Whereas most of the world designates people as givers and takers, with interdependence we strike the perfect balance between the two.

A few years ago, Mannix and his partner Nick Nicholson recommended that every person in the company, from Rose to the receptionist, write down the six items that they considered the most important parts of their jobs. "There were no processes established to aid in getting the work done," recalls Mannix. "Whoever happened to walk by Rick's or Gordon's door got the job. The company was growing so fast that they hadn't taken the time to figure out who should be doing what." (See Dataflex Quality "Climate" chart below.)

Associates were then asked to rank the items based on which they would do first if they had only twenty minutes to work. But instead of merely handing in the list to some boss's office where it would gather dust in an IN box on a desk, the exercise continued (See Motivation Process chart). Each manager was required to compile a list of priorities for each of the associates in his or her department. Then the manager sat down with each associate individually and hashed it out until their two lists agreed.

"My list of priorities for the salespeople was exactly the opposite of what they put down," notes Rose wryly. "The salespeople said they needed to prospect more, but I said they should service their present customers more thoroughly. After discussion, it became apparent that we were essentially after the same thing. But my point

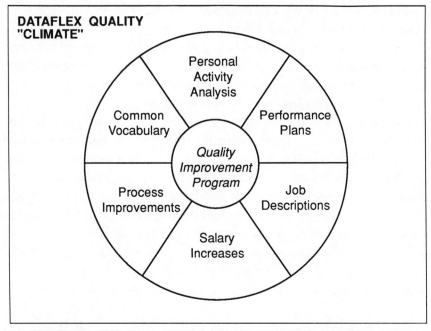

DATAFLEX QUALITY "CLIMATE"

- Personal Activity Analysis
- Common Vocabulary
- Performance Plans
- Quality Improvement Program
- Job Descriptions
- Process Improvements
- Salary Increases

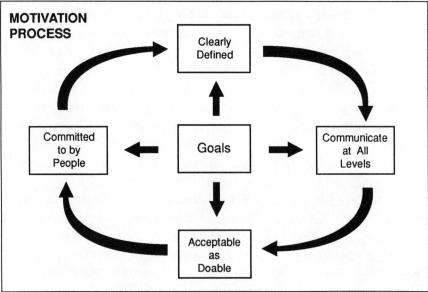

MOTIVATION PROCESS

- Clearly Defined
- Committed to by People
- Goals
- Communicate at All Levels
- Acceptable as Doable

was that they could more efficiently generate new business from existing clients.

"That exercise taught us many things. One, it helped people understand each other's jobs better. Two, it demonstrated that what may seem important to you may not really be the most critical thing for the company. Everyone came away with a much clearer under-standing of how their work affects the company as a whole—the big picture."

Once the list was established for each associate, graphs and charts that illustrated the performance of each worker were posted. Only the top one or two items are continuously tracked for all the world to see. That's part of helping people focus on the most important aspect of their jobs, says Rose. (See examples of Quality Process charts from various departments below.)

"In business too many people leave work and have no idea whether they've done a good job that day or not," asserts Rose. "By letting people establish what they will be measured by, we eliminate that frustration. Individuals can see on a daily basis whether they are giving 110 percent.

"We use measurements not only to help people feel good about themselves, but because it's good business. We use measurements in our selling. When a customer asks about the level of support we offer, for instance, we're able to say, 'If by good support you mean handling one hundred calls a day and solving problems in an aver-age of less than fourteen minutes, then the answer is yes.' "

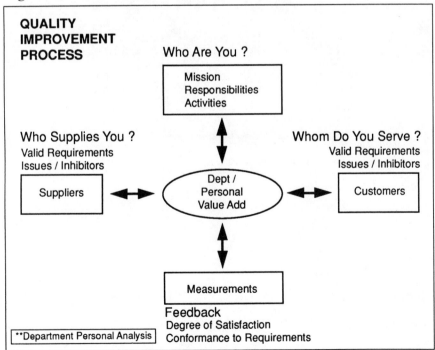

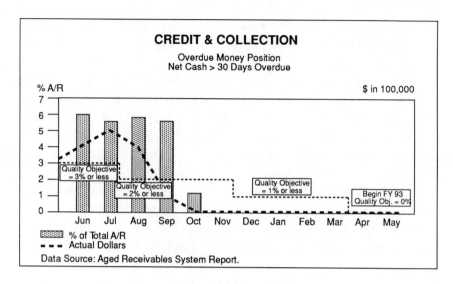

CREDIT & COLLECTION

Overdue Money Position
Net Cash > 30 Days Overdue

% A/R $ in 100,000

Quality Objective = 3% or less

Quality Objective = 2% or less

Quality Objective = 1% or less

Begin FY 93 Quality Obj. = 0%

Jun Jul Aug Sep Oct Nov Dec Jan Feb Mar Apr May

% of Total A/R
Actual Dollars

Data Source: Aged Receivables System Report.

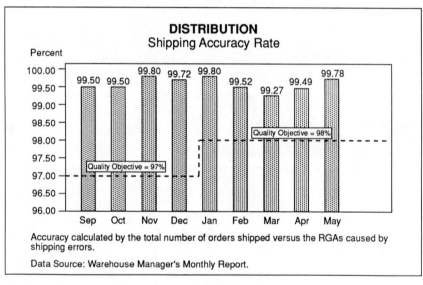

DISTRIBUTION
Shipping Accuracy Rate

Percent

	Sep	Oct	Nov	Dec	Jan	Feb	Mar	Apr	May
	99.50	99.50	99.80	99.72	99.80	99.52	99.27	99.49	99.78

Quality Objective = 98%

Quality Objective = 97%

Accuracy calculated by the total number of orders shipped versus the RGAs caused by shipping errors.

Data Source: Warehouse Manager's Monthly Report.

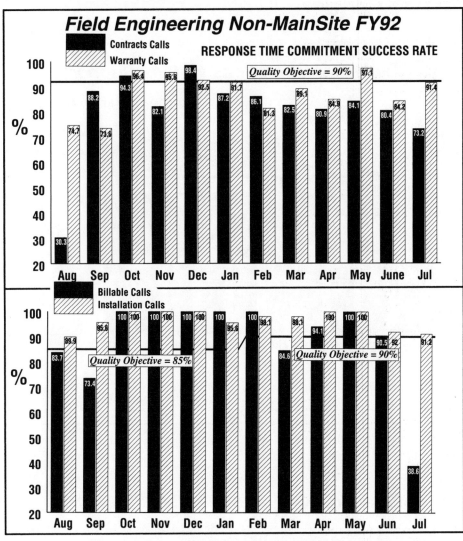

Field Engineering Non-MainSite FY92

■ Contracts Calls
▨ Warranty Calls

RESPONSE TIME COMMITMENT SUCCESS RATE

Quality Objective = 90%

Month	Contracts	Warranty
Aug	30.3	74.7
Sep	88.2	73.6
Oct	94.3	96.4
Nov	82.1	95.6
Dec	98.4	92.5
Jan	87.2	91.7
Feb	86.1	81.3
Mar	82.5	89.1
Apr	80.9	84.9
May	84.1	97.1
June	80.4	84.2
Jul	73.2	91.4

■ Billable Calls
▨ Installation Calls

Quality Objective = 85%

Quality Objective = 90%

Month	Billable	Installation
Aug	83.7	89.9
Sep	73.4	95.6
Oct	100	100
Nov	100	100
Dec	100	100
Jan	100	95.6
Feb	100	98.1
Mar	84.6	98.1
Apr	94.1	100
May	100	100
Jun	90.5	92
Jul	38.6	91.2

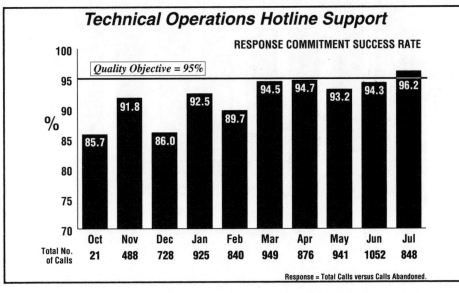

Technical Operations Hotline Support

RESPONSE COMMITMENT SUCCESS RATE

Quality Objective = 95%

Month	%	Total No. of Calls
Oct	85.7	21
Nov	91.8	488
Dec	86.0	728
Jan	92.5	925
Feb	89.7	840
Mar	94.5	949
Apr	94.7	876
May	93.2	941
Jun	94.3	1052
Jul	96.2	848

Response = Total Calls versus Calls Abandoned.

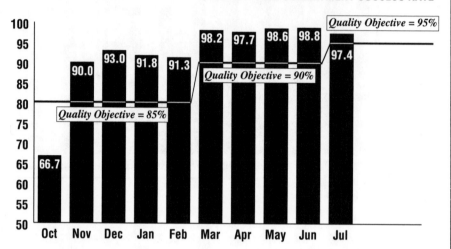

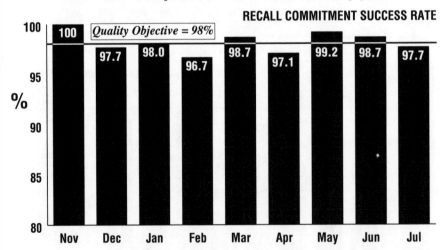

Recall = Same problem on the same machine within 30 days of the original call closure.

That six-point list serves as a job description and is the basis of quarterly—not just annual—reviews. Says Rose, who abhors bureaucratic systems, "It has eliminated paperwork, and there are no surprises at review time." (See departmental analysis checklist below.)

Measuring performance has boosted quality, too, by rewarding people for doing their jobs right the first time. "I have observed that for every day you do it right, you get one day on the other end that goes well," says Rose emphatically. "But for every day you do it wrong, you pay for it with three days of torture on the other end. Seventy-five cents of every dollar companies spend on quality assurance actually goes to correcting mistakes. Do it right the first time."

Department Analysis in the Drawer ?

The analysis should be the basis for

- Performance Plans

- Job Descriptions

- Department Measurements

- Salary Increases

- Recognition and Awards

- Process Improvements

- Organizational Changes

- Ongoing Performance Reviews

- New Hire Orientation and Education

- Common Vocabulary

Fendrick rushes into Rose's office and takes out his wallet. He hands Rose a crisp one dollar bill. Rose gives the bill a cursory glance and then asks, "What do you want to know?"

"Where do you see me in my career in five years?" asks Fendrick, taking one of the two chairs facing Rose's desk. The president scribbles Fendrick's question on the face of the dollar bill and adds it to a growing cache of dollar bills that are neatly squared on his highly polished cherry desk.

Then, elbows resting on his desk and fingertips touching, Rose leans forward and says, "You're going to have to take a step backward to get where you need to go. You'll have to get out of the golden handcuffs of sales."

That comment provokes a philosophical discussion that lasts about fifteen minutes. Rose notes that one of the pitfalls of being excellent in sales is that you become dependent on a large commission check. Accepting the cut in income that moving into management demands—even though it's short term—calls for a good deal of soul-searching. But he goes on to explain a three-step plan that will eventually lead Fendrick to preside over another location and concludes by saying, "Above all you must continue to be the number one sales rep and be the best at what you're doing." Satisfied, Fendrick lopes back to his cubicle.

To an outsider, seeing a salesman pay a dollar to the president of a company for a moment of truth may seem odd or even slightly unsavory. But Rose realized that one of the hardest things to instill in the people around him was the idea that they had a right to ask questions and to expect a truthful answer. On a whim one day, Rose announced at the weekly company meeting that for one dollar you could ask him anything and get the truth.

"I'd give people the truth whether they paid the dollar or not, but the act of paying the dollar seems to make people feel more like they are owed an honest answer," observes Rose. "I especially wanted to teach the salespeople to ask tough questions and expect answers. Professional salespeople must know how to stick up for themselves."

After returning a few phone calls and perusing a stack of papers that his assistant, Liz Massimo, left for him the previous night, Rose gets restless. His schedule, posted on the door of his office, shows no appointments until a company tour for some potential clients at 11 A.M.

Although he moves through his day at a rapid clip, one of Rose's talents is being able to zero in on whomever he is speaking with. You may get only fifteen minutes of his time, but thanks to his intensity and focus, those who drop into his office rarely leave feeling shortchanged or rushed.

Rose's zeal has served him well. In the first five years after he and McLenithan devoted themselves to creating the best company in the industry, both worked seven days a week, arriving at 6:30 A.M. each day, except Saturday and Sunday. On those days they allowed themselves the luxury of coming to work at 8 A.M.

Explaining why they drove themselves so hard, Rose says: "We didn't invent the formula for Famous Amos chocolate chip cookies. We didn't have patents on anything. In fact, we didn't even make anything. All we had were our attitudes and our work ethic. And we both believed in leadership by example."

To Rose, leading by example certainly doesn't mean leading from some lofty perch. Rose subscribes to the Henry V school of management: Leading means getting down in the trenches. In the early days, he appeared in the warehouse one morning and declared, "I'm going to be working here with you for the next month, and I want you to teach me everything about the warehouse." He did the same thing in each department, putting the time in to learn how to order equipment, how the computer system worked and was programmed, how the company shipped products, how the accounting system worked, and how to sell Dataflex's products and services. In the process, he also ferreted out incompetence and spotted unwieldly systems that needed improvement.

"Rick used to want to get all kinds of reports," recalls McLenithan. "He'd insist on loading the system himself, and invariably he'd crash it. It drove me crazy, but nobody was going to tell him not to do it. Finally, the sales department complained so much about the system crashing on an almost weekly basis that he stopped." McLenithan chuckles.

Asked to describe himself, Rose replied, "I'm an agitator. You can have soap, water, and clothes in a washing machine, but nothing happens until the agitator starts." He doesn't give lip service to "management by wandering around," a concept featured prominently in Thomas Peters and Robert H. Waterman, Jr.'s classic, *In Search of Excellence.* Both he and McLenithan practice it daily.

In search of some action, Rose leaves his office and walks back down the gray carpeted hallway toward the finance department. The finance director, Ann Marie Bernet, catches his eye and asks him to come into her office. He stands in the doorway. A colored spreadsheet glows on her computer. Bespectacled and conserva-

tively dressed, she says quietly, "Listen, Rick, morale in my department is low. They feel unappreciated. They definitely don't feel like
part of the team. Nobody understands what we do."

Rose listens attentively and then asks, "So why don't you have an
open house? Give your people a chance to talk about what they do
with the rest of the company." Bernet brightens and nods her
agreement. She immediately calls a meeting to start planning.

Another voice calls out from an office, "Hey Rick." Prasad Srinivasan, the credit manager, likes nothing better than being the bearer
of good news. When Rose appears in his doorway, he continues,
"You know that letter and the dozen long-stemmed roses we sent
to Nynex, thanking them for being so punctual paying their invoices? Well, they called us up this morning. They couldn't believe
it. They said nobody had ever done something like that for them
before."

Rose grins and wags his head, "Yeah, the thank-you letter was a
great idea, and the roses were a nice touch."

"I'd like to make that a regular thing each month," says Srinivasan, "like a Customer of the Month. We'd give the honor to the
accounts payable department that proves the most cooperative.
What do you think?"

Says Rose, "Go for it." He pauses at a graph that shows the
percentage of invoices that were right when they went out to clients.
That's a critical measurement because incorrect invoices cost companies thousands and even millions of dollars annually in terms of
delayed payments. Hmmm, the percentage looks pretty good—96.6
percent—Rose thinks to himself. For comparison's sake, that figure
at IBM hovers around 82 percent. Next he studies a graph charting
forecast dollars versus collected dollars.

Bernet taps him on the shoulder. "How does Thursday sound for
the open house? Any conflicts?" she asks.

"Nope," says Rose over his shoulder and continues on his
rounds. He greets people by their first names, asking about vaca-
tions, kids, and the other things that people care about. In the
warehouse department, he pauses to ask Dexter Jasper a question
he typically poses as he moves through the ranks, "Is there anything
we can do to make your job easier?" Rose knows that sometimes
people are so focused on getting the job done that they don't take
time to call attention to problems unless they are asked to point

blank. That is the beauty of management by wandering around: You jolt people out of their comfort zones.

Jasper puts down the box he's carrying and says, "Rick, believe it or not, our printer doesn't work since we put up the new computer system. We're having to hand write. . . ."

Rose interrupts, throwing up his hands, "Stop." He turns on his heels and heads for the office of Greg Coccetti, director of information systems.

Rose asks Coccetti to get the printer fixed. "They need their printer working. Those guys are receiving $500,000 worth of equipment a day," Rose exclaims. "We're going backward, not forward."

Now some management gurus might argue that Rose's actions undermine the authority of others, but at Dataflex the emphasis is on getting problems fixed as soon as they are uncovered, no matter who spots it. Says Rose, "I don't want to be encumbered by bureaucratic channels when I'm trying to solve a problem, and I don't want anybody else to be, either. I want to create an environment where people feel safe about getting things changed."

McLenithan shares his conviction on this topic and says, "People have empowerment here, but if they don't use it, someone else will solve their problem for them."

Fifteen minutes later, the printer is working, and Rose is back at his desk when several of the warehousemen come in and thank him.

Liz Massimo sticks her head in the door to let him know that the group for his 11 A.M. appointment is early. He smiles to himself, knowing that they will have plenty of time to read the letters and the articles displayed prominently in the lobby. In fact, several of the salespeople have been known to let clients wait a few minutes after they've been announced, expressly for that reason.

To Rose, the success of Dataflex lies in the degree to which he is successful in fostering a team spirit. In an organization that is sales driven, that is an especially delicate task. Traditionally in business, salespeople have been treated almost as a breed unto themselves. Companies treat them either as a necessary evil or as prima donnas to whom the rest of the company must bow and scrape. Either way, other employees usually view salespeople with loathing and jealousy. In some companies, those attitudes emanate from the executive suite.

Worse still is the cutthroat attitude that pervades most sales forces. Unfortunately, sales is often a world where sales managers award the chosen few the plum territories. Less experienced salespeople, often in desperate need of guidance, are left to their own devices to scrap for the crumbs. By contrast, at Dataflex no one is assigned certain accounts or territories. Everything is up for grabs. And salespeople often team up on accounts, splitting commissions accordingly. Says Rose, "The whole point is when someone owns an account they can take on a lackadaisical attitude about it. At Dataflex you constantly have to justify your right to maintain an account."

Shaped by two decades of work in sales, Rose is determined to devise an environment where sales and operations cooperate with and respect each other. To that end, each new salesperson does what Rose himself did: Salespeople spend the first several weeks of their time at Dataflex working in different departments, so they can learn how the company works. And more important, the exercise instills respect for the people who enable them to pick up their commission checks.

Another critical ingredient of the utopia Rose envisions is something called team-order processing or TOP. Like so many ideas at Dataflex, team-order processing was a concept that developed from a meeting, and its implementation was almost instantaneous. During a budget meeting in 1987, the department managers were discussing the resources they would need to support the Dataflex goal of doubling revenues the following year. Sales administrator Heidi Gray informed Rose that to process the additional orders would require eight more people to supplement her staff of ten. Bob Wallace, the warehouse manager, said he could get by with seven more people to pull and prep the orders. Kerry Mutz, systems-integration manager, chimed in with a request for six new hires. By the time all the managers had stated their needs, Rose realized they were asking for thirty new associates.

"Wait a minute," Rose said. He stood at the head of the conference table and began pacing, hands behind his back, as he often does when the wheels are furiously turning. "There is something inherently wrong here. Think of this, Heidi. You alone are asking for eight people. Let's pick an all-star team and put the best at every position. How many orders could we process then? How much technical support could we give?"

There were blank looks around the table, so Rose plunged ahead, waving his arms excitedly as he spoke. "Who's the best salesperson around here?"

"Well, you," stammered Gray.

"Fine. I know how to sell. I know what this company can and can't do. I know how to use its resources. Who's our best sales administrator?" Rose demanded.

Gray replied firmly, "I am."

"Alright, Heidi," said Rose. "You're going to be our sales administrator. Who's the best inside sales representative? The best warehouse guy? The best tech-support person? The best prep person?" Now there were smiles around the table as the room nominated an all-star team.

Pausing dramatically, Rose asked, "If we all worked together and all we had to do was process our own orders, even though next year we plan to grow 80 percent, if that team worked together, could we do it?"

The group agreed enthusiastically.

An experiment was born. Declaring department heads and himself ineligible, Rose and the managers carved an all-star team choosing one person from each of the various departments that are involved in processing an order.

What struck Rose full force that day was what he hoped was the answer to the problems that had dogged him throughout his sales career: First, how to give salespeople the tools to do more than just make promises and then hope the company delivers on those promises. As it stood, salespeople spent about 70 percent of their time chasing down administrative details within the company—time that could have been spent with clients and potential accounts. And second, how to get operations to share the urgency of the sales staff.

In any organization sales is a horizontal department. So is sales administration, warehouse, prep, inside sales, and all the departments you need to coordinate and process an order. If you look across any organization, what you'll see are departments performing tasks independently. Although ultimately the departments must rely on each other to get the job done, nobody has stepped back to analyze how those tasks are interrelated. Such a structure is inherently unwieldy; nobody understands the next person's priorities. It encourages people to be autocratic and isolated. Interdependence is stymied.

Yet that is the American way of setting up companies. During his tenure as a salesperson, Rose had come to joke that the operations department should be renamed the sales-prevention department. The jokes were the only way to defuse his anger at a system he felt powerless to change.

"Under the old system, when Alan gave a $100,000 order to the warehouse, there wasn't an individual he could talk to if a problem developed," Rose reflects. "If the customer asked him to speed up the process, he'd check with the warehouse manager and inevitably get this answer: 'It's here in the warehouse some place. We don't know who's handling that, but we know it's here. We'll find out for you, but it will take some time.' "

The process failed miserably in two ways:

1. There was no vehicle for communicating priorities. The salespeople were boiling with frustration at operations, and the feeling was mutual.
2. There was no consistency because the same person didn't do the same customers' orders every time. No one other than the salesperson had a sense of ownership.

Even now that Rose was in charge, he still hadn't found a way around that process. He was caught hiring more and more people to fuel the engine of growth, following conventional wisdom. That is, until the moment of inspiration struck, and he cut the engine.

Here's how it worked.

Top performer, Diane Katz, whose customers include Merck, Shering-Plough, Price Waterhouse, Chubb/Federal Insurance, Prudential, and Guardian Life, was selected as the salesperson for the all-star team. And a top performer from each department was given the job of working exclusively with Katz to service her clients. The challenge the team was presented with was twofold: to double sales and slash processing time in half without increasing the staff. The team was given sixty days. Of course, the members were also expected to maintain high-quality service.

The carrot was good, old-fashioned green stuff: $1,000 for each member if the team succeeded. In the first sixty days, virtually all orders were shipped within three working days, down from five working days previously. Even more impressive, more than 70 percent of the orders were shipped the day after they had been received. Quality and customer satisfaction also increased. Before the team concept was initiated, customer satisfaction (based on getting an order on time and in working order) had peaked at 97 percent. Customers of the all-star team rated it a near-perfect 99.2 percent. Soon turnaround time was further reduced to two days.

With team-order processing, Katz also found that for the first time, she had enough breathing room to allow her much more contact with key customers like Merck. Now she was able to call with follow-up questions the day she received an order. For example, she'd ask if the company wanted partial shipments if only part of the order was in stock. Under the old system, Katz would never have had the leisure of making that call. She would have been too busy following the order through a myriad of channels.

During the second thirty days in the sixty-day trial period, management designated Fendrick coordinator of a second team. Team 2 was given the benefit of learning from Team 1. "People gain *experience* through hard work and trial and error," says Rose. "People become *wise* quickly by learning from the experience of others. It takes less time to become wise."

The two teams competed to see who could process the most high-quality orders in the shortest time. Again, the results were startling. Three weeks into the second thirty-day period, Team 2 achieved parity with Team 1. Ultimately, both teams reduced the turnaround for processing orders from five days to two days.

Rose distributed $1,000 checks to the team members at the company meeting that week. Everybody in the company started clamoring to be on a team. Rose carved out teams for the entire sales force.

McLenithan and Rose also developed an innovative way to compensate salespeople. They decided that salespeople who had been with the company for more than a year would still be paid solely on a commission basis, but the commission would be based on their team's gross profits. The average sales veteran winds up with a six-figure income in commissions a year.

Furthermore, a team's gross profits also determine bonuses for the team members (the $1,000 bonus checks were given only during the testing stage), and salespeople are encouraged to think of creative ways to reward their respective teams for helping them make good on their promises.

"Profits are the way to keep score," declares Rose. "You can sell your way straight into Chapter Eleven. We want people to have the same goal the company has: to make a profit. Don't get caught up in selling for the sake of selling."

And that's how team-order processing became the new order.

On the other side of the building, Sophia Cathcart, the prep technician on Fendrick's team, is examining the latest order from one of their bank customers. But something doesn't look right to her. The machine's storage devices don't appear to be configured correctly. She alerts Fendrick to the problem and contacts technical support. Within an hour, tech support tells her that her instincts were right. If the equipment had been shipped as it was, it wouldn't have worked at all. Those delays would have been costly for the customer and costly for Dataflex's reputation with that customer.

Before team-order processing, Dataflex was losing money on more than a few orders because of internal and customer errors. As Fendrick points out, "TOP added another measure of quality without slowing delivery time."

Rose estimates that team members catch at least one error a day.

"The equipment they get reflects on the job that I do," says Cathcart. "If their machine isn't working properly when it arrives, that's my fault."

That's TOP in action.

The seed for TOP was planted by Tim Mannix, who was an executive on the IBM team that rolled out Big Blue's personal computer in a division that went from 13 people to 10,000 in three years. In the two years that he worked with Dataflex as a consultant, Mannix tested a theory he called "connective management." The crux of his theory, which he began to develop as IBM's director of quality and systems assurance, was to help people understand how they contribute quality to the end product.

Mannix, whose level of calm serves as a perfect foil for Rose's nervous energy, says, "If you can show the warehouse guy how his work fits into the big picture, then all of a sudden he's more than some strapping fellow who wears lumberjack shirts and big, heavy boots to work. It's like the old story about the worker who says he's laying bricks, but he doesn't know what he's building. The next worker is also laying bricks, but he's doing it with great care and proudly tells people that he's building a cathedral.

"The problem with most quality programs is that most companies apply the concept only to customer satisfaction. We've got to understand that we have customers and suppliers inside these four walls, too. How can we expect to get it right on the outside if we don't have it right on the inside?"

Mannix is proud of TOP. "TOP dovetailed with our overall drive to promote ownership," he says. "Before, if the warehouse made twenty shipping errors, those errors were attributed to the group. With TOP, errors show up specifically associated with the person responsible. When a person does well, he or she knows it."

One measure of productivity is attained by dividing a company's total sales by the number of workers. Since TOP was instituted in 1988, that number has moved up significantly. In fiscal 1991, it was $566,934 per employee—more than double the $247,000 of fiscal 1987. Profit per employee was $26,000, net income after taxes. The year TOP was instituted Dataflex hired less than 10 percent of the people that the managers initially said were needed.

The difference TOP has made in the sales department is astounding. The average commissioned salesperson who has been with Dataflex more than twelve months now sells more than $10 million worth of equipment and services a year. In the industry as a whole most salespeople do that kind of business in a *decade.* TOP frees the sales staff at Dataflex from many of the administrative duties that used to nibble away at their time, so they are able to spend almost 100 percent of their time selling. The two-hour meetings take place, for the most part, before their competitors begin their days. Fendrick, for example, has quadrupled his business, but has added only one member to his team.

*   *   *

It's now 11:15 A.M., and Liz Massimo, who is slim and impeccably dressed, welcomes the three visitors from a major prospect and leads them down the hall toward Rose's office. Ken Constantino rings the bell as they arrive at Rose's open door, and Rose appears to congratulate Constantino on his latest coup: a mainsite contract—$256,411 worth of business—to service a large New Jersey bank. Constantino worked on the account for four years, determined to make this moment happen. Says Rose, "So I guess I owe you a pig roast with all the trimmings."

Donning the sport coat he'd shed earlier in the day, Rose introduces himself and Constantino to the trio and gives a quick explanation of the pig roast and the bell ringing. "Ken bet me a few years back that he'd win this business *someday,*" he states. "I told him if he ever did that I'd throw a pig roast for him and invite the whole company. At company meetings each Friday, I used to rib Ken with updates on the pig's health, like 'The pig's getting fat' or 'The pig is not worried.'

"As for the bell, we ring it any time we get a new client or make a sale over $50,000. I hope I go home with a headache every night."

Rose escorts the visitors into the small conference room connected to his office. On the walls of the conference room are framed copies of the annual reports of dozens of Dataflex customers, all on the Fortune 500 list. He talks to his guests about Dataflex for five minutes.

Then Rose says, "Let me show you around."

He starts with the sales department, lingering by the board. Applause and the sounds of delight erupt in the corner of cubicles occupied by Katz and some of the women on her team. Katz has just won $11,000 from an IBM-funded contest for doing the most trade-ins during a ninety-day promotion. But instead of taking all the money for herself, she announces that she'll divvy it up among her team members—$1,000 for Christina Estok, her senior inside sales rep, and $500 apiece for the others. "You deserve this money," she says to the gang crowded around her desk.

Rose once commented that if you don't enjoy taking people on a tour of your company, something is seriously wrong. He learned the importance of company tours from Dennis Cagen, the founder of DJC. "We were a small company, but whenever clients would visit, Dennis showed them through our cramped offices as though he was ushering them through a palace," he recalled. "We only had eight offices, and he would spend fifteen minutes in one of them. He would be so cranked up talking about the company that by the end of the tour they were envisioning our future and how they could be a part of it. Dennis had effectively painted a picture of where we were going. That enthusiasm played an important role in propelling the company from $5 million to $50 million in the time I was there."

The maze of portable gray walls that form a network of cubicles makes you think of a honeycomb with busy bees swarming among the cells. Rose stops short at Constantino's cubicle, which has a pop-up scene of an unnamed Caribbean island. A small, thatched-roof building bears the sign Ken's Bar. A miniature hammock dangles languidly beneath two plastic palm trees. A tiny plastic beach ball that probably went with some kid's Barbie lies on the beach.

"This," announces Rose with a flourish, "is what gets Ken Constantino out of bed in the morning." At that moment, a bullet from a Nerf air gun whizzes by, barely missing one of the visitors. Rose doesn't flinch. He laughs and ignores the quizzical looks that pass among the three. "One of our associates, Jayne Banach-Walther, recently took up a collection and bought these Nerf air guns for whoever wanted one."

The thrill of not knowing what to expect is an integral part of the culture at Dataflex. Pranks and wisecracks are played out constantly against the pressure-cooker environment of sales. Banach-Walther, who has been selling for the company for less than a year, darts back in her cubicle, just missing being struck by a Nerf dart fired by Glen Koedding, a salesperson and the target of her wayward shot. In a dark, dress-for-success suit and with dark hair pulled back in a severe chignon, Banach-Walther makes a singularly unlikely Nerf sniper.

Rose leads his guests into the lunchroom and offers them coffee or soda. He keeps a running dialogue going while he dumps out coffee grinds and puts on a fresh pot of coffee. There is enough coffee to pour the two cups that are requested, but Rose doesn't like to leave the pot empty for the next person.

He moves on to the systems integration and product training and support departments, sprawled in an area equal to the floor space devoted to sales. One entire row of cubicles is filled with different computer systems that are set up so the specialists can quickly trace a customer's path and thus respond to questions more easily. "Our specialists provide the best support in the business," says Rose. Charts show that in the past month, customers who called in with a problem got a technician on the phone, rather than voice mail or a busy signal, 92.5 percent of the time. They were able to get their problems resolved within fifteen minutes 85 percent of the time. And no one called back with the same problem within that thirty-day period.

One man questions why he sees primarily Macintosh computers on desks throughout the company when Dataflex consistently wins awards as a reseller for IBM. "We use Macintosh because their ability to reproduce graphics and color was superior to IBM machines when we originally started writing this program," Rose answers. "IBM has now caught up, but we already bought the Macs."

As Rose strides ahead to the warehouse, the three guests murmur among themselves. They appear especially impressed by the technical support Dataflex supplies. A plaque memorializing Jimmy Seccafico, a warehouse manager who passed away in March 1988, hangs above a slot for a computerized security pass. Seccafico came with Rose from DJC without even asking what his new salary or his job would be.

The warehouse is swept clean, and one man whizzes by the visitors on a forklift. Well-muscled men in T-shirts and jeans greet Rose by his first name and go on about their business. Several of them are wearing Walkmans and nodding to the beat of their own private concerts. "This warehouse contains more than $15 million worth of equipment in any given day, and these are the people responsible for making sure it gets out to our clients correctly and on time," Rose explains, giving his guests time to observe the bustling activity.

In the next few minutes he breezes through the systems preparation, customer engineering, product repair, and marketing departments. He concludes the tour at the finance department, saying, "When I was a teenager, I raced motocross bikes. I was tinkering with my bike down at the track one day, debating whether I should add something else to it. An old-timer bent down next to me and said. 'If it doesn't make it go forward fast, don't put it on your bike.' Everybody here at Dataflex understands that principle. We don't make a move unless it will accomplish one of three things: decrease costs, increase revenues, or improve customer satisfaction. In other words, we don't want it on our bike unless it will help it go forward faster."

The company tour has taken exactly forty-five minutes. Rose bids the three visitors good-bye at the lobby, shedding his jacket and loosening his tie again as soon as they are out of sight.

ACTIONS

☑ Be willing to take chances.
☑ Don't just say you believe in people—show them.
☑ Don't mistake compliance for commitment.
☑ Treat people decently without any hidden agenda.
☑ Treat people as partners.

The secret is to make sure they don't have the same skill set you do because then you're just asking for a conflict. If you hire people who are good, leave them alone and let them do their job. Everything doesn't have to be discussed. If it comes down to a disagreement, always go with the manager you hired to make the decision.

I never cared about whether I personally got credit for being the best. I just cared about doing the best job, period. It became evident to me that the best way to accomplish that was to surround myself with talented people. Ultimately, I believe that together we produce something far better than if I had attempted to achieve my goal alone.

I wouldn't do homework by myself. Instead I would gather people together who had different sets of skills. One would be really creative, another a deductive thinker, another a comprehensive thinker, and another would have a photographic memory. We would study together, and collectively would be better at the subject than if we had studied alone.

☑ Measure what counts.

☑ Do it right the first time.

☑ Encourage people to stick up for themselves.

☑ Don't worry about jealousy in the ranks. The type of people who resent others' success won't stick around this kind of corporate culture long enough to merit your attention.

☑ Profits are the way to keep score.

☑ If you wouldn't be proud to have your best customer tour your company, there is a serious problem. Visitors should see not only what you do, but, more important, how happy the people are who do the jobs.

☑ Make sure you allow salespeople to do what they do best: *Sell!*

MORE ON TOP: TEAMS MANAGE THEMSELVES

- TOP trains people to become leaders. Although the salesperson often emerges as the group leader (because salespeople tend to be leaders in the first place), the title team leader may shift among team members. For example, an engineer may have 200 systems to prepare. He or she may assume the role of the team leader and call a meeting to discuss the task at hand and how to speed up the process.

- Teams become self-policing. They live and die as a unit. They examine their weakest links and give those members help. A team member who isn't pulling his or her weight can be thrown off the team, which effectively gives teams hiring and firing power. Only one person who has been thrown off a team has remained with the company. About 5 percent of team members have been terminated in this manner since TOP went into effect, and management does not interfere with this power.

- These teams are highly individualistic. No two operate alike. They are designed to service their set of customers' needs.

- Absenteeism has markedly decreased since TOP was instituted because associates know their teammates will have to pick up the slack.

2

Lead with Muddy Boots

It's lunchtime. At this time of day the kitchen area is filled with men and women from different departments throughout the company. It is also filled with laughter. The atmosphere is relaxed and casual. The smell of slightly burned microwave popcorn hangs in the air.

Rose heads for the kitchen, where a half-cheese, half-pepperoni pizza awaits him. He has no formal lunch plans, but he invites Kim Kenderes, a twenty-three-year-old former hairdresser who works in human resources, and Cindy Styron, a twenty-two-year-old administrative assistant, to sit down with him. They sit at one of a half dozen small tables at one end of the room. He exchanges pleasantries with the two young women who are perfectly at ease having lunch with the president of the company.

"Hey, Kim, do you have time to give me a trim after lunch?" Rose asks.

"Sure, Rick," she replies.

Always pragmatic, Rose encourages associates to go to Kenderes for haircuts, reasoning that it's that much less time he and others have to spend on errands. Besides, he says, she does a great job. In return, an associate will usually treat the young woman to lunch. In a conversation later, Kenderes expresses how amazed she was when Rose took the time to talk to her during the interviewing process three years before. "Here I was a hairdresser with no experience in the corporate world, and the president cared enough to talk to me about his company," she says softly.

Rose eats heartily, offering slices of pizza to anyone who he notices doesn't already have a packed lunch or something from one of the local fast-food places spread before them. Many associates bring their lunches from home and put them in the full-size refrigerator.

The lunchroom at Dataflex contains a scattering of tables and chairs and two vending machines. Kevin Denecour, one of the resident technical gurus, reprogrammed the soda machine's computerized message, which originally read "Have a nice day," to flash this message: "JWP, Computerland and Valcom suck canal water." A foosball table against the wall in the back of the room is a favorite diversion of some of the warehouse guys.

Two things make this common area different from that of many companies. One, the walls are covered with professionally framed collages of photos taken at the many company events that Dataflex sponsors. Dataflex spends about $30,000 a year on its summer Friday-afternoon barbecues, a day at the horse races, an evening at Atlantic City, and other events. That money comes from a pool made up of prize money awarded to the salespeople by various manufacturers.

The second thing you notice is how clean the place is, especially in light of the extensive use it gets. Several months before, Rose walked into the kitchen after lunch one day. He saw dirty mugs in the sink, empty sugar and Sweet'n'Low packets littering the counter, and an empty carton sitting in a small puddle of milk. He spent several minutes cleaning up the mess.

At the next company meeting, Rose said, "The kitchen in this place is disgusting. You wouldn't treat your own home this way. Don't treat Dataflex like this. Have respect for your co-workers."

One of the talents that makes Rose a great leader is his ability to hone in on the big picture. But, although he doesn't get bogged down in niggling details, he recognizes the ones that can distort the picture and signal a looming larger problem. Despite the fact that he describes himself as a disorganized person, order and neatness rank high with him. And what he saw in the kitchen that day disquieted him. It wasn't about a couple of empty sugar packets. It meant a lack of caring.

Rose asked Massimo to have homey aphorisms from Robert Fulghum's *Everything I Needed to Know in Life I Learned in Kindergarten* blown up and put on the walls of the lunchroom. Signs exhort associates to Play Fair, No Hitting, Share Everything, and Clean Up Your Own Mess. The counter and tabletops are always clean now.

Dataflex reflects Rose's belief that work should be fun. Although the place is frenetic, it is also friendly. The heart of his business philosophy is simple: Treat people decently for the sake of treating people decently—whether they are customers, vendors, or associates.

RICK ROSE: There's no such thing as Dataflex. It doesn't do anything. The associates who work here do. That's why you have to put individuals first. I take a personal responsibility for the 200 families of the people who work here. Ultimately, my job is to make sure everyone is treated decently. That goes way beyond the profits and awards this company achieves. Those tangible measures of success are secondary to whether people are treated decently. My goal is to provide an environment where people look forward to coming to work. These should be the best eight hours of the day, not the worst.

When I joined the David Jamison Carlyle Corporation in 1979 as its vice president of sales, one of the first things I noticed was that the founder, Dennis Cagen, hired people for their expertise and then let them do their jobs. The culture he established was based on friendship and mutual trust. It was a small company, and Cagen went out of his way to make sure everyone was equally appreciated for his or her contributions. Titles were for outsiders. People worked hard to take the company from $5 million to $50 million in sales in four years because they felt they were a part of the team.

I follow Dennis's example at Dataflex. No one person is more important than another here. We just have different skills. People get paid different salaries based on the laws of supply and demand. But we strive to help everybody believe that his or her contribution is important. Harmony must be pervasive for a company to thrive. We have titles here only so that people on the outside know what our job functions are. Within these walls, I'm just Rick. We call each other by our first names. It's a small thing, but it sends the message that we're all just people. I'm nobody special because I'm the president. In the military, people salute the uniform, not the individual. Here we want people to respect the individual.

One day I asked one of my salespeople to check on an account. He immediately said he'd have his sales assistant do it. There was something in his tone that made me wonder about his treatment of those around him. So I watched the way he spoke to the support people. Sure enough, he was bossing people around with a superior edge to his voice. I told him, "You can't talk to people like that. She's helping you out, not the other way around. All you're accomplishing is making people want to spit in your eye." He didn't change his behavior, and he's no longer part of the company.

At Dataflex, inflated egos aren't rewarded with fancy offices, preferential treatment, and deference from subordinates. We don't refer to people as employees because the word has taken on a cold connotation. We chose the word associates to describe the people who work here because we're proud that they've chosen to be associated with Dataflex.

I have always made every business decision by asking myself: If the situation were reversed, would that person do it for me? If the answer is yes, then I do it. Once people see that you consistently deal with them in a fair manner—of course, you want fairness for yourself—the tension of the workplace melts away. They don't have to be guarding their own interests. Instead they can channel that energy into the pursuit of making the company thrive.

Most people don't make decisions that way. They have the paranoid view that people are out to get them. Actually, in the face of layoffs and at a time when CEOs are taking home huge checks while their companies are going down the tubes, that view is the norm. But if you want harmony, it can't be you or me. It has to be us.

I've loaned money to people in this company personally. I knew that they were having trouble with their car or paying off a bill, and I'd offer to help out. Sometimes I knew that I'd probably never see my money again. In some cases people left the company owing me money. Others would say, "I can't believe you did this."

"Why?" I'd ask.

"People are taking advantage of you."

My response: "You're absolutely right."

You have to make a choice. During the course of business, people are going to take advantage of you. There's no question about it. But if you choose to live your career protected, anticipating that a few people are out to get you, you'll miss out. There will be far more wonderful opportunities if you choose to trust than if you concentrate your energies on avoiding getting nailed.

Every business person has to choose whether to be fair and share the wealth. I want people to participate in the prosperous nature of this business.

The final arbiter in this process is your own reflection in the mirror. Whatever you do during the course of the day should be based on a simple question: Is this the right thing to do? For the customer? For myself? For the company? For my family? I mention the latter because ethics aren't something you can turn off and on like a faucet. Your code of honor is who you are on the job and at home.

Rose takes only about twenty minutes for lunch and then goes back into his office, leaving the door open behind him. He checks his voice mail and finds an urgent message from Ken Constantino. Rose calls him promptly to let him know he's back. Five seconds later, Constantino is at the door and says, "Rick, we've got a problem. Remember that half a million dollar order? Now the client is insisting that we deliver an upgraded machine since the other systems are still on back order. I just can't believe he's pulling this stunt."

The customer in question had given Constantino a purchase order for 100 systems on a particular date to take advantage of a manufacturer's rebate before it expired. However, the customer actually didn't need the systems until several months down the road. The salesman was up front about the fact that the systems wouldn't be delivered for a few months because the manufacturer had them on back order. The customer assured him that it was no problem, saying he didn't need the systems right away.

The ink was barely dry on the contracts, however, when the customer started making noises about wanting the product deliv-

ered pronto. First, he threatened to cancel the order. Then he insinuated that Constantino and Dataflex had failed to live up to their
promises. What he was demanding now would mean a $40,000 loss
on the order for Dataflex. Giving in to his demands for a more
expensive system would also take about a $4,000 chunk out of
Constantino's commissions, not to mention the hit on his team's
all-important SG & A (sales general and administrative expenses).
The kicker was that Constantino had gone all out for the account.
And by this point he knew beyond the shadow of a doubt that this
customer wouldn't give Dataflex repeat business.

Constantino, his brow deeply furrowed as it always is when he's
under pressure, is seething with frustration and the sick feeling that
comes when you know you're getting the shaft on a deal. Rose's
eyes narrow to a squint as he listens intently. Gradually the heat
rises in his face, and his jaw sets. He is absolutely livid about the
latest twist in the plot.

But Rose thrives under pressure. The hotter it is, the better he
likes it. The words are barely out of Constantino's mouth before he
swings into action. First, Rose makes another call to the manufacturer. Constantino has been in almost constant contact with the
supplier since he realized what the customer was up to. But the
manufacturer claimed it couldn't deliver the systems any faster. On
this day, Rose goes straight to the top, explaining the bind Dataflex
is in and asking for help. Still, the manufacturer says it can't break
the logjam that is delaying the order.

Pacing the small expanse behind his desk, with his hands jammed
in his pockets, Rose pauses long enough to punch the automatic
dialer and calls Dataflex's lawyer. When he gets the lawyer on the
speaker phone, Rose does his own dramatic interpretation, complete with hand gestures, of the events of the past few months. He
does all the parts, including Constantino's, as he's relating the story:
"And so the customer said to us, "If you can't deliver that product,
you deliver the next most expensive product and you eat it. You
made a deal with me."

For the next hour the three men discuss the options. Much of the
time Rose spends venting his wrath. Finally, he terminates the call
and plops down in the chair on the other side of his desk, beside
the one Constantino is occupying.

"You know what," he says. "We could tell these people just to forget it because there's nothing in it for us." His words hang in the air, but Constantino doesn't answer because he senses something else is coming.

"But," Rose says, pausing for impact, "is that treating people with integrity and sincerity? We made a deal, and the deal wasn't ever contingent on them continuing to do business with us. This decision is going to cost us $40,000, but we'll just have to eat it. We owe them the delivery of the next most expensive product.

"We will do what is right. The fact that they do not extend us the same courtesy isn't any reason to reject our basic beliefs."

Constantino slowly nods his head in affirmation.

Not sure that Constantino is quite sold yet, Rose's resolve stiffens and he adds, "We're not trying to be the cream of the crud around here; we're trying to be the cream of the crop."

Constantino laughs for the first time in an hour and says, "Thanks, Rick." He is still rankled over the whole deal, yet when he walks back to his desk he feels lighter somehow.

He sits down at his cubicle and his phone rings. It's Rose. "Hey, Ken. I just thought you'd like to know I've got two eighty-five-pound pigs on order for your pig roast."

That afternoon was a turning point for Rose. "It made me take a look at these basic beliefs that hang on the wall, and it reconfirmed that nothing would ever separate us from them," he reflects.

Dataflex's basic beliefs are:

- People are entitled to an excellent working environment.
- Customers deserve to be treated with sincerity and integrity.
- We want to be the best company we can be.

Rose continues: "If I hadn't stuck to my guns, Ken would have gotten the message that our basic beliefs applied only when it was convenient. Treat customers with sincerity and integrity is number 2 on the list. Basic beliefs cannot be conditional. They are the fiber from which our company is woven.

"But everybody has to believe them. In most companies, the average worker doesn't have the foggiest idea what those basic beliefs are and how they pertain to him or her. Worse, the worker sees contradictions and hypocritical actions day in and day out. It comes down to taking a stand: You either walk the walk or you don't."

Rose readily admits that in that situation his ultimate decision to stand true to his creed was a real struggle. His first impulse was to attack. Intensely competitive and quick tempered, he constantly battles the desire to shoot first and ask questions later. Occasionally he loses the internal battle and fires off a few shots. When he first came to Dataflex, he used to take out quite a few innocent bystanders along with his intended target, say those close to him. But he has largely learned to control his trigger-happy self. And, to his credit, as quick as he is to anger, he's also become quick to apologize.

"I have a tendency to be like George Carlin," Rose laughs. "He says, 'Anybody going faster than me is a maniac, and anybody going slower than me is a jerk.'"

In an executive meeting recently, Rose chastised the vice president of customer engineering, Peter Galati, for allowing his engineers to get into selling situations. Later in the meeting, the discussion was on the need to turn away small business that was administratively intensive but unprofitable. Rose cracked, "Why don't we just send some of Galati's people out there with the contracts. There's no way they will ever do business with us then."

"Hey, I don't appreciate that," Galati said.

Rose whirled on him and said, "You know what I don't appreciate? Having something I have specifically asked to be stopped keep happening over and over again."

After the meeting, Galati confronted Rose about the remark. "I don't mind if you tease me, but other people may construe that I have a bunch of knuckleheads in my department, and that isn't true," the manager said.

"You are absolutely right," said Rose. "And I will publicly apologize at the next executive meeting."

Rose is hard on himself, constantly looking for ways to improve his leadership and managerial skills. He seeks feedback from his associates daily, and what separates him from many leaders is that he listens and sincerely tries to change his actions. About once a month, he holds what he calls the president's luncheon. He randomly selects several associates in the company and invites them to have lunch with him in the conference room.

During one of these lunches, Rose tossed out a general question about whether there was anything he could do to make life better at Dataflex. Veronica Cassiba, a credit analyst in the finance department, spoke up: "I hate it when you joke about the finance department being the dungeon. I understand that we're quiet, and we're kind of looked at like the bookworms of this place. But I think that nickname makes the stereotype worse and divides us from the rest of the company.

"And another thing that bugs me is that you don't spend any time in our department. You make a beeline for Gordon's office, and that's it. It would mean a lot if you could come by every once in a while."

Cassiba was floored the next day when he marched into the department. "He started jumping up and down like some kind of nut and then went around sitting in people's laps and cutting up with everybody," she says. "Since then he walks through regularly and talks with us. It may seem like a small thing, but it's given the whole department such a boost."

As hard as Rose is on himself, he expects the same from his associates: "My father always said to me, 'Don't do anything to embarrass this family.' It wasn't: Don't embarrass yourself. In other words, I was a representative of my brothers and my sisters and my parents and my grandparents, my cousins, my religious affiliation, and my high school.

"We must first recognize the chords of our interdependence before we can achieve harmony with those around us. What my father was saying was, 'Don't take that connection lightly.' What you represent is far more than yourself as an individual.

"That realization delivers a heavy sense of responsibility. You can't be a loose cannon out there. The only plea I make to our associates is: 'Please, don't embarrass this company.' "

He offers this example: "Early in his career, Alan Fendrick was asked by a customer to take a return, which would mean a $3,000 loss. That's a costly thing for our company because we can't resell the systems once they've been in place. Alan exploded in anger and behaved inappropriately.

"Afterward, I explained how he could have gotten some marketing mileage out of the situation if he had let the customer know that it was going to cost the company time and money, but that he would do it for them. He would have saved himself the embarrassment of the outburst, and he might have saved the account. The outcome would have been the same monetarily; we lost money on the deal either way. But, in that instance, we lost more than that: The Dataflex name was harmed.

"Salespeople are in contact with people all day long. You can't control what they do or say out in the field. But you can teach them to remember not to embarrass the company."

Like any company, Dataflex has its own set of rules, its own standards. "We spent about six months in 1988 discussing all the various things that we thought this company stood for. This need was brought to our attention by our consultants who asked: What are you trying to do or say here? What do you stand for?

"We looked at different options and talked about not only what Dataflex was, but what it wasn't. One of our basic beliefs is that customers are to be treated with sincerity and integrity. That does not mean that people can take advantage of this organization by demanding that we provide services and products that are not profitable.

"Our salvation is that we know who we are and we know who we aren't."

Once the executive committee decided on the basic beliefs, it set out to communicate them and get people to buy into them. "We review our basic beliefs with everyone in this company at least once a year and at every management meeting, which we hold four times a year. People are taught the basic beliefs of Dataflex when they come on board the company.

"We ask ourselves, 'Do these still hold true or have they changed?' I don't know how I would explain that we've decided not to treat people with sincerity and integrity." He laughs at the absurdity of the thought and then plunges ahead: "The point is that these beliefs don't have to be set in concrete. However, most of our beliefs are based on values that have survived many civilizations."

Rose asserts that most companies fail miserably in communicating their beliefs to their workers. Part of the failure stems from the fact that management rarely takes the time to get associates involved in the early stages, he says. "Our mission statement declares that 'this is what we want to be when we grow up.' That statement comes from the individuals who work here. It's not just something I dreamed up. Too many companies spend time and energy designing a mission statement, but then top management is the only group that really believes it.

"In many companies, a group called the board of directors gets together and comes up with a mission statement over some period of time. I've heard of it taking six or seven years to devise companies' basic beliefs. They put down these wise and almost overwhelming statements about the mission and community service. Then they tack the mission statement up on bulletin boards and people are supposed to respond.

"We don't relegate our basic beliefs to a few bulletin boards. We've plastered them prominently all over the walls. Our associates shouldn't have to think too hard to be able to recall them. We routinely have buttons printed up with key phrases that serve as reminders of our basic beliefs. For instance, we have one button that simply has the word *the* printed on it to remind people of our mission statement. Another button says '110% or bust.' I wear these buttons, and so does everyone on the Dataflex team."

Assuming the mission statement is clear in your company, Rose offers this advice: "After you've communicated your basic beliefs effectively, encourage your staff to be open if they disagree with anything. We tell people to give managers the courtesy of going to them directly and confronting any differences of opinion head-on.

"If it's not resolved, both parties go to the next level of manager, and they can take it before the board of directors if they want to. If a person feels so strongly about something that he or she no longer looks forward to coming to work, we want to get it changed. And if the person can't get it changed, it means that person has a basic philosophical clash with the management of this company. At that point the person should go work somewhere else where his or her philosophy is in harmony with the company's philosophies.

"Your mission statement is crucial to establishing a path to greatness. Otherwise, you'll find yourself and those around you wandering. If you don't know where you're going, any road will get you there."

It's 2:30 P.M., and Massimo ushers Joe Spencer, a senior partner of Price Waterhouse, into Rose's office. As a public company, every year Dataflex goes through a detailed audit with Price Waterhouse, one of the Big Six accounting firms. On behalf of his firm, Spencer signs the audit statements vouching for the accuracy of Dataflex's statements. He hands six crisp dollar bills to Rose. There are questions written in neat script on each one of them. "What are you doing?" asks Rose.

"I heard from Gordon that for one dollar you'll tell anybody the truth, and I have six questions for you," Spencer answers.

"You're kidding."

"No, and the first question is: There's a loan on the books to you, Gordon, and Jeff from the company. Do you really intend to pay it back, or are you just going to bonus yourselves the money at some point? I gave you my dollar, so I want my answer."

Rose laughs with delight and replies, "We fully intend to pay back that loan, and it would be unfair to have the company bonus us the money."

"Fair enough," says Spencer. "What do you see for fiscal 1992 gross profits and pretax profits?" Rose answers that question and the remaining four.

When Spencer finishes the last question, he comments, "This is the easiest I've ever had it. I wish all my clients had such an approach."

It's 3 P.M. Rose walks with Spencer to the lobby and says goodbye. Nancy Rotundo, a sales administrator, is watching her tiny, redheaded daughter Stephanie take a few wobbly steps. Her husband brought the child to the office because these steps are a first, and he wanted to share the excitement. The president pauses to applaud the one-year-old's efforts, kneeling down to her level.

Rose loves children. For years he coached Little League football. The walls of his office are literally covered with photos of his three sons: Scott, 20; John, 7; and Charlie, 5. In the center of one collection is a photo of Rose and his wife, Linda, a pretty brunette with laughing brown eyes. The couple looks relaxed and happy. Wayne Isbitski, director of systems integration, took the picture at an associate's wedding and gave it to Rose as a gift.

Most of the photos of his children were taken by Rose. "I had a lot more up in my old office," he told me one day. "But the decorator who did this office said she thought it was too much." Rose prides himself on hiring professionals and then trusting them to do their jobs. But in this case, he put his foot down. They wound up compromising. Rose kept most of the pictures up, but he agreed to get them professionally framed and let the decorator do the arrangement.

The decorator was brought in at Liz Massimo's insistence. Liz says, laughing, "It wasn't until Tim Mannix was hired and he ordered new furniture that I convinced Rick to get some. He doesn't really care about that sort of thing. He would have been content with the banged-up old furniture from the old office."

Rose relies heavily on Massimo, who started at Dataflex as the receptionist a few weeks before his arrival, to attend to the details of his life. She confides that when he first asked her to be his assistant, she turned him down flat. Then she says, "It took him two weeks to wear me down before I agreed."

As assistant to the president, she organizes the many special events sponsored by the company, keeps Rose's calendar, and handles the bulk of his correspondence and all his files. She also straightens his desk each night. As part of managing the office of the president, Massimo, in her mid-forties, manages the ten people who provide administrative support for the entire company. At Rose's urging, Massimo, a Brooklyn native who married her high school beau and promptly had two children, takes classes at night toward a college degree in psychology. "Rick pushes you to do things you never expected to do," she says. "You may not always agree with his tactics, but he gets results. He's a big, tough guy, but he sincerely cares. Between appointments he goes around socializing, and I can tell by the noise level what part of the company he is visiting." Massimo teases Rose that she chose psychology as her major so she can understand him better. Massimo shares Rose's love of sales. She sold Amway for seven years and was an Avon representative for nine years. In 1982 she was named the number one Avon sales representative in a district of 6,000 reps.

Rose frequently bellows Massimo's name across the hall to her office. Recently, Joe Rizzo, the vice president of corporate marketing, presented him with a bull horn with a note that said he was tired of hearing him yell. Rose taped a small sign on it that says Voice Mail and uses it.

At exactly 5:30 P.M. Rose leaves his office and walks out the side exit, saying goodnight to the handful of associates who have gathered outside to take a smoke. (Smoking is not allowed inside Dataflex.)

Gordon McLenithan, Peter Galati, and several other people from the customer engineering department are standing in the parking lot, waiting for a few stragglers before they leave for dinner. McLenithan, who is responsible for 120 out of the 200 associates at Dataflex, is taking the customer engineering department out to dinner tonight to congratulate them on their excellent customer response times. He often treats entire departments to a night out.

"Have a great time," says Rose, as he climbs into his black Lexus (the license plate is DFLX, the company's ticker symbol) and puts on his seat belt. He pops in a compact disc for the forty-five-minute ride to his house in Rumson, New Jersey.

The house was a standard colonial when the Roses purchased it three years ago. But during that time it has undergone a complete transformation: The style is now English country, and the Roses have almost doubled the house's size to six bedrooms. Last summer they added a pool. Linda Rose laughs and says, "Dealing with the contractors is practically a full-time job." Rose likes change no matter where he is, and the house reflects his and Linda's need to improve things constantly.

Rose, whose taste in music ranges from jazz to country rock, likes his music loud. Today he is listening to Eric Clapton's *Wonderful Tonight,* recorded live, a compact disc that his son Scott, who attends Union College in Schenectady, New York, gave him for his birthday.

The parking lot is still more than half full even though quitting time is officially 5 P.M. Although like most of corporate America,

Dataflex's declared hours are 9 A.M. to 5 P.M., associates' work schedules are flexible. If a team completes its work early, it's not uncommon for the team leader to call it quits at 3 P.M. or so. Rose may be a stickler about punctuality, but he's not a clock watcher. There are no time clocks at Dataflex. Rose doesn't care what hours an associate keeps, as long as the person keeps his or her commitment to the company.

"The Marine Corps is known for its effectiveness and efficiency," Rose declares. "In the Marines when you get a job done, you get the day off. In other branches of service, when you get the job done, you get another job."

Rose and McLenithan agreed about two years ago to stop putting in sixteen-hour days and to cut out coming to the office on weekends (although Rose says he suspects McLenithan still comes in on Saturdays sometimes, and the CFO confirms it with a smile.) "It was a question of quality of life," says Rose. "We could be here twenty-four hours a day, but at some point your efficiency diminishes. Besides, after spending half my life on a plane during all those years as a salesman, I wanted to have more time at home with my wife and kids."

Since Rose goes to the office so early, he has no qualms about calling it a day at a reasonable hour. Still, he rarely leaves this early, but tonight is special. Maurice Scaglione, one of the salesmen, is coming to dinner at 7 P.M. For Christmas each year Linda Rose gives Scaglione a coupon good for "one eight-pound leg of lamb dinner with Rick, redeemable with five working days' notice."

That night at dinner the conversation focuses on travel and gourmet cooking, passions of both men. Rose shares his secret for roasting garlic with his guest. When associates come to Rose's house, the topic of Dataflex doesn't come up much. But toward the end of the meal, Rose asks Scaglione what his goals are.

"Actually, Rick, I want your job," Scaglione says cooly. He is dark haired, five feet nine inches tall and often wears his white Dataflex jacket emblazoned with "the wheel," an emblem used in company advertisements and promotions to communicate Dataflex's different services visually. Scaglione proudly wears the garment the way an athlete shows off a letter jacket. (See the Dataflex Wheel below.)

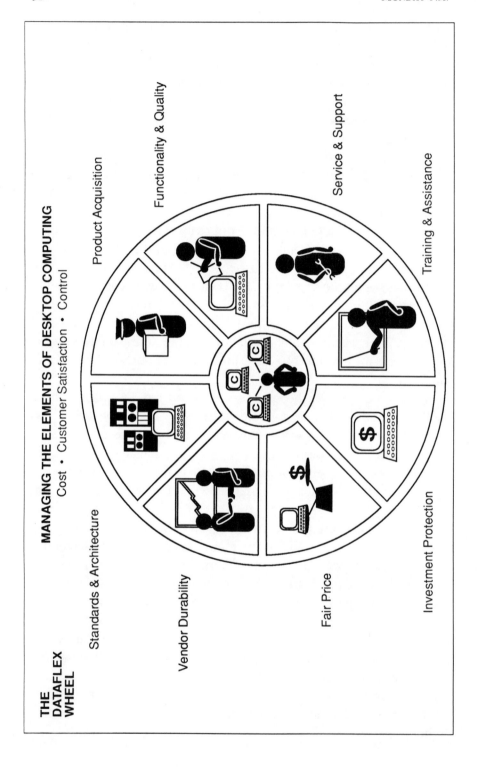

Like Rose, Scaglione has an intense desire to improve himself. When he first came to Dataflex five years ago as a salesman, his peers told him during one of the pond-scum meetings that his voice was weak and grating. Fendrick told him that he sounded miserable on the telephone and that he'd never make it at the company. The next week he hired Liz Dixon, one of the top voice coaches in New York City, and paid seventy dollars an hour to achieve the pleasant voice he now has.

Scaglione, who has supported himself since he was thirteen years old, also shares Rose's competitive nature. At NCR Corporation, he was considered one of the top experts in the nation on the company's distribution software. His nickname was Database, and the young man thrived on the recognition.

At Dataflex, he was just another sales rookie, albeit the first true techie on the sales team. And after his first ninety days at Dataflex without a sale, he couldn't take the internal pressure and resigned. Rose told him to take the rest of the day off to think about it. While he was out, a company he had been prospecting called to place an order. Diane Katz took the call for him. That client was Consolidated Railroad. The next morning when Scaglione arrived for the morning meeting, Rose handed him a $100 bill in recognition of his first sale. With that $100, sales reps were traditionally expected to buy pizza for everyone. Scaglione, who always likes to put his own stamp on things, bought not only pizza, but several cases of soda, too. The Consolidated Railroad account has since brought in about $10 million in revenues for Dataflex.

Rose stops chewing his lamb and grins: "So, are you planning to bump me off, or do you have another idea?"

Scaglione, who came to Dataflex in April 1988 at age twenty-three, has from the moment he arrived talked of wanting to make his own mark. And he's not content with his berth among the top four salespeople each month. He wants to be the unquestionable top dog, and he's tortured by the knowledge that Fendrick and Katz have too big a lead on him in Edison. For the past two years he has wrestled with his need to prove his mettle and his fierce loyalty to Dataflex and Rose. Scaglione's father died when he was young, and Rose is the male role model Scaglione never had.

Scaglione straightens his glasses and then says, "Rick, you keep saying you'd like to open a Dataflex office in Connecticut someday.

Well, I think that day has come. I want to help head up that office.
I'd have a great chance to test my skills as a leader. And I could bring
the spirit of Dataflex to that location. Besides, I have fallen in love
with someone up there, and our relationship would have a better
chance of progressing if we lived in the same state."

Rose doesn't look up from his plate. "Sounds reasonable to me."

"So what do you think?" Scaglione asks.

"We'll start the ball rolling tomorrow. Anything else I can do for
you, Mo?" Rose asks, using the affectionate nickname he has given
the young man.

"That's it for now, Rick."

ACTIONS

- ☑ If you want to know what's really going on in your company, make yourself accessible to people.
- ☑ People are entitled to an excellent working environment.
- ☑ Customers deserve to be treated with sincerity and integ-
  rity—even when they aren't acting that way.
- ☑ Basic beliefs have to be believed. Ask yourself: What are the
  core values that you want for your company? More impor-
  tant, do you really believe them? Can you communicate
  them? And will people buy into them?
- ☑ You have to walk the walk, not just talk the talk.
- ☑ Don't embarrass the company.
- ☑ Make dreams come true whenever you possibly can.

SEEK HARMONY, NOT DOMINANCE

How can you tell if you are moving toward harmony? How do you treat
the newest members carved on the totem pole? Some of our new hires
are eighteen years old, fresh out of high school. How would you react
if some young whippersnapper started making suggestions a few days
after being hired?

We love it. In fact, the best ideas come from people who join our
company and have the guts to speak up within the first thirty days.
That's why I personally sit down with new associates and ask them for
their help. I explain that we suffer from a malady called inbreeding, and
they are the cure.

The second week Maurice Scaglione was with the company, he was working in the warehouse as part of the training we instituted to help people empathize with other people's work loads. One of the things that caught his attention was the fact that we filed our pickups for the United Parcel Service manually. At the end of the day, Maurice came to me with five suggestions. From working at NCR Corporation selling high-end distribution software, he knew about an automated UPS system that would save our company thousands of dollars. We did a study on it and bought the machine.

He commented on the less-than-professional image conveyed by our hand-cut packing slips sent out with our hardware. In the sales class we designed a new slip that is still being used. Scaglione also noted the dead inventory in the warehouse and suggested that a stagnant-inventory report be given to the sales staff. Now on a quarterly basis, Rich Dressler, vice president of materials management, puts together the report, so the salespeople can deplete the older items. Thanks to this program, only about 1.5 percent of the inventory we have in the warehouse is slow moving, according to Dressler. With new models and new technology constantly being introduced, being caught with the old stuff can be a killer. We have heard of competitors who have as much as 10 percent of their inventory classified as dead.

We practically force people to talk. This business is constantly changing, and we need new blood. But if we don't glean the fresh insights immediately, no matter how hard we try, the set of principles under which we work tend to creep in. People start to think, "I love it here so much, everything Dataflex does must be correct." And it's far from correct.

Think about how many times you've heard managers make statements similar to these:

- That's just the way it's going to be.
- It's my way or the highway.
- No one's paying you to think.
- Your idea is no good, but I can't tell you why it's no good.

Sound familiar? If people in your organization are regularly making these kinds of statements, they are brutalizing people.

Forging a relationship of equality is the only answer. When a subordinate relationship is set up, both parties are cheated: The subordinate person is frustrated, and the dominant person is not living in reality because he's surrounded himself with people who are afraid to tell him the truth. These kinds of relationships aren't rewarding in either case.

3

How to Pick a Racehorse and Keep It from Being Tied to a Plow

Maura White, the new director of sales, is standing at the board this morning. More than two-thirds of the chairs around the conference table are full. "The word for the day is *innumerate,*" she announces. "Can anyone use it in a sentence?"

Whippet thin at five feet four inches tall, White has short, brown hair and sharp features. She stands ramrod straight, poised by the board, grease pencil in hand. Like Mannix, she is an ex-IBMer. In her first three years at Big Blue she was ranked in the top three of all sales people nationwide. White, who went to IBM at age twenty-four, spent ten years of her career there, achieving four promotions. Her last position at IBM was as its consulting marketing representative to Dataflex.

After a year of working closely with Dataflex, during which time she had her first child, Casey, she knew she'd found her next challenge: to step into Rose's shoes as sales manager. Convincing the three amigos that she was the person for the job was another matter. A graduate of Pennsylvania's Bucknell University with a double major in music and business, White watched from a distance

63

as they interviewed several other candidates over a three-month period in early 1991, before finally coming back to her with an offer in May. Their hesitancy had nothing to do with her abilities and everything to do with the knowledge that whoever stepped into the role that Rose had molded to himself would have a monumental task ahead.

Rose, sprawling in a chair near the head of the table, replies to her question, "I think that it is the setting up of sequences. 'When you enumerate, it's a sequence of priorities.' "

"No," says White, "that's a different word. The definition of this one is negative. It's 'marked by an ignorance of mathematics and of the scientific approach.' "

Maurice Scaglione, who slightly resembles Microsoft billionaire Bill Gates, shoves his glasses back on the bridge of his nose and gives this answer: "One would get the impression that our competition is innumerate when it comes to market share and profit." Everyone laughs.

Next, White introduces Nick Corcodilos. Corcodilos represents a new era for Dataflex. First, he is the only sales person who wasn't hired personally by Rose—White has taken over that responsibility—and, second, unlike all but one other salesperson in the room, he has had several years of computer-selling experience. He worked for Clancy-Paul/Valcom Mid-Atlantic for four years and before that as a headhunter for positions in computer engineering in Silicon Valley.

About five feet seven inches tall, Corcodilos, aged thirty-seven, has short, curly, dark hair and a small mustache. His wire-rimmed glasses give him a professorial air. His nails are perfectly trimmed, and, like most people on their first day, he is slightly more dressed up than anyone else in the room. He appears good-natured and laughs when someone promptly nicknames him Crocodile. But he shares that same intensity that marks all ten of the salespeople at Dataflex.

To begin the class this morning, a vendor comes in to talk about his product, but the man can't begin to answer the questions the group asks. Even the basics seem to elude him. Of course, he's facing a tough audience that spends several hours each week working on presentation skills. After the salesman leaves, Rose bursts out: "What a waste of time. That guy couldn't even answer simple questions about his company's financial position. He did not even know what Dataflex does. I sat here for twenty minutes, and I got about thirty seconds worth of information on his product. I almost walked out, but I kept thinking he'd get to the meat of his presentation.

"Meetings are too valuable to spend time listening to someone who obviously hasn't done his homework. People should come in, make an effective presentation, and get out."

The convivial atmosphere typical of the early part of the meetings returns when White asks the group to nominate two people to send on a trip to the Tour de France. The sales department won the trip from Pacific Data Products for selling the most font cartridges during a two-month period. The salespeople follow the example of Rose and McLenithan who eschew taking such gifts for themselves, preferring to pass them on to their associates as bonuses to show their appreciation. In the past year or so, the sales staff has given away a cruise to the Bahamas, a Windjammer cruise to the Caribbean, and several trips to Cancun to associates in positions from the warehouse to product training and support to administrative support.

When a salesperson nominates someone, he or she has to give the reason the person deserves the trip. Two women who are accounts-payable administrators, Terry Pallosi and Donna DeVito, come up winners. "If our customers don't get billed correctly, nothing else matters," says Diane Katz.

Like many of the sales meetings, the agenda includes reading and discussing several passages of a book. You can often tell which book is being scrutinized by listening to the salespeople talk. During the weeks Stephen R. Covey's *The Seven Habits of Highly Effective People* was being discussed, their speech was littered with phrases like *emotional bank account, win/win,* and *identifying your center.*

Today the book that will be spotlighted is *The Age of Unreason* by Charles Handy.

White gives a brief synopsis of the book, stating that she hopes it will make the class think about change. She begins reading from the first chapter, entitled "The Argument":

The scene was the General Synod of the Church of England in the 1980s. The topic being debated was the controversial proposition that women be admitted to the priesthood. A speaker from the floor spoke with passion. "In this matter," he cried, "as in so much else in our great country, why cannot the status quo be the way forward?"

It was the heartfelt plea, not only of the traditionalists in the church, but of those in power, anywhere, throughout the ages. If change there has to be, let it be gradual, continuous change. That way, the cynics might observe, nothing changes very much.

Continuous change is comfortable change. The path is then the guide to the future. An American friend, visiting Britain and Europe for the first time wondered, "Why is it that over here whenever I ask the reason for anything, any institution or ceremony or set of rules, they always give me a historical answer, 'because'; whereas in my country we always want a functional answer, 'in order.' " Europeans, I suggested, look backward to the best of their history and change as little as they may; Americans look forward and want to change as much as they can.

Circumstances do, however, combine occasionally to discomfort the advocates of the status quo. Wars, of course, are the great discomforters, but so is technology, when it takes one of its leaps forward as it did in the Industrial Revolution; so is demography, when it throws up baby booms or busts; so is a changing set of values, like that which occurred during the student unrest in 1968, and so are economics.

Circumstances are now once again, I believe, combining in curious ways. Change is not what it used to be. The status quo will no longer be the best way forward. The best way will be less comfortable and less easy, but no doubt more interesting—a word we often use to signal an uncertain mix of danger and opportunity. If we wish to enjoy more of the opportunity and less of the risk, we need to understand the changes better. Those who know why changes come waste less effort in protecting themselves or in fighting the inevitable. Those who realize where changes are heading are better able to use those changes to their own advantage. The society which welcomes change can use that change instead of just reacting to it.

There is a slight pause when she finishes and Rose then says, "The main goal that I have for Dataflex Corporation in this fiscal year is to prepare the company to expect change. If we welcome change and are not afraid of change, then when change comes, we'll just do what we have to do. The British writer views Americans as this unbelievably spontaneous group who want change. From his perspective, I would agree.

"As an American in this company, I know there is such a resistance to change that it took us over two years to talk about what we deem painful. Think of the wars that we went through trying to believe that our salespeople could sell services and not just rely on hardware."

Then he prods, a slight edge of irritation in his voice, "Why has no one in this room applied for other jobs within the company? Why hasn't someone formed a team that is so excellent that other salespeople will want to use it? You are highly resistant to changing anything." His eyes sweep the room expectantly, almost as though he thinks someone will jump up and ask to be shifted to another department.

Mannix, sitting at the opposite end of the table, says, "It's human nature to be resistant to any type of change, no matter how good or bad it may seem. A wall comes down in Europe, and you still have people out there saying, 'I wish the wall was back up because I'm afraid of what may happen.' "

Diane Katz says, "What everybody does is look at what they're successful at and then look ahead and say, 'Well, chances are that if I keep doing those same things, I'll continue to be successful. If I change, there's a chance that I may not.' "

"Realistically," Rose says, "there are people sitting in this room who are not going to be that successful in their sales careers. Not everybody is a star! Yet I wonder how many times the alternative of doing something different within this company, which may be far more satisfying, occurs to you. Having been a salesman myself, I know that there were times that I was very uncomfortable selling all the time. Yet I did not have the guts to try something else.

"You may be thinking, 'Compared to Maria, our receptionist, who answers the phone out there, we're really ambitious.' And I will make a case that she is much more willing to change and take risks than are the majority of the people in this room. She left being a homemaker to come back into the work force, wanted to work part time, has accepted a full-time position, and has taken on more and more responsibility."

White jumps in, "Change is a survival tactic. We're not going to have a choice. Those who don't like being the instigators of change are going to be left behind."

Change is a critical topic at Dataflex. Its industry is still young. The company itself has seesawed between selling hardware and selling services. It is also grappling with rapid growth, having hired more than 100 people in two years. But Rose knows that no matter what, human nature causes people to seek comfort zones. And although the topics he pegs the meetings upon are important, Rose's primary goal is to shake the participants out of their comfort zones, in his own words, "to teach people to stick up for themselves." That's why, on occasion, he unleashes his aggressive nature in these meetings because he says, "They aren't ever going to face a customer tougher than me. If they can stand up to my point of view in these meetings, I know they'll do fine on a sales call."

The president cups his hands behind his head and cocks back in his chair: "I've been having these meetings for about seventeen years, and we've been having them here for eight years, and they haven't changed that much. Know why? Because no one wants to change them, including myself."

White continues reading from Handy's book:

> George Bernard Shaw once observed that all progress depends on the unreasonable man. His argument was that the reasonable man adapts himself to the world, while the unreasonable man persists in trying to adapt the world to himself.

Rose interjects, "In other words, if you're unreasonable, you will be out trying to get your own way all the time."

"Imagine being told, 'You're being unreasonable' and answering, 'Thank you!' " says White. She laughs and then proceeds:

> Therefore, for any change of consequence, we must look to the unreasonable man, or, I must add, the unreasonable woman. While in Shaw's day, perhaps, most men were reasonable, we are now entering an Age of Unreason, when the future, in so many areas, is there to be shaped by us and for us—a time when the only prediction that will hold true is that no prediction will hold true. A time, therefore, for bold imaginings in private life as well as public, for thinking the unlikely and doing the unreasonable. The purpose of this book is to promote a better understanding of the changes which are al-

ready about us, in order that we may, as individuals and as a society, suffer less and profit more. Change, after all, is only another word for growth, another synonym for learning. We can all do it, and enjoy it, if we want to.

The story or argument of this book rests on three assumptions:

1. that the changes are different this time: they're discontinuous and not part of the pattern; such discontinuity happens from time to time in history, although it is confusing and disturbing, particularly for those in power;
2. that it is the little changes which can in fact make the biggest differences to our lives, even if these go unnoticed at the time, and that it is the changes in the way our work is organized which will make the biggest differences in the way we all will live; and
3. that discontinuous change requires discontinuous upside-down thinking to deal with it, even if both thinkers and thoughts appear absurd at first sight.

Says White, "We are going to have to require some upside-down thinking, looking at things differently from the way we have before."

Rose asks, "What are some of the small changes that have taken place in this business?"

"There are changes in what are called alternate channels," offers someone. "You're starting to see the exploration of additional methods of distribution."

"There are some changes in the microprocessor."

"What else?" Rose prompts. "I'm talking about in Dataflex."

"We're getting a lot more publicity," says one of the saleswomen. "Our company's reputation is out, and people are looking at us."

"Think of changes even smaller than that," urges Rose. "Changes like Maura leading this class today. Women are becoming more prominent, as managers and as leading salespeople. I am spending less time with the company on a day-to-day basis; we're starting to run out of room again; the summer is over, and we're supposedly coming into our busiest time, yet there are no indications that that is going to happen; and August, traditionally a terrible month, was one of the best months of all time."

The discussion moves back to larger changes in the industry. White says, "I think of IBM. For years people looked at that company as infallible. Yet, the other day you asked the question, 'Will

IBM be the big player?' No one knows, but they will have to make some significant changes to maintain their position of power."

Fendrick asks, "So you're saying that if IBM's going to continue, they've got to change?"

White replies: "One of the big differences I've noticed is how highly motivated you all are. The compensation plan here promotes that high level of motivation. At other places, including IBM, it's more the norm that the sales force is operating against quotas."

Wayne Isbitski, director of systems integration says, "I've got a short story just to emphasize Maura's point. Last night I was talking to a childhood friend of mine named Mike who lives in California. A few of you may actually have interviewed him for a sales position here at Dataflex. He works for a biotech firm, and he is their top rep in the country. Their fiscal year ends October 1. He has been designated their top rep this year, his second year with the company, because he was 127 percent of quota.

"I said, 'Mike, that's terrific! You must be making a ton of money!' He said, 'You know, I get paid only up to 105 percent of quota. I have some huge orders sitting here. I've asked my customers, 'Please don't place them until after October 1, so I can get the credit on next year's plan.' "

Rose asks, "Why would someone do that?"

Fendrick bites, "More specifically, why would the president of a company that has a salesman with 127 percent of quota let him go?"

Rose says, "One reason it happens is that the majority of companies aren't run by marketers and salesmen. Their view of what a salesperson does is perverted. They look at a sales rep almost as an unskilled worker and operate from the standpoint that since they're overpaid to begin with, therefore, the loss of any one or all of them is no great loss to the company. Because the executives were never in sales themselves, they have no appreciation for the discipline.

"At military school, the first year and a half there they make you take eight weeks of every sport. I fenced. I had to do gymnastics, boxing, tennis, lacrosse, golf, rugby, and some really weird stuff that I never would have played in my life. But when I watch a fencing match now, I have some appreciation for how skilled and disciplined and graceful those people are because they put me in that seat and made me understand that you just don't get out there with a sword and a mask over your face. Someone will rip you to shreds if you don't know what you're doing and don't have all those moves."

Rose hurtles on: "That's why I get upset with certain people here. I don't care if you are the leading salesperson, if you're doing only 50 percent of what you're capable of I have a problem with you. Don't show me how well you're doing. Let's talk about the potential.

"Who is going to reset some paradigms at Dataflex? Wayne, you have a question?"

"I reset a major paradigm here," Isbitski replies. "When I first told sales that we needed to charge customers for sending out a technician to load software and configure systems, everyone said that we had to do it for free because our competitors do. Finally, we agreed that salespeople would have the prerogative whether they charged the customer or not, but if they didn't, they had to take a hit against their gross profits. The sales staff quickly learned to sell that service, and now we even make a small profit on it."

"Anybody else?" asks Rose. The room is silent.

"Well, you can see we're all struggling with this. I'm sure everybody is wheeling through their library, 'Gee, did I ever reset a paradigm?' If we spent enough time thinking about it, each of us could probably come up with one or two examples. But in general, it's tough, isn't it?

"How many times have you had them reset for you? People get their paradigms reset pretty good when they come to work here! I think they find out, 'Whoa! It doesn't have to be like it was at my previous job.'

White interjects, "My paradigm of what a sales meeting is all about certainly got changed once I started sitting in on these."

Rose says, "Like what you can or can't do and should or shouldn't talk about."

White replies, "Before, meetings to me were for downloading information, and nobody liked going to meetings."

"Now," asks Rose, "is resetting a paradigm behavior modification? I say it is."

White comments, "It leads to a change in behavior."

"I think they are one and the same," Rose says.

The new salesman, Nick Corcodilos, who has a master's degree in psychology from Stanford University, looks thoughtful and says, "Behavior change precedes attitude change. You can't change someone's behavior by first changing their attitude. You change the behavior first and the attitude follows. That's what brainwashing is. You start with little, minute things and build them up. You don't ask someone to buy a statement that says: 'I hate my country and it's wrong!' You ask them to turn their back on the flag first. And then you go from there."

Rose looks at Corcodilos approvingly, pleased that he's injected himself into the discussion. "Ah, an educated man among us," he says, winking at Corcodilos. "This whole class has been a form of behavior modification to get you to admit that perhaps the way you did it before wasn't correct. To get you to try little things a step at a time, to get you to change your behavior, so that your attitude will follow.

"Our consultant Nick Nicholson said that there are two ways you can get people to change. One, get them to think about the way they should act, and then they will ultimately act that way. The other is to get them to act that way, and it will change their thinking. He said that it's much easier to get people to act a certain way and have their attitude follow."

White, "Think about inventors. Do they change a behavior before they invent something? No! They changed the way they thought about something and then created something, and as a result of that invention, behavior changed. I would argue that we are at a time where we can't afford to rest on our past successes: Changes in behavior will get us to point X. We've got to get to point X."

"You mean," asks Rose, "that this book may be saying that the traditional way of changing an attitude—change your behavior a little and your attitude will follow—is not good enough in today's day and time? And that we have to work on how to change an attitude so the behavior follows because that's the quickest way? But then the question becomes: How do you change your attitude?"

"What we're talking about is erasing prejudice. Because if we did not have prejudice, we would accept any attitude given to us. Now why would a lack of prejudice be good or bad in business?"

Fendrick responds, "I did things six years ago, when I first started, because I had total spontaneity and because I was so naive, that I wish I could do now. But I can't do them now because I have all this knowledge of what's good or bad."

Rose jumps up and waves his arms as though he's flagging down a car and says, "When people first come here, they say, 'I have faith in this program. It seems like there are some successful people here. I'm going to do what is asked of me,' and they reach tremendous levels of success. But then the fear of changing kicks in. From this company's perspective it sounds like we would be better off taking away every one of Alan's accounts, giving them to someone else, and saying to him, 'Please go find some more.'

"The best thing Alan could be doing, if he had confidence in his ability to do it, would be to go out and build another base of accounts. We're not doing the right thing for the company, and we're not doing the right thing for him by allowing him to maintain the status quo.

"I still have to remind myself almost daily that I can do anything I want. I get into a situation where there's something that I don't like, and I think, 'I wish it wasn't like that!' And then I have to remind myself, 'You can do anything you want!' We don't operate under hard and fast rules. The only rule around here that I know of is: You had better have enough food at a Dataflex event."

There is laughter around the table, as Rose continues, "And that you cannot be vindictive toward other people who work in this company. Outside of our basic beliefs, I know of no rules under which we operate. And yet we have burdened ourselves with all these things that we can and can't do. No one has ever gone after the small-business market because we have said, "The Fortune 500 is our target market." No one has talked about opening a super store. Yet they are standing in line to get into these places. Let's challenge each other to change."

White says, "We've talked a lot about the role that having a purpose plays in all this. When you have a purpose, it eliminates the fear and the insecurity."

Fendrick adds, "You push everything out of the way to get to a goal. Once you're there and know how hard it was to get there, you start defending your turf. You don't want to change."

"So what Alan's saying," says Rose, "is that the very thing that got you there is the very thing that you stop doing because you want to protect your position. That's why when people get what they want, you must manage them properly because that's when they are most likely to crack!"

Fendrick adds, "What I was suggesting was that people who are successful are the people who are most willing to change."

Salesman Russ Schultz drawls, "My only question is, 'Alan, who will be getting your accounts?' "

The room explodes with rollicking laughter. Rose sprints over to the door and swings it open: "Time to get out there and sell."

Rose waits by the door until the new salesman, Nick Corcodilos, walks by. "So what did you think?" he asks.

"I attended a few of these meetings during the interview process, so I knew what to expect," Corcodilos replies. "You and Gordon were out on the road meeting with investors when I was here before. But I thoroughly enjoyed this morning."

White and Rose walk down the hall with Corcodilos. "Nancy Ebery, our human resources manager, will introduce you to everyone," White says.

Rose stops at the door of his office and adds, "But be back in the conference room by 10:10 for your orientation with me."

An announcement reverberates through the building: "Attention, Dataflex. Attention, Dataflex. John Quarry, Jr., a seven pound two ounce boy was born this morning. Congratulations to the new parents," Maria Infusino, the receptionist, informs the company.

Rose immediately sits down at the PC stationed behind his desk and dashes off a congratulatory note to the family. He sends personal notes to Dataflex associates congratulating them on big events in their personal lives, as well as work accomplishments. If, for example, a customer writes, praising a certain employee, Rose will usually send kudos, too. He sees that personal touch as part of the recognition he believes people need.

Rose likes what he's seen of Corcodilos so far. Until this point, building the sales team has been entirely his baby. Turning over what he views as such an important part of the sales process to White has been tough for him. He derives a tremendous amount of satisfaction from transforming those with only a modicum of sales experience or none at all into members of what he calls the "sales elite." He never tires of telling people the stories of his top three salespeople: Fendrick, the stand-up comedian; Katz, the medical secretary; and Tom Beer, a prison guard and semipro baseball player.

But now, Dataflex is in a position to afford to hire more experienced people, and with the industry in the state it's in, there are some good people looking for places to go. White and Rose have discussed the pros and cons of hiring experienced versus inexperienced salespeople over the past few months. But to Rose it remains a big question mark, and he still leans toward hiring less experienced people.

RICK ROSE: Over on my left hand, I have a handful of very experienced salespeople. They've worked in this industry for competitors. I have to pay them a lot of money for their experience. And they come to Dataflex with a ton of prejudice. They think they know the answers, and most of them are not necessarily open to change. And I'm going to have a pretty good fight on my hands in trying to get them to see it my way, which is radically different from anything they've been doing.

On my right hand, I have highly motivated, somewhat experienced salespeople, not necessarily from my industry, but they have sold something. They know what a sales cycle means, they understand that you go through a process from looking for people who have a need for your product and service, to actually providing it for them, to the ongoing service and support that's associated. They understand that there is a cycle that one goes through in selling. They know that you don't sell to everybody who has a potential need for your product, and they have an understanding that sales is a process with extreme highs and lows. These people have worked someplace that did not allow them to reap the rewards if they happened to make a big sale. And they never had any formal training in sales. Their employer just tucked the product under their arms and said, "All right, kid. Get out there and knock 'em dead!"

So I have these people over here at my right hand. Oh, by the way, you don't have to pay these people a lot of money. They're just looking for an opportunity. They realize that with formal training, the proper environment, the right operational systems, and their desire to sell, they could be enormously successful.

The question to ask is: "What percentage of this group is successful compared to that group?" The answer is, "The same percentage." Those who have experience when they come to Dataflex have the same chance of succeeding as do these highly motivated people who are looking for training and a chance. About one in twenty make it—from either category!

The next question to ask is: "If the same percentage succeed, what is the degree of success? Do these experienced people sell $20 million worth of services and hardware a year versus $5 million a year for the inexperienced people?" Believe it or not, the degree of success is the same. Now, as a business person, which one do you choose?

In my twenty years in the computer industry, I hired the experienced and watched how many succeeded, their degree of success, and I hired people who brought with them only a great attitude and a willingness to learn. And I found out that in both categories, the percentage of success and the degree of success were the same. So what was the difference? With the experienced people, it doesn't take as long to find out if they're any good or not. With novices, you have to invest about a year to eighteen months in training.

The one Achilles' heel that *Forbes* highlighted in its December 10, 1990, article on Dataflex was that the company depended on a relatively small number of salespeople, and Matthew Schifrin, the writer and a senior editor at the magazine, speculated that Wall Street was nervous about what would happen if one of the star performers left. (At the time Dataflex's stock was languishing at around six dollars a share.)

Two years later Dataflex has yet to lose a single top performer, which speaks volumes in a high-turnover position like sales. Second, of those salespeople who have made it through the first year, only one has resigned. Rose instills in the sales department an understanding that the salesperson doesn't own the accounts—that the magic comes from being backed up by the Dataflex team.

"Sales is usually set up in one of two ways," Rose said one day. "Either the salesperson is so good that he or she floats from company to company, taking all the accounts to the next job. Or the company has all the power, and the sales staff really isn't much more than a bunch of order takers. What most people call selling is more aptly described as glad-handing, account administration, telemarketing, or public relations. Selling is not only all the above, but a constant conceptual learning business.

"I don't want either the all-powerful salesperson or the order takers at Dataflex. I want professional salespeople who recognize the value that the Dataflex name imparts.

"I also don't feel threatened when people here get job offers. That comes with the territory when you have trained people well and they begin to get recognized in the industry as being winners. I always tell associates that one way to measure how good you are is by how many job offers you get. If nobody wants you, why should we?"

The morning after the article on Dataflex appeared in *Forbes,* Rose arrived at headquarters at 6 A.M. to find a young man in a three-piece suit sitting by the front door of the building. "How long have you been sitting here?" Rose asked, as the man scrambled to his feet.

"Since before dawn," said the man. "I wanted to make sure I was the first person you saw if there are any openings in your sales department." The man was a stockbroker who wanted to join Rose's sales team. The stockbroker-would-be-salesman scored high in three critical areas: chutzpah, sense of humor, and creativity. Rose ushered him into his office and interviewed him immediately. However, when Rose offered some criticism, as he typically does in an interview to see how the person responds under pressure, the man bristled. Ultimately, Rose didn't offer him one of the sales positions he coveted.

"From his response, I knew then and there that that guy wasn't going to be able to take the intensive training and constructive criticism we dish out to people," says Rose.

If you put the ten salespeople who make up the Dataflex team in a lineup and tried to figure out the common denominators, few would surface immediately. In looks and temperament, they are widely divergent. However, if you talked to them long enough, you would find that, like Rose, each one grew up in families where cash was short. Almost all come from dysfunctional homes, and all are fighters who have had to struggle to get what they want.

Besides Katz, Fendrick, Constantino, Scaglione, and Beer, the other veteran is Russ Schultz. Tall and bearded, Schultz, aged thirty-four, has the voice, low-key manner, and looks of a young Kris Kristofferson. In high school, he developed a passion for sailing and, after attending the Florida Institute of Technology, he moved to Annapolis in 1980 to sell sailing yachts.

Six years later, Schultz, then a newlywed, determined that selling yachts would never afford him his dream of owning one, so he began night school for computer repair and landed a job at Wang Laboratories as a field technician, servicing mini- and microcomputers. When he expressed an interest in moving to the sales department at Wang, he was denied an interview because he lacked a four-year degree. Disillusioned, he soon left Wang and bounced between sales jobs at three start-ups in the computer industry. "Without that four-year degree, none of the big companies would look at me," he recalls.

Finally, a small ad in the *Newark Star Ledger* caught his eye. Schultz did some homework and concluded that Dataflex was what he'd been looking for. Rose didn't bring up his lack of a college diploma. "If you weren't interviewing here, what would you be doing?" Rose asked during Schultz's interview.

Without hesitating, Schultz said, "If I don't succeed here, you'll find me on a sailboat somewhere between St. Croix and St. Lucia." Rose liked his candor. And after Schultz passed muster with Katz, Fendrick, and Beer, Rose gave him the job.

On the shy side, Schultz didn't attract much attention when he first came aboard, but when Rose took the entire company on a snow-skiing trip one weekend, the salesman became the target of a prank. When he and his pregnant wife went back to their room after dinner, their bed was neatly turned down with mints on the pillow. But their mattress was missing. Only the boxsprings were left. Schultz was furious and called the front desk, demanding to speak to the manager. "The chambermaid stole our mattress," he bellowed into the phone. "I want my mattress back immediately."

"Sir, are you with a group?" the manager asked.

"Uh, yes," stammered Schultz, realizing that he had been had. "Oh. Never mind." He learned later that Fendrick had pickpocketed his room key and enlisted Constantino to help him swipe and hide the mattress. That was a turning point for Schultz. He felt somehow that he'd been initiated into the group and for the remainder of the trip exhibited a wicked sense of humor.

Shortly thereafter, he took honors as the Salesperson of the Month and Performer of the Month.

In January 1990, Rose announced during a sales meeting that he wanted someone to take over as sales manager and that he didn't have time to bring someone in from the outside. Schultz, who had been with the company for three years by that time, was elected by his peers. For a year he worked from 7 A.M. to 7 P.M. six days a week trying, as he puts it, "to get his arms around the sales administration, the development of sales reps, and the training of new ones." Rose kept reassuring him, but finally Schultz—who has a daughter, aged four, and a son, aged two—convinced Rose that he wasn't suited to the job, and he went back into sales as an account executive. Says Schultz, "In retrospect, I should have concentrated on bringing in new reps and training them. I was trying to do too much, and Rick casts a mighty long shadow."

Schultz has earned Rose's respect and admiration because he's willing to step out on the wing and try some maneuvers that are uncomfortable for him. Schultz is once again stepping to the forefront. He told Rose recently that he'd like to carve out a sales team that would concentrate solely on selling services and that he'd like to lead that team.

Elaine Mosher, who has shoulder-length, brown hair and blue eyes and is also thirty-four, backed her way into the sales department. She was hired by Wayne Isbitski of systems integration as an Apple product specialist. She had developed her Macintosh expertise during a two-year stint selling computers for Transnet Corporation in Ocean, New Jersey.

A blithe spirit who grew up a few minutes from the Jersey Shore, Mosher supported her wanderlust by waiting on tables. She earned an associate degree in social sciences in between a backpacking trip in Europe for several months and other forays to far-off lands. After spending her early twenties traveling, waitressing, and helping out in her father's retail drapery store, Mosher decided she didn't want to spend the rest of her life "asking people how they wanted their steaks." She launched a blitzkrieg, working three jobs and going to school full time, and received her degree in management at age twenty-nine. One of her first acts after getting her diploma was to retire her waitressing uniform.

During Mosher's first year at Dataflex, she was restrained from selling by a noncompete contract with her former employer. However, in June 1990, Schultz promised her that if she found some business and flipped accounts to the sales reps, she'd get a chance to become a full-fledged sales rep herself. "I don't think they expected me to do it," says Mosher. "But I did." And she smiles.

Likewise, Glen Koedding, the youngest on the sales team, proved his mettle in other positions within the company before becoming a sales representative. An enterprising young man, as a high school junior on Staten Island, he ran a blackjack operation in the lunchroom to get money for college. "I went to school with the sons of mobsters, where kids got Corvettes for passing math," he laughs. "I made $150 the first day. I was amazed at the kind of money they would bring to the lunchroom."

The summer before his senior year in college in Buffalo, New York, Koedding cast his eye toward the future. He wanted to work for a midsize, but growing company in the tristate area and one in a hot industry. Eight companies met all his criteria, and he sent letters and a résumé to the CEOs of those companies seeking summer employment in marketing. He was shocked when Rose called him for an interview the following week.

The first question Rose asked him was whether his school was "NCAA accredited."

Koedding stammered, "I think so."

Rose said, "Listen, you're just over the border from Canada. Take a ride over there and buy me a box of Tueros cigars, and I'll give you a job." Rose was testing Koedding's sense of humor, as well as his willingness to go out of his way by asking him to get the Cuban cigars.

"Are you serious?" Koedding asked. He heard a chuckle through the phone line.

"I'll see you next week," Rose answered.

Koedding flew home the next weekend and raced to the interview. Rose hired him to work in the marketing department, which was practically nonexistent in the summer of 1988. By the end of the summer, Koedding knew he wanted to be in sales and asked Rose what he needed to do. The answer: "Get sales experience and gain product knowledge."

When Koedding returned to college, he promptly changed his curriculum to marketing and computer science from engineering and got a part-time job doing telemarketing to improve his phone skills. During the winter break, he prospected for Fendrick, and one of his leads turned into an account. He called Fendrick religiously each month from school to monitor the progress of the leads he'd generated, hoping that Rose would be impressed by his initiative.

After graduation, he worked on Fendrick's team as a sales administrator, putting in ten- and twelve-hour days to learn the business. Still, Rose was skeptical about whether Koedding could make it as a sales rep. But Koedding had a champion in Mannix, who admired the tenacity Koedding brought to problem-solving. When Mannix suggested that Koedding be promoted to the sales force, Rose protested, "But he looks like he doesn't even shave yet."

"Yes, but I like his thought processes. When it comes to processing data, he's probably the best we've got," Mannix replied. "You tell him something, and he'll work at it, and if he makes a mistake, he listens to criticism."

Schultz, who was the sales manager then, promised Koedding that if he could make a presentation on every one of Dataflex's products and wow the sales staff with it, he could have his shot.

For three months Koedding worked on the project and then presented it to the sales staff. Even Rose was impressed and offered the ambitious young man a position selling services. In the next six months with "no tools, no rules—just pencil and paper," the fledgling salesman called on fifty to seventy potential clients a day. During that time he made enough to pay off his entire four-year student loan and brought in two accounts that became major customers for Dataflex. He won his spot on the sales force on April 1, 1991.

Despite all his hard work, Koedding still seems somewhat detached from the sales team. He doesn't go out to lunch with anyone, preferring to eat lunch at his desk and to make calls in between taking hasty bites of a sandwich. His cubicle is right beside the board, which shows the ranking of the salespeople, and he is often turned in that direction when he's talking on the phone. Koedding is the person whom Liz Massimo, who often works late, frequently has to chase out before she turns off the lights at night.

When jokes and pranks are flying all around him, Koedding will sometimes laugh, but it sounds strained. Most of the time, his young face bears an expression that betrays his ferocious need to show the world what he is worth. As a child, he remembers being in his backyard building treehouses and other things while all the other kids were playing football together. Now he's busy building a future, blocking out any distractions around him.

"My father," says Koedding, measuring his words, "is a very successful sales rep in Pennsylvania. My parents divorced when I was young, and my mother has lived on an inheritance for all these years, but that's running out. I want to make a lot of money, so I can support my mom. I also have a sister who has two little kids who I will probably need to help."

The last newcomer, before Nick Corcodilos, was Jayne Banach-Walther, who has the distinction of being the only salesperson with extensive experience hired by Rose. Hard working, serious, and corporate with a capital *C,* Banach-Walther worked for six different resellers over the past ten years. Her last position before she came to Dataflex was as an account executive for Businessland in Springfield, New Jersey, where her annual sales quota was $4.5 million. Banach-Walther, who has a degree in marketing and computer science from Fairleigh Dickinson University, had tired of the reselling industry and wanted to get a position at Microsoft.

Dataflex was virtually the only reseller in the area that she hadn't worked for. A colleague who once interviewed at Dataflex told her that the place was run like a small military academy. "You'd have to be crazy to work there," he said. "Who wants to go to meetings at seven-thirty in the morning and then put in twelve-hour days?"

But she kept hearing high praise from IBM reps, and her curiosity got the best of her. She decided to interview with Rose. She was impressed with the fact that the warehouse was on site and that Rose makes himself accessible. At Businessland, Banach-Walther had initiated an approach similar to team-order processing, but she didn't have the support she needed from headquarters to make it click. She was also drawn to the camaraderie fostered by Rose. "When he took me on a tour of the company, it was evident that he genuinely cared about people," she says. "I was also impressed by his integrity. He was open and honest about what it would be like to work here. People sometimes paint a picture that they think you'll like, but he obviously wanted me to understand the life of a sales rep at Dataflex."

After talking to her for several minutes, Rose said, "I'd like you to work here because I certainly don't want to compete against you, Jayne."

The scariest part of the interviewing process for Banach-Walther was knowing that the other salespeople had a voice in whether she was hired. When she visited a sales meeting, Diane Katz threw a pretzel at her, shouting, "If you can catch this, you can have a job." Banach-Walther caught the pretzel, but thought to herself that this group was "so bizarre."

The message that she needed to relax came through loud and clear one day when she was on the phone with an executive director of a large drug company. People were talking loudly and cutting up in the cubicles around her. Banach-Walther cupped her hand over the receiver and yelled, "I'm on the phone, so cut it out." Rose poked his head over her cubicle and said, "So what? Better lighten up."

"Now, I'm not as stuffy as I used to be," she says. "I even shoot people with my Nerf air gun."

Banach-Walther has already weathered some tough times at Dataflex. In October 1991, the month she married, a $5 million deal that she'd been working on for months fell through. She was devastated, but her peers and Rose rallied around her. As she says, "If I had been anywhere else, I don't think I could have taken the disappointment. Rick was so supportive and never made me feel inadequate. In the meetings you could tell that people honestly cared about how I was doing."

Banach-Walther quickly distinguished herself as one of the most effective salespeople in terms of working with a team. She gives her team members full authority to talk to customers and has taken them all out to see customers. "It's caused problems at times because they've made mistakes, but their learning curve is going to be a lot shorter, which will give me more time to sell in the long run," she says.

Scientific in her approach to sales, Banach-Walther is the picture of calm and knows exactly what she needs to get the job done. Unlike Koedding, she doesn't make hundreds of prospecting calls a week. Instead, she carefully targets a few customers.

Banach-Walther is careful to treat those around her with the utmost respect. "When I was working my way through college, I often didn't have enough money to buy food," she says. "My friends would buy me meals on their meal plans. I vowed then that I would always give back to people. The perception of salespeople is that they have ulterior motives and are sleazy. No matter what company I'm in, I want to be seen as a good mentor to whom others can turn."

At 10:10, Rose meets Corcodilos in the main conference room. Every new associate is given an orientation, usually by Rose. The president likes to set meetings at odd times to help drive home the point that minutes count. His jacket is off again, and he has rolled up the sleeves of his monogrammed white button-down shirt. A gold Rolex watch gleams on his wrist. Corcodilos takes a seat in the middle of the conference table, near the white board.

"Today we're going to talk about what business we're in," Rose says, standing by the board. He draws a simple chart on the board that shows the manufacturer and the end user with the dealer (Dataflex) in between. "Ninety percent of the presidents of the companies we compete against don't understand what business we're in.

"How so? The manufacturer builds the computer and ships it to the dealer. The dealer gives money to the manufacturer, allowing the manufacturer to invest in raw materials for a smooth rate of production so it can reach its goals. But the problem is that dealers don't realize that they're in the inventory-management business. Customers say, 'Why should I have to wait six months? You ought to be able to deliver in two weeks!'

"If we as dealers don't offset this cost of investing in finished goods, we don't deserve to exist. And if IBM incurs this cost, it will have to raise its prices some 50 percent. That's why IBM is 20 percent to 40 percent higher than everybody else: It's absorbing the cost of finished-goods inventory because the dealers are so bad at inventory management."

Rose strides over to the phone and dials an extension. He puts it on the speaker phone.

"Alan Fendrick," says a voice on the line.

"Hi, Alan, it's Rick. What business are we in?"

"We're in the business of inventory management."

"Thanks a lot."

"Hi Mo, it's Rick Rose here. Do you know what business we're in?"

"The inventory management business."

"All right, thank you very much."

He makes a few more calls and gets the same answer consistently. "If we get this right, we have an opportunity to make money," Rose says. "We turn our inventory 9.6 times a year, versus the industry average of 5.5, which means I can make the same profit as my competitors at almost half the gross margin on a sale." Like the inspiring teacher almost every person remembers fondly, Rose has the ability to deliver material that he's gone over hundreds of times before with a verve and enthusiasm that's contagious. Even though he has an audience of one, he is putting as much energy into his presentation as he does for 200.

Corcodilos, who has been working in the computer industry for twelve years, listens intently and respectfully.

"The reason that manufacturers have us manage their inventory is simple: We can do it for less than they can," continues Rose. "You may say, 'Wait. I'm a sales executive here, an account executive. How can you say I'm an inventory manager?' "

Replies Corcodilos, "Because I'm being paid on profitability."

Says Rose, "My responsibility is to make sure that we are as effective and as efficient as we can be. We have only two major costs around here: people and inventory. The desks, chairs, lights, and the building aren't really worth anything compared to the inventory and the people.

"As a sales representative, I make promises to customers. When you think of inventory management, don't just think of an IBM PC. We have a lot of inventory around here that's not hardware. It's called resources. Russ and Wayne, very smart guys, are part of our inventory, our resources. One knows how to support a customer technically, and the other knows an awful lot about local area networks and systems integration. If you misuse them and have them out chasing leads that are never going to develop into business, you're not being a wise inventory manager."

He goes on to enumerate the other resources of the company, concluding, "So don't think of being an inventory manager as just managing boxes. That's only part of it. After roughly forty minutes of discussion, you've found out that you've chosen the inventory-management business. If you get that right, you have an opportunity to make a profit. If you don't, you're out. An interesting discussion, isn't it?"

Corcodilos says, "You're right. Nobody's ever put this business to me that way. I once read a book called *Money Love.* It was about why you try to make all the money you possibly can and why it's all right to want to make a lot of money. The only point the book made was that the money that you make is not money. It's nothing. Money represents your love for other people. And I thought, 'Yeah, that's a nice, California-type of. . . .' But the logic was that you have family you love and care about, so you work. You make money, and that all translates into a love for your family and those people you care about. So working and money mean something very specific, and money's not just a symbol itself.

"It's only a method of keeping score," agrees Rose. "Change the word *inventory* to *resources* in your own mind. And if you'll take that personally and make every decision here as if you owned this company, then you and I will have a wonderful business relationship. I have to trust the people I work with to do everything that's in the best interest of the company and the customer. If you manage the resources as if you owned Dataflex, then that's good enough for me.

"If at some point I don't like your judgment and your decisions are translating into losses, upset customers, and increased overhead, we'll have a discussion. If you can convince me that there's a method to what you're doing, fine. If not, I'll say, 'Maybe you ought to run someone else's company because I think you're putting us out of business.'

"But you will always have an opportunity to speak up. If you think you're any good and you have some ideas that you want to try, I beg you to do it here!

"I'll be glad to give you all I have, but I'm asking the same thing in return. Please teach me and make me better. Come up with ideas, challenge my thoughts. Then this will be a very stimulating environment for all of us."

Corcodilos smiles and says, "Thanks for putting it out on the table."

Rose says, "You will be most valuable in these meetings for about

the first three months that you're here because you have no prejudices. Unfortunately, we suffer from inbreeding. Right now, your
ideas aren't ours. So the most valuable thing is what you did
today—speak up immediately before you get any prejudice about
what we're supposed to be doing."

"This morning was really enjoyable," says the salesman, looking
far more relaxed than when the orientation began. "It was incredibly stimulating for me. The same thing happened when I came in
about a month ago."

Rose puts down the grease pen he's been holding and says, "So
Mr. Inventory Manager, I wish you luck. You and I have to have one
more discussion. I need to take you through our marketing strategy.
It's another half hour, but we'll schedule an appointment for early
next week."

Rose has patiently and painstakingly built a foundation at Dataflex
to make sure it offers value. As much time as he's spent building a
dream sales team, he is equally devoted to the rest of the company.
"There's no sense in buying a race horse if you're going to hitch it
to a plow," says Rose, whose speech is sprinkled with down-home
analogies that reflect his southern roots. "In other words, why have
a dynamic sales force if the rest of the company can't fill the promises made by them?"

Some may say that Rose took a big risk by relying so heavily on
raw talent. The average age in the company is twenty-eight; a few
years ago, the average worker was twenty-six. But when Rose and
McLenithan cleaned house in the beginning, there wasn't much that
they could offer new recruits. "We couldn't offer above-average
salaries because there wasn't much money left in the kitty," Rose
recalls. "We didn't have prestige associated with the name Dataflex.
All I could give them was a vision for what I was trying to build."

Rose pursued the same strategy in laying the foundation for the
company that he used in building the sales team. But he says he
would have recruited the same people, whether or not the company
had more money to spend. "Look at the military," Rose commands.
"They don't hire experienced people and try to make them soldiers.
They hire people who are highly motivated and want an opportu-

nity. These people don't come into the service with prejudices about what it's supposed to be like. And the military turns them into a fighting machine, a team of confident, organized individuals."

Ann Marie Bernet, for example, was twenty-six years old when she was hired in 1984 as a junior accountant. Rose and McLenithan quickly recognized her as a star, promoting her four times in her first four years with the company. Bernet kept her head in tough situations and had a knack for understanding processes. Today she is director of finance and sits on the executive committee.

"I'm just like the young person we hired back then," Rose exclaims. "Every time we sell $1 million more, it's new ground for me. I've never managed this large a company before, so I have no prejudices."

Instilling his dream in the handful of people who remained after the purge was a towering task because their views had been tainted. Normally, restoring the morale at a company that has experienced extensive firings can take months. But Rose sifted through the people at Dataflex with the same critical eye that he was casting upon newcomers. He set up time with each person and conducted extensive interviews with them all.

One young man, Rich Dressler, came in at his appointed time and announced that he was sick of Dataflex and was leaving. He said he wanted to devote more time to playing with the rock-and-roll band he led. Rose asked the disgruntled twenty-six-year-old shipping clerk what he would do differently. Dressler, gold chains at his throat and dressed in a T-shirt and cutoff shorts, asked, "You really wanna know?"

Rose nodded.

For the next half hour, the tall, muscular young man sprawled in a chair and detailed a litany of complaints. But he also put forth solutions for several of them. Rose knew from Dressler's personnel file that he was an initiator. After two years in college, Dressler had dropped out to take over a one-person tailoring business in 1979. Three years later, revenues had grown from $35,000 a year to $75,000 before a contract dispute closed his doors.

Rose saw past the young man's lack of polish; he saw in Dressler the traits he wanted in the new Dataflex: fearlessness and caring. "Rich, I don't blame you for being unhappy here," Rose said when Dressler concluded. "If you weren't unhappy here, I wouldn't want you to stay. But would you do me a favor and give me three months? If you don't like what you see after that, then I'll honor your resignation letter."

Rose briefly transferred Dressler to the sales department, but the young man noticed Rose doing purchasing himself one day after he'd fired the person responsible for procurement. Dressler offered to take over the responsibility with the promise that he could jump back into sales whenever he wanted. "My predecessor was buying cables for fifteen dollars each," Dressler recalls in his thick New Jersey accent. "I found them for six dollars." By April 1990 Dressler had five promotions when Rose made him vice president of materials management.

In an office two doors down from Dressler, Joe Rizzo, director of marketing, toils. Rizzo holds an M.B.A. from Baruch College in New York City and is one of a handful of M.B.A.s in the company; the only two salespeople with M.B.A.s from Ivy League schools that Rose had ever hired resigned after a few months. The director of marketing was also hired by Rose, who chuckles, "Rizzo makes me look laid back."

Dressler and Rizzo could not be more opposite from each other, except that they both lift weights and enjoy Fridays, because it is dress-down day. "I hate wearing shoes," says Rizzo. "I'm lobbying to make Thursday Sneaker Day."

While Dressler's respect for Rose runs deep, Rizzo, aged thirty-four, frequently clashes with Rose and is one of the most likely people in the company to disagree with him. "Rick flies by the seat of his pants," says Rizzo, before taking a swig from a two-quart container of water that is always within reach on his desk. A two-day growth of beard darkens his face, and his feet are propped on his desk, which faces the wall, leaving Rizzo's back to his door. "I'm always saying, 'What does the customer say? Let's let the customer dictate our direction on new services and products. Let's get more data.' But I can't fight the results. Besides this is his ball game, and I respect that."

But, like Dressler, Rizzo thrives on the constant challenge Dataflex provides. "There's no playing polite here; if there's a problem, it's immediately out in the open," he says. "Another thing I like is that Rick basically leaves me alone to do my job. I don't have to report every decision to him. Working at Dataflex gives me an opportunity to do those things that I always thought were the right things to do. That's what drives me. I'm able to contribute in a big way. It's like being given a petrie dish and growing an organism. It's your experiment, but you stick out like a sore thumb if you aren't producing."

Rizzo was interviewed at the end of March 1989. At that time, there was no formal marketing department; like so many tasks, Rose handled it himself. Rizzo had launched his own small marketing consulting practice after working for Wakefern Food Corporation for five years. But he realized he wasn't making the kind of money he wanted and targeted a few hot-growth companies with his résumé. "I saw immediately that Dataflex was quite different from other companies. It is truly sales driven, rather than marketing driven," he says.

McLenithan and Rose asked Rizzo to come back the next day with a presentation on what he thought they needed. He came back a day later with a concept that evolved into the Dataflex wheel. He was hired the next day, April 1, which is *the* big holiday at Dataflex.

"Last year at review time, Rick never called me in," Rizzo recalls. "Finally, I went into his office and said, 'Hey, Rick, what about my review?' You know what he did? He said, 'You're doing a great job, Joe,' and then he walked around the desk and gave me a big hug." Rizzo smiles slightly and shakes his head.

For several years, Rose interviewed each new associate personally, and McLenithan was the last interviewer for associates. But once the company grew past 100 people, the interviewing process was taking an inordinate amount of their time. So Rose and McLenithan trained managers to look for five qualities when they were interviewing potential workers:

1. A drive to give 110 percent commitment. As Rose says, "Experience doesn't matter. Commitment does."

2. A willingness to learn. "Some people don't have the desire to be taught," observes Rose. "This kind of person stunts the growth of a company."

3. Flexibility, meaning a desire for a loosely defined position. "Because this company's management is relatively flat, we need people who are looking to create their own ideal job and to take on more and more responsibility," Rose explains. "We don't want job-title seekers and those who expend energy trying to limit their responsibilities."

4. A creative flair. "If you're not finding things wrong, you aren't doing your job," Rose states flatly.

When Rose interviewed Prasad Srinivasan for his job as credit manager, Rose told the Indian native, "You have a thick accent. People are going to have a hard time understanding you. How could you overcome that obstacle to doing the job?"

Srinivasan didn't miss a beat and answered, "Because I have an accent, people have to listen more closely to what I'm saying. And if I have their attention, they will realize that I know what I'm talking about."

Rose says, "Prasad showed grace under pressure and gave a creative answer. I knew then that he was right for the job."

5. The confidence to take the initiative.

Rose sees getting "the right people in the door on the front end" as a critical factor in Dataflex's success. "When you're building a house, you can't say, 'I'll go back and correct the frame later.' One thing depends on the other. We had to get it right from the foundation up."

Some may question why a company president would take time to interview someone who won't work with him directly, yet, to Rose, that time is well spent. If he particularly likes a candidate, he's been known to drop everything and take the person on an impromptu company tour. "We appreciate the fact that people take the time to learn about our company," he says. "We want to sell them on why they should come to work here. If we get everybody excited about working here, we'll have the pick of the crop."

Peter Fasolo, Ph.D., an industrial psychologist who has been consulting with the company for three years and recently accepted a full-time staff position with Squibb, gives Rose high marks for communicating to new people a realistic picture of what those expectations are. The company's voluntary turnover rate is substantially lower than the industry percentage. Look at the following chart.

	INDUSTRY '90	DATAFLEX '91
VOLUNTARY		
Management	5.2%	0 %
Technical	6.1%	5.45 %
Nontechnical	6.8%	8.05 %
INVOLUNTARY		
Management	12.8%	0 %
Technical	15.5%	2.5 %
Nontechnical	13.2%	3.15 %

After his orientation with Corcodilos, Rose goes to the office that Fasolo occupies on Tuesdays and Thursdays. Anyone in the company can visit the psychologist on a confidential basis to get help with business and personal problems. Fasolo, a handsome man with brown hair and blue eyes, estimates that about 80 percent of the associates have come to see him at least once. But while most companies with employee assistance programs report that a high percentage of inquiries come from people with alcohol or substance abuse problems, that is not the case at Dataflex. In three years, only two associates have approached Fasolo about substance abuse. Mannix says, "We have a system here that's self-policing because associates are keenly attuned to each other's performances. A problem like that wouldn't go unnoticed for any length of time."

Fasolo attributes the low number to the screening on the front end and Rose's drive to convey to his managers exactly the type of people with whom he wants to work.

"Most of the time companies call me in when there are problems," says Fasolo. "Rick took a proactive approach and brought me in to help make things better. Many entrepreneurs can't build businesses because they are less interested in developing the people side than they are in selling their product or idea. Rick absolutely believes in developing people."

Once a year Fasolo conducts an attitude survey throughout the company. The survey asks associates detailed questions about their satisfaction with their pay, supervisors, work relationships, benefits, communication, and resources and their degree of commitment to the organization. Today the results are back, and Rose is eager to see them. "So what's the word, Peter?" asks Rose, as he takes a seat. The previous year an annual survey of salaries that Fasolo also conducts had shown that Dataflex's salaries were slightly below the range of other companies in the area. By the next pay period, salaries were increased to bring them up to par with the competition's.

"Overall, everyone seems pretty happy," says Fasolo.

"What about commitment," asks Rose. "I've felt lately that there are some people here I would not have hired in the beginning."

Fasolo says, "Ninety-two percent of the associates indicate that they are committed to the philosophies and values of the company. That's a pretty amazing number."

Rose stands up and starts pacing. "That is not good enough. I want 100 percent," he says. "But I've been thinking about this feeling that something's not quite right a lot lately, and I have an idea about how to fix it." He spends the next hour discussing his latest dream with Fasolo.

ACTIONS

☑ Always give the benefit of the doubt and the chance a person deserves. All job openings are posted, and 98 percent of the jobs are filled by promoting from within. I want people to know that I believe in them. No jobs are open to the outside unless everybody in the company agrees that we can't fill it from within. If somebody at Dataflex thinks he or she has the talent to do a job, why should I go to the outside and put my faith in somebody based on a nice résumé?

☑ Let the shrinks roam free. We have psychologists who come in once a week to see people. Associates are free to discuss any problem on an absolutely confidential basis. It doesn't necessarily have to be work related. People's problems are rarely centered on work. They may need help with a family member, or maybe they can't balance their checkbooks. Again, this step lets our associates know that we value them and that we want to provide them with all the tools possible to make their lives better. You can't say you want to build a family atmosphere or a team strategy, but ignore whole chunks of a person.

TOP SALESPEOPLE AREN'T BORN, THEY'RE MADE

Good salespeople are success-hungry, quick thinkers who have the ability to grasp an idea conceptually. None of those characteristics requires experience. Successful Dataflex salespeople sell ten times the industry average, yet none of our million-dollar-a-month performers was a heavy-hitting sales pro when I brought him or her on board.

A recent study of the turnover of sales representatives by Learning International of Stamford, Connecticut, showed that the main reason salespeople leave their jobs is that they don't get support from their managers. We invest many, many hours of training in our salespeople, and we want to hang on to them. Indeed, we've only had one salesperson who made it through the first twelve months leave the company. That is in marked contrast to the turnover in most sales organizations. Our interviewing process is designed to make sure we make the best decision on the hiring end.

Soon after new salespeople come on board, I pull them aside and tell them that if they are waiting for me to take them into the corner and whisper the secret of sales in their ears, it's not going to happen. I tell them that it's going to take hard work on both our parts. What it doesn't have to take is a tremendous amount of time. Most sales managers approach salespeople with the attitude that it will take years to teach them to be truly professional salespeople.

I didn't buy that.

In fact, I decided that if I could figure out how to impart the hard-won wisdom I'd gained over my career in two years instead of in twenty, then those around me would be way ahead of the game. I'd be more successful, and they would be more successful. What prevents other leaders from sharing those invaluable nuggets of truth? Two things. First, the fear that there is only so much victory to be spread around, and if I let you in on my secret, you may get a bigger bite of it than I do. Second, that vague thought that whispers in our ears: "I came up the hard way. Why make it easier on anybody else?" Personally, I'd rather save someone else the pain of bumping up against the barbed-wire fence of experience. Studies have shown that if a picture of an event is painted vividly enough for a listener, the human brain cannot distinguish whether the person actually experienced it or not. That's why we spend so much time in training classes.

What makes a salesperson successful?

- Confidence in his or her own abilities.
- A willingness to take calculated risks.
- Nimble thinking. That doesn't mean a genius IQ. It's the ability to take the available information and formulate the best possible response instantaneously. To do that, you have to be a conceptual thinker, somebody who can answer any question on a given topic because you completely understand it. Many companies train their people off a script, but to be a true professional, you can't afford to depend on rote responses.
- A great sense of humor.

To spot great potential in inexperienced salespeople, make them run the gauntlet during the interview process. At Dataflex it starts when they answer the Dataflex ad. My assistant, Liz Massimo, has been instructed to give any callers the brush-off.

"When I called, Liz tried three times to tell me why I wasn't what they were looking for, but I was persistent," recalls Fendrick. "I stood my ground and said, 'Look, I really think I have what it takes. It's at least worth a few minutes of Mr. Rose's time.' " He cleared the first hurdle.

I am deliberately adversarial in the first interview. It gives me a clear idea of what candidates would be like with customers. In the first interview I give constructive criticism and challenge them. I put them on the spot, try to see if they have convictions, embarrass them. If they're too sensitive, they aren't going to do well around here.

My first words to Fendrick were, "Why in the world do you have performing stupid human tricks on the 'Letterman' show on your résumé?" Then I asked him, "Aren't you supposed to look nice for an interview?"

Alan came back with a zinger. He looked me dead in the eye and said, "Are you talking about me or you?"

I tell people, "Forget about what you think I want to hear. Forget that this is an interview." I try to shake them out of the standard interview mode. If they persist in giving rote answers, even after I've told them point-blank that that's not what I want, I know they aren't right for the job.

After candidates have been in my office for about five minutes, I will tell them bluntly that I'm not very impressed—even if I think they're terrific. I'm looking for their response. I want them to try to convince me that I'm wrong about them. In sales you either believe in what you're doing or you don't. Good salespeople must believe in themselves.

When I interviewed for a sales job at Applied Digital Data Systems, I forgot to pack a tie and was wearing black-and-white wing-tip shoes, which were in vogue in Florida in 1971 but raised eyebrows in New York. The secretary put my résumé upside down on the vice president of sales' desk. He was eating a tuna-fish sandwich when I came in. Failing to find a napkin, he wiped his hands on what he thought was a blank sheet of paper, but was actually my résumé. He asked me several questions and insinuated that I was not packing the goods to do the job. I remember feeling almost a violent reaction to that challenge. I was thinking, "Someday you'll not only eat my résumé, but those words as well." I ended up selling more equipment than the rest of the sales force combined, which was eight people. To this day, I don't know whether his goal was to challenge me or whether he really thought I couldn't do the job. But I learned the value of being challenging in an interview from that man.

Next in an interview, I ask for a definition of sales. Then I pose the clincher question, "Have you unquestionably, without a doubt, 120 percent, decided on sales as a career?" If they answer no, the interview is over.

If they say yes, I ask why they've chosen sales. A common response? "I want to help people." My comeback to that: You want to help people? Go be a nurse. Another line people toss out: "People tell me I'd be good at selling." When that one comes up, I'll point outside my office window, "See that lawn out there. If people told you that you'd be good at mowing lawns, would you be interviewing for that job right now?"

Then comes the real test. I'll say, "If I told you I'd give you $1 million to mow that lawn over there, would you do it?" I am looking for people who are honest enough to admit they are motivated by money because that is the motivation for a salesperson. You'd be amazed at how many candidates try to dance around that fact. About half the potential salespeople are eliminated at this juncture because they won't shoot straight with me. Instead they persist in saying what they predetermined would win them the job.

Why is being direct a critical trait? Customers smell it when you aren't giving them a straight answer. We have built our reputation on being honest with people to the point that if we make a mistake, every manager who had a chance to catch that error and didn't calls the client and apologizes. If somebody isn't straightforward in this company, they've got a real problem.

I'll often ask a question to test a person's honesty. I asked Alan Fendrick, "Do you have some deep burning desire that you want to accomplish."

"You may think this is stupid," he replied. "But I'd like to make more money than my father makes."

I didn't think his answer was stupid at all. Most sons are competitive with their fathers, but it took guts to be honest about it.

Next I give applicants for sales jobs a little test to see if they are able to grasp concepts. I tell them they can ask me as many questions as they need to once I've explained the subject to them.

"He told me he wanted to teach me about something called a statistical multiplexor and then he wanted me to explain it to him," recalls Fendrick. "He talked for about fifteen minutes, giving me all this technical detail. I garbled the explanation something awful, and he told me so. Rick also told me I should have asked more questions. I said, 'You're absolutely right.' "

Conceptual selling—the ability to help a customer visualize how your product or service will fit into his or her life—is a key to becoming a professional salesperson. It's applicable whether you are selling computer peripherals or top soil. Many people are good at memorizing or following a deductive reasoning pattern, but if you understand something conceptually, it doesn't matter where you come in, you can figure out what's going on. You've got to understand your product conceptually to be able to sell it. Sensing a winner, I gave Alan a second chance, and he passed the test with flying colors.

I conclude the interview by telling candidates to go home and call me after they've thought it over. I tell them I'll do the same. About half never work up the nerve to call back or, I suppose, just aren't interested. Alan, however, wouldn't leave the room until he had the promise of a second interview. I knew that tenacity would help him close tough sales. He was the only person, before or since, who has ever done that.

Nobody gets hired until he or she gets the nod from the people in the department where the job opening is. Why would anybody want to come to work at a place until he or she met the staff? All our salespeople spend fifteen minutes or so with any potential salesperson who comes back for a second interview. I want all the associates to enjoy the people they work with.

The time the person spends with sales staff isn't a cakewalk. Alan will, for example, ask, "Does it intimidate you that during the past five years, we have seen thirty people come and go?"

Some potentials will walk away right then. That doesn't bother me in the slightest. Our salespeople are an elite group. We'll sell about $100 million worth of product and services this year, yet we have fewer salespeople than we had when I joined the company eight years ago at the $5 million sales level. The interviewing process is structured to rule out the squeamish and the uncommitted. Anybody who is willing to put himself or herself through it is a decent prospect.

Finally, interviewees are invited to participate in a week's worth of sales meetings. The emphasis is on the word *participate*. The same rules that apply to our regular sales staff apply to the prospects. They'll get kicked out if they don't participate. We want to see how they handle pressure because that's what sales is. If the interviewees survive our interview process, we know they have the extreme confidence it takes to thrive in sales. It all boils down to something simple: People who take more risks sell more.

4

Icebreakers

Prasad Srinivasan is sitting at his desk stunned. Nothing like this has ever happened before. The credit manager prides himself on collecting exactly the amount he estimates. And he's never collected less than 97 percent of his estimate. But this . . . this is a catastrophe. He had promised the executive committee that he would collect $1.4 million today, which would have been a new record for Dataflex. But the check log shows that only $18,000 is in house. It's an absolute fiasco.

A native of India and an aeronautical engineer by training, Srinivasan started at Dataflex in April 1990. At that point, more than $2.3 million were overdue on the books. Within a few months he had collected the entire sum. "We analyze customers' credit worthiness the way a bank should analyze customers," says Srinivasan, who garnered an M.B.A. from Pace University in marketing and finance in 1985. In his previous job as credit manager for London Fog, Inc., U.S.A., he saved the company hundreds of thousands of dollars by refusing to do business with the Campeau Group of companies, which eventually went bankrupt. "Nobody can entice us to do business with promises." He draws great satisfaction from the fact that "nobody owes us money beyond thirty days."

Rose calls Srinivasan one of the most brilliant people at Dataflex. But today Srinivasan is having his first Dataflex crisis. There are messages on his voice mail from his boss Ann Marie Bernet and from Gordon McLenithan telling him how disappointed they are. He paces his office, practicing breaking the news to Rose. Finally, he decides to wait until after lunch.

"The group who plays together, stays together, right?" says White, proudly showing off a group shot taken during a Skirmish weekend.

"Wow, Maura," says Rose, fresh from his meeting with Fasolo. "You look great in camouflage."

Skirmish is a game in which teams divide up and then try to shoot each other with paint-gun pellets. It's similar to kids playing army. You play it in the woods, and when you're hit with paint, you're dead. The participants dress in camouflage gear, and serious players develop elaborate battle strategies. Three women are pictured among the twenty-five players in the photograph: Chrissy Zielinski, a sales assistant; Pam Beer, Tom Beer's wife; and White. "I got nailed only twice on Saturday," says White. "You should have come, Rick."

Jack Neary, a marketing-support specialist, who is strolling by, says, "Yeah, I thought Skirmish sounded like the silliest thing in the world until I found out that I had the opportunity to shoot a sales-person."

"I promised to take the boys golfing," Rose replies. "Alan, Scott, and I are going to eat sushi. Do you want to come, Maura?"

"No, I can't. I've got an appointment with Elaine to see a client in a little while," says White.

Rose holds out a packet, imprinted with the words: "Rattlesnake eggs. Caution: Keep in cool place." "Have I ever shown you my snake eggs?" he asks. "I got them when we were out in Arizona last year for the sales-recognition event."

White looks dubious, but takes the packet and cautiously peeks inside. A buzzing, like the sound a rattler makes before it strikes, brings a shriek from White, who drops the packet and simultaneously falls back into her chair. She clutches her throat dramatically and then joins the guffaws of Rose and Neary. The trick was a paper clip and rubber band strategically wound to emit the terrifying noise.

After regaining her composure, White asks, "Rick, can I talk to you for a minute in your office? I need your input."

"Sure," says Rose and walks the few steps across the hall. On his door someone has taped a copy of this quote: "In a single day, Samson slew a thousand Philistines with the jawbone of an ass. Every day, thousands of sales are killed with the same weapon."

Rose opens his desk drawer to return his snake eggs to their lair. Besides the usual supplies, the president's drawers are filled with props for pranks and mementos from funny moments in Dataflex's history. Watching him peruse the contents is reminiscent of catching a small boy emptying his pockets after a day at school. You never know what will turn up.

One of Rose's prize possessions is a piece of cardboard with a scrap of yellow silk stapled to it. Tucked into a coat pocket, it appears to be a perfect pocket square, a must for power dressers. It came from a dry cleaner, and the cardboard bears a message congratulating the owner for being so canny as to wear this corporate emblem of good taste without having to bother with buying an entire handkerchief. On Wayne Isbitski's first day on the job, Rose suddenly whirled during the sales meeting and said to him, "Wayne, you aren't wearing one of those silly, fake pocket squares from the dry cleaner are you?"

As Isbitski, whom Rose has nicknamed "Mr. Politically Correct," blushed crimson, Rose grabbed the yellow silk and whipped it out of the man's pocket for all to see. His hunch proved correct, and the sales force collapsed in laughter. The next day, Isbitski bought fourteen yellow silk handkerchiefs.

RICK ROSE: During my first sales job, I became friends with the top salesman at the insurance company where I worked. He was always number one out of 35,000 agents. I discovered that he loved fishing for dolphin, so I asked to go along as a mate on his boat. Pretty soon he took me under his wing and on some of his sales calls. Travis Young was a tall, affable country boy from Opelousa, Louisiana. He was soft-spoken, certainly not a hard-sell kind of guy.

I quickly learned from watching him that humor is a great tool. People like to be around humorous people. He weighed a situation in the wink of an eye and then wielded his wit when it was appropriate, never overstepping his bounds. He put people at ease, and he used to say, "If people like you and believe you, they'll buy." I never forgot that lesson.

Part of helping people fulfill their potential is helping them see that there is more to life than work. At Dataflex, we go hot-air ballooning and to baseball games, basketball games, and all sorts of happenings together. Once a year, the entire company spends a day at the horse races. We barbecue chicken in a special place beside the track and have our own area where we can mix and mingle. Having fun together is an important part of working together. You are creating history and a sense of camaraderie that makes the day-to-day stuff more fun. Furthermore, business is intense. Most people around here do the work of three people, and the frenetic pace is pressure packed. Humor allows a welcomed release from that pressure.

A sense of humor is critical to success—especially in sales. Robin Williams would be a great salesman because he's quick. In sales, the key is to formulate the available information and give the best possible answer quickly. A joke isn't funny if the delivery isn't instantaneous. Customers expect the same from salespeople. That's why April Fool's Day is one of the biggest holidays at Dataflex. It's also the anniversary of Rizzo's employment here. To help him celebrate last year, we filled his entire office with those plastic peanuts you use for packing.

The *Wall Street Journal* reported recently that several well-known companies, including some of our customers, have been bringing in humor consultants to teach their employees how to lighten up. After assigning a task force to the issue, Eastman Kodak opened a "humor room" in its Rochester, New York, headquarters. That sounds to me like they're approaching this thing a little too seriously.

Although you won't find a humor room in our Edison, New Jersey, headquarters, humor permeates the corporate culture at Dataflex, and it isn't confined to these walls. To make sure people are really reading our proposals, we'll slip in goofy answers on the question-and-answer pages that accompany them. For example, in a section of a proposal we once submitted outlining how differences will be settled, the response was: "We hereby promise to square off in a twelve foot-by-twelve foot ring and duel using the marquis of Queensbury rules."

We've inserted codicils in contracts that say if either party signing the contract is declared legally insane, the contract is considered null and void. In a product announcement, we'll talk about IBM memory and all the fantastic additions to some new products. Then we'll attach a question-and-answer sheet that will ask: "What do I do if I can't wait the six months until this product comes out?" and the answer: "Marry a city slicker, move to a trailer in the middle of Kansas, and it will be the longest six months of your life." We wanted to see if anybody was reading our material.

One of our most successful salespeople, Alan Fendrick, you'll recall, was a stand-up comedian before he came to us. He's still a stand-up comedian. He just gets paid for it much better now. Humor is so important that we've devoted entire sales classes to it.

Practical jokes, one-liners, teasing—nothing is off-limits here. It's part of the process of nurturing creativity. In a friendly environment, teasing helps people to overcome sensitivity about an area that may detract from their ability to sell.

We tend to come up with sniglets—made-up words that describe actions—in sales meetings during the process of helping each other to become better salespeople.

One salesman sat in his cubicle and prospected for sales, but he never exhibited any excitement about his work and, subsequently, didn't generate much from his clients. Finally, one day I gave him my Ranger Rick fire hat that I used to wear whenever I was dealing with a crisis to signal the staff that today was not the day to ask for a raise. I suggested that whenever he prospects, he should stand up in his cubicle and don his fire hat. Now when he puts on that fire hat, he literally goes through a Clark Kent–Superman transformation. It has changed the way he talks to his customers, and he has gained recognition from his peers for taking a risk.

There are all kinds of jokes going on at Dataflex. People are laughing and enjoying themselves. They're more willing to do whatever needs to get done because it's a fun place. If you look forward to going somewhere, whether it's a social event or whatever, you're going to have fun. If it's your job, and you go in and have fun there—which most people don't—you'll be far more productive. Dataflex is a place where there are no rules. Where else can you see styrofoam bricks, like guided missiles, flying through the halls? Or the president of a company walking around showing people his snake eggs?

As White slips into one of the chairs facing Rose's desk, she says, "There's a situation on which I wanted to get your opinion." She then explains that she wants to move a team member who has expertise in local area networks (LANs) from the team of a junior salesperson to that of a sales veteran. The rub is that one of the senior salespeople is notorious for failing to develop people on their team. She is leaning toward giving that salesperson a chance to prove a stated desire to change and putting this highly talented expert on their team. However, other people who are selling more LAN contracts arguably would benefit more quickly from having a LAN expert on their team. Rose listens and asks her to explain her logic. Then he explains what he would do, which differs from her instinct, and why he would take that course of action. But he does not try to force his opinion on her, leaving the decision up to her.

Rose rarely leaves the office for lunch, but his twenty-year-old son Scott, who has been working in sales administration, will be going back to college soon, and he wants to treat him. Fendrick has a passion for sushi, too, so he comes along. The Japanese restaurant is a short drive away in a strip mall. The three men sit at the sushi bar, and Rose, always adventurous, orders à la carte. "Try the spicy tuna," he urges, eating hungrily. He keeps the sushi chef busy.

Scott Rose, good-looking and athletically built, strongly resembles his father and has the same cheerful confidence. The elder Rose has an easygoing friendship with his son. Although he is obviously proud of Scott, he doesn't give that sense of pressuring the boy to fill his shoes. Rick Rose is content living his own life without trying to live his son's life, too. Scott has worked in the warehouse during school breaks since he was twelve years old, and his foray into sales administration has been a real eye-opener, he says. Fendrick's conversation centers on the antics of his new son, and he hauls out a raft of pictures of the tiny, dark-haired infant.

Rick Rose's attention is evenly divided between both men during the lively conversation that ensues during the thirty-minute meal. He is polite to and undemanding of the service staff of the restaurant and quietly picks up the tab.

After lunch, Fendrick picks up his new car phone and rushes back to the office. He says, "Rick! I just got my car phone installed! I can't wait to try it out! Let me go to the parking lot and call you."

"No problem, Alan," says Rose amicably. A few minutes later his phone rings.

"Hello?" he answers.

"Rick! Isn't this car phone great?"

"Hello, hello, hello?" Rose pretends the car phone isn't working and slams down the receiver. He grins mischieviously, his eyes squinting. In no time flat, Fendrick is back in his office.

Rose keeps a straight face, rubbing his chin in a puzzled fashion, as he says, "I didn't even know it was you. I just thought someone dialed the wrong number. I couldn't hear a word."

Fendrick interrupts, "Well, let me try again!" And he dashes back out to the parking lot.

After four tries, the account executive comes running back into Rose's office. He's out of breath and starting to sweat. Rose can no longer contain himself and starts to laugh. Fendrick gives a tight smile as he suddenly realizes he's been had. Then he doubles over in laughter, too.

Fendrick has been a frequent target of Rose's practical jokes since his first week at Dataflex. The cocky young comedian barged into Rose's office one morning to show him his new pen. Fendrick sprayed ink all over Rose's crisp, white shirt. Rose turned red as a beet and roared, "Get out of my office."

Fendrick stammered, "But, Rick, it was just a joke. It's disappearing ink."

"I said get out," Rose hissed between clenched teeth.

Fendrick slunk back to his desk, wondering if he'd crossed the line.

The next morning at the sales meeting, Fendrick felt even more concerned when Rose came into the room and wouldn't even look at him. "The topic of the day," Rose announced, "is professionalism." Fendrick sank even lower in his chair, staring at the table.

"Take, for instance, Alan here," said Rose. Fendrick looked up just in time to see Rose pull an Uzi water pistol out from under the table and shoot a stream of water in his direction. Fendrick dashed out of the room and grabbed a plant mister that he'd seen in the office. Pretty soon most of the sales staff were drenched.

The lunch hour is over. Ken Constantino is sitting at his desk. He has to make a phone call he's been dreading. Stacey Bernstein, the sales-operation manager, has just informed him that the manufacturer of a popular line of laserjet printers said it will be at least two months before it can deliver any of the printers. Constantino takes something out of his desk drawer and places the call to the company that has been waiting patiently for the now-delayed product. He says, "This is Ken Constantino at Dataflex. Name your favorite tune."

"Excuse me?"

"Just give me a group!"

"What?"

Constantino starts playing "New York, New York" on his kazoo that he keeps handy for just such occasions. His customer starts giggling on the other end. After Constantino hangs up the phone, he reflects on the environment: "We know we can do whatever we want. It's freedom."

Not everybody is crazy about the freewheeling attitude at Dataflex. It's another point on which Joe Rizzo differs with Rose. "I try to lay low when it comes to joking around and pulling pranks," he says. "I made a conscious decision not to hang around people from work because I can't afford to get too deep in the forest. I've got to be able to see things differently—not necessarily always as the contrarian, but just differently. They think I'm antisocial because I don't like to go on the sales-recognition event. For one thing, I hate to fly, and I also don't want to get that close to the sales force. If I'm friends with them, it could influence business decisions that I have to make."

Ken Cavanagh, product training and support manager, spent the first ten years of his career at such corporate behemoths as Marsh and McLennan, Inc.; Shearson Lehman Brothers; Milliken & Co.; and Philip Morris Companies, Inc. His last position at Philip Morris was as a senior sales-systems trainer, developing and supporting training services for a national sales force of more than 4,600 before he joined Dataflex a year ago. Even though he had been a client of Dataflex during his tenure at Milliken, he still gets a jolt from the antics that go on at the company on occasion, and he knows it is a big shock to many clients. "Clients from the big corporations we serve who visit the company usually have one of two reactions," observes Cavanagh. "If they come from a straitlaced corporate environment and aren't happy with their jobs, you can see the disapproval on their faces. I've overheard those kinds of people mumbling about the 'juvenile' atmosphere. Others have a live-and-let-live attitude about it. They may not understand it, but you can tell they think it's fun. Sometimes you see an expression of wistfulness when they're walking around on a company tour."

Mannix takes issue at times with Rose's style. "I believe in humor, but not at someone else's expense," he asserts. "Salespeople tend to have that kind of banter, and a lot of positive bonding takes place in the sales meeting. Sometimes it can get out of hand. I think having new associates walk the table at the company meeting is a ritual that is fun and harmless. The bows and arrows break up a pressurized atmosphere.

"This company isn't the place for people to stay in their shell. There's no place to hide. And one of the great things about Rick is that he really does set a tone. Humor has been an enormous part of his success as a salesperson. You don't have to be a wisecracker to be a company president, but you ought to allow people to have fun and smile. The attitude in corporate America is 'Have fun, and that's an order.' "

Rose loves telling stories about pranks that he has pulled and that have been pulled on him at Dataflex. "When we do our annual budgets, all the vice presidents come and make a presentation on their required funding for the next fiscal year," he says. "Tim, Gordon, and I ask questions and challenge them. Peter Galati is one of the more sedate managers we have here. He's up before Wayne Isbitski, who is always nervous about doing his budget.

"So Peter was on from 9:30 to 10:00 A.M., and we asked that when Wayne opened the door at 10:00 A.M., Peter should pretend he was quitting the company.

"The hour came and Wayne swung open the door to the conference room to hear Peter say, 'I can't believe you guys are talking like this. I did a lot of work here. I presented a fine budget, and if that's the way you feel about it, I quit.' Peter is the sort of guy who you would never expect to do this. Wayne's mouth was hanging open. Peter was packing up his overheads and materials to leave. Finally, Wayne said, 'Why don't I come back in a little while.' We answered, 'No, you're up next, Wayne.' Then Peter turned around and said, 'My heart has not beat for the past twenty-two seconds.' And he started laughing."

Despite Rizzo's efforts to avoid drawing attention to himself, he also has had a fair number of pranks played on him, says Rose. "At the first recognition event, he had arranged to leave early to catch a 7 a.m. flight," Rose recalls. "Alan and Ken decided to torment him by calling his room at 2:30 a.m. Rizzo answered the phone on the first ring, said, 'Thank you,' and hung up. They rang his room a second time and got the same response. Then it hit them: Rizzo thought it was his wake-up call.

"The following Monday, back in the office, Alan casually mentioned having a problem with the hotel wake-up call in front of Rizzo. Well, Rizzo went crazy, and said, 'You wouldn't believe what those jerks did to me! They gave me my wake-up call at two-thirty in the morning. I got up, packed, and took my shower. I was down in the lobby before I saw a clock that said it was only 3 a.m. Then they had the nerve to deny it, but I recognized the night manager's voice.' Alan never did tell him."

Fendrick and Constantino give out joke awards at the sales recognition event each year. At the last recognition event, Christina Estok, a senior inside sales representative, was given the Travel Excellence award for losing her airline ticket for the second year in a row. Another classic that the duo likes to tell dates back to the recognition event in Boca Raton. A band was playing during an elegant dinner at the Boca Raton Hotel, but no one was dancing. Finally, Constantino and Fendrick took the dance floor—together—cheek to cheek. A few minutes later the maître d' sidled up to them and hissed, "Gentlemen, please." When they went back to their table, their waiter confided that the maître d' had instructed him to cut the men off from the bar. The maître d' was dumbfounded when the waiter retorted that he hadn't served them anything yet.

Why the emphasis on storytelling? "Friendship is shared experiences," Rose comments. "In order to have a supportive atmosphere where people are vulnerable, they have to be able to be open and honest without information being used against them. Storytelling encourages that feeling. The sales staff frequently exchange war stories. Storytelling is a way of giving information and honing communication skills simultaneously. I like seeing associates talk because I assume they are sharing good news."

As you walk around the company, you will frequently hear people making plans for gatherings after work. Lunchtime is lively, too. Rarely do people eat alone, unless their work load is particularly heavy that day. Occasionally, there is some friction in the product-support department over scheduling lunch breaks, but only because someone must be on hand to answer the phones at all times. The atmosphere in that department is sort of like what you would find at an Emergency Medical Service dispatch operation. Although they aren't dealing in lives, they are answering calls that often involve thousands and even millions of dollars worth of equipment.

What you won't hear as you walk around Dataflex is the petty gossip and backbiting so prevalent in many corporations.

"It's pretty difficult to have hard feelings toward someone if you spend time with them outside the office," Rose comments. "I think tension and frustration in the workplace usually boils down to a lack of openness among co-workers. People don't empathize with each other because they have no idea what others are going through in their lives. Executives who hold themselves above others are viewed as cold and aloof. Then they wonder why there are problems. You can't hide behind a big mahogany desk forever." He shakes his head and sighs.

Asked to name his best friends, Rose ticks off the names of several people, all associates at Dataflex. Indeed, several associates and their families recently joined Rose and his family on a skiing vacation in Beaver Creek, Colorado. He says, "I extend my friendship to every single person who works here, but some people don't seem to be able to get around the fact that I'm the president." He appears genuinely befuddled by that attitude.

Office romances are openly encouraged by Rose, a self-described romantic. "There are a bunch of young people here," he says. "We are an equal opportunity employer: The staff is divided almost 50-50 female to male. People spend most of their time at work. It's only logical that they are likely to find someone here who they are interested in."

Rich Dressler recalls being summoned into Rose's office one day. Dressler had been seeing a young woman who works in the finance department, and he was afraid he was being called on the carpet for unprofessional behavior. Trudging to Rose's office, he racked his brain for something he might have done or said that was out of line but was coming up with nothing.

Rose said, "Rich, I want to ask you a question about your relationship with Antoinette. How come I never see you talking to her or being anywhere near her? If you guys like each other, it's abnormal that you wouldn't want to be together. I don't want you acting any differently here than you would outside work." Rose has even offered to pay for the wedding of any associates who want to get married on the premises.

Srinivasan called together his staff to try to figure out what happened to the money Dataflex had been promised. The credit manager's Indian accent grows thicker when he is upset, and today he is clearly upset. No one seems to know what the problem is. There are long faces in the finance department. Srinivasan knows he can't put off breaking the bad news to Rose any longer. He comes into Rose's office and apologizes profusely. Rose echoes Bernet's and McLenithan's disappointment. Says Srinivasan, "I'll get in my car right now and try to collect the money personally. I still have a few hours before 5 P.M."

He stops by his office on his way out and is surprised to see his staff gathered there. Beaming, they hand him $1.8 million worth of checks—a new record for daily collections. The whole company knew about the prank and claps and cheers wildly when an announcement is made over the PA system about the new record. Srinivasan takes the rest of the day off.

At 4 P.M. six people from Dataflex knock off early. IBM is hosting its annual Top Gun Dealer Sales Representative Event this evening to honor the top 10 percent of the salespeople in the region. Out of seventy dealers, Dataflex has three salespeople who qualified: Katz, Constantino and Fendrick. In addition, Kevin Denecour is one of three technical advisers to be honored out of the seventy in the region, and Wayne Isbitski is invited in recognition of his success with LAN. White and Rose have been invited as well. Ironically, the gala was the brainchild of Maura White when she was IBM's marketing manager. Gerry Zagorski, Dataflex's new IBM representative, is also attending. This year the event is held on a yacht that sets sail from Weehawken, New Jersey, and sails around the Statue of Liberty and halfway up the East River. It concludes the journey by taking the revelers for a close-up of the Statue of Liberty.

Fendrick takes the Top Gun award for number one salesperson in the region for the second year in a row. At one of the banquet tables, Fendrick and Rose start regaling their dinner companions with Dataflex stories. One man leans over and says to Fendrick in a hushed tone, "I only wish I could pull a prank like that on my boss, but I'd be in big trouble."

At one point one of the people at Fendrick's table asks, "What does your president think about all these pranks?"

Fendrick shrugs and says, "I don't know. Ask him. He's sitting right next to me."

They thought Rose and Fendrick were both a couple of sales guys.

About halfway through the dinner, Isbitski excuses himself and slips the announcer a note. A few minutes later, a booming voice says: "Let's all join in and sing 'Happy Birthday' to Rick Rose, president and CEO of Dataflex Corporation. He's celebrating the big Five-O today. Yes, he's 50 years old." Rose turns crimson as the entire room breaks into song. The others from Dataflex convulse with laughter when several people stop by the table to congratulate Rose on "looking great for fifty." Not only is it not his birthday, but he's still seven years away from the half-century mark.

ACTIONS

- ☑ Remember that people want to do business with friends.
- ☑ Get associates to participate in sports and fun activities together.
- ☑ Be a good sport when a prank is pulled on you.
- ☑ Encourage storytelling.

How to Use Humor Effectively

At Dataflex, we use humor in four ways:

- To break the tension that arises in a company where productivity and the drive to excel are constantly in high gear.
- To tease each other about little habits that can inhibit our sales abilities.
- To teach creative thinking and quickness to our salespeople.
- To have fun and encourage friendships.

This business is fast paced, and there's a lot of self-induced pressure that comes with the territory. It's especially evident among the sales force. When things aren't going well, Ken wrinkles his forehead. So I got a thick rubberband and told him to put it on to keep himself from looking stressed out. Every third or fourth day he'd wear this rubberband around his head. Eventually he began to give it to other salespeople who looked distressed.

His first few years at Dataflex, Constantino folded under pressure. He talked about the problem in the pond-scum meeting one Friday afternoon. He wanted to change. After that plea for help, when his associates saw him start crumbling in the face of a crisis, someone would call out, "Hey, Cave-in Kenny."

We could have taken another course and said seriously, "You're caving in again." But that would have made him feel more pressured. This way it became funny and allowed him a chance to take a step back and laugh at himself and adjust.

Constantino believes the approach was his salvation: "What would have been destructive was if my co-workers were talking about my problem behind my back. Unfortunately that's exactly what happens in most companies."

Another one of Constantino's shortcomings was his tendency to ramble during sales presentations. During the daily sales meetings, the class was role-playing, and Rose was the customer. Finally, in the middle of Constantino's dissertation on nothing, I said, "Excuse me, sir. What is your point?"

Constantino's mouth fell open, and then he said, "I have no point."

Tim Mannix quipped, "Oh, it's a Kennybunkpoint."

So now any time a person in the class says, "Kennybunkpoint," it gently signals the speaker that he or she is rambling. In a sales presentation, a salesperson can't afford not to make a point.

Says Constantino: "If we didn't talk seriously about these things in our pond-scum meeting, the teasing wouldn't be funny. Because you can't razz people for their shortcomings without letting them know that you care about them. It should only be brought up in a humorous way, because you want to help them."

Another salesman stuttered. He knew he stuttered, and his associates all knew he stuttered. He finally said one day in a pond-scum meeting, "I stutter."

About half the salespeople in the room said, "That's easy for you to say."

Everybody laughed. The pressure was off. And over a period of months, he stopped stuttering because he knew that his peers cared about him and accepted him regardless. In another environment, he never would have felt comfortable bringing his stuttering up publicly. And people would have been talking behind his back about the fact that he was hired as a salesperson in the first place.

Dataflex is a "no slack" environment. If somebody misses an opportunity to inject humor, we are all cheated! That pressure to be on promotes quickness, a key ingredient of being a professional salesperson. You have to come up with a pertinent comment on the spot. You can't be funny five minutes later. It just doesn't work.

Even in our prospecting calls, we have fun. When I was selling, I'd call and say, "Hi. This is Rick Rose and I'd like to speak with Mr. Smith."

"Mr. Rose, who are you with?"

"Oh, I'm just by myself today, thank you."

Or another question I'd get all the time was, "Where are you from?" to which I'd retort, "I'm originally from Boston, Massachusetts. Where are you from?"

One time a secretary said, "Oh, I don't think he's quite in yet." I said, "What, is he halfway through the door?"

We're looking for anything to differentiate ourselves and to make this workplace more enjoyable.

5

Fire Prevention

"The word of the day is *gauntlet,*" says White.

Rose queries, "The thing at the end of the quest?"

"A challenge?" asks Glen Koedding.

Fendrick suggests, "Isn't that where you have two rows of people with whips and sticks and they make you walk down between them. . . . Isn't that called running the gauntlet?"

"In football practice," says Rose, "a drill that offensive backs do is go through these guys who are trying to whack and slap you and knock the ball out, so you're not only feeling the sensation of them trying to rip the ball out of your hands, but. . . ."

White interrupts, "The first definition is 'a double file of armed men who strike at one man who runs between them.' The second definition is 'a series of trials and tribulations.' The road to the White House is a challenging gauntlet of processes, primaries, debates, and interviews."

"Our industry," says Maurice Scaglione, "is a bit of a gauntlet because you've got vendors beating us up on one side and customers beating us up on another, and we've got to get through."

Says Corcodilos, "The road to becoming a primary vendor is like a gauntlet in a large corporation."

Besides the salespeople, Tim Mannix, Rose, and White, there are three other additions to the meeting. Kerry Mutz, the hard-working systems-integration manager, has been attending the meeting almost daily for the past seven weeks. He called Rose at home one night to say that he didn't think he understood sales the way he needed to: "I don't know what we're promising our customers." Rose reminded him of the open invitation for anyone in the company to attend the morning sales meetings and suggested he come. Stacey Bernstein, the sales-operation manager, and Bethann Wapinski, the twenty-one-year-old senior inside sales rep on Constantino's team, are also on hand.

Bernstein, aged twenty-six, who started as a receptionist during a summer break from college in June 1987, appears uncomfortable, but starts talking, "I attended a human resources class last Wednesday on interpersonal relationships. I was the only person who represented the sales end of this company. All the other facets of the company were represented. We did an exercise on interpersonal relationships in which we wrote down who our problem person was in the company and then wrote down how we resolved the problem anonymously. Five out of the seven problem people cited were salespeople.

"The main perceptions were that someone in sales will say, 'Jump' and the associate has to say, 'How high?' Other sore points were salespeople who say, 'We have to get this done. I don't care how you get it done.' These associates feel that they have their own responsibilities and all of a sudden we impose our priorities on them, and we compound the ill will by speaking to them in a derogatory manner."

No one speaks for a moment or two after she has finished. Rose remains silent, arms crossed and resting on his chest. He looks at the faces around the table. Finally, Rose explains that Bernstein, who has worked on a team with both Fendrick and Katz, talked to him yesterday about how disturbed she was about these perceptions. He had asked her to relay her concerns to the sales staff.

"I know exactly why these attitudes fester," says Rose. "Diane went nuts the other day because the customer couldn't get their software properly loaded on the system. She went through this place like a total maniac. So we invested $15,000 in a LAN to download programs automatically that no one uses."

Katz gives no response while Rose continues his story: "That's why people get upset with salespeople. Most of the time when you come in to tell me about a problem, what happens? I am out of my chair, dragging you with me to get it solved before you can even finish an explanation of what happened." There is nervous laughter from a few. "What kind of attitude do you think that shows to the rest of the company?"

"Urgency?" says Koedding, who has had his shiny, black locks shorn close, giving him the appearance of a young soldier.

Rose says, "No one likes it because it challenges their competence. We've been talking about failure, that there are only two ways one can fail: You either quit or you do not try. If you can equate failure with errors, wouldn't you agree that one fails because they make errors? I read a statement the other day that said, 'All errors are based upon either intent or incompetence.' Would you agree that failure comes about by quitting or not trying? And that failure is really a result of errors, and errors can be caused only by intent or incompetence?"

Says Scaglione, "There can be a level of success and a level of error as well. The way you described it sounds like it's black and white. When we enlist you, the message is: 'I can't get the job done, so I have to get Rick.' I went around with you once, and I didn't like what transpired. You lose more than you gain when you enlist Rick Rose to solve all your problems."

Fendrick dives in, his words tumbling out in a rush, "My experience in having been dragged around by Rick, not always willingly, when I brought a problem to him was one, the problem gets fixed and two, you leave a bunch of angry people in your wake. Rick has a way of doing things where he makes sure you don't go through the experience again. And you fix the process."

"Yeah," says Katz, "but you shouldn't have to bring Rick around."

"You shouldn't, but sometimes you have to," argues Fendrick. "When is it okay to get upset? There has to be some point when you have a right to get angry at somebody.

"I always look at everything that goes wrong as 50 percent my fault," says Rose, "and 50 percent the other person's fault."

White says, "We had a process meeting with Diane's team about a month ago, and it was incredible how the different members were not aware of what was going on with the other functions. Once everyone understood what was going on from the customer's perspective and why requests are so urgent, they pitched in and really started to iron things out. All the customer sees is Dataflex as one entity. The customer doesn't see an individual's work or problems.

"I don't think there's anyone in here who didn't have a parent who said, at one time or another, 'Do it, just because.' Weren't you incredibly frustrated? Didn't you wonder, 'What do you mean: Just because?' But the only answer you got was, 'Because I'm your father, or I'm your mother.' "

Rose shakes his head, saying, "But this isn't a democracy. Throughout my career, I had to do many things for which I did not get an explanation."

White replies, "We can all relate to the frustration of being bossed around. We've got to make servicing customers something that everyone wants to do as much as we do. And it takes only thirty seconds more."

Banach-Walther adds, "There are times that we have to do something that others don't understand, but that's where team-order processing comes in. That's where the trust comes in; if you build relationships, your team trusts you even if you don't have time to explain. And they'll do whatever they have to."

Rose shifts in his chair and says, "That's the basis of military operations. You can't have soldiers asking, 'Why?' when you say, 'We're going to charge that hill.' "

"But," says Banach-Walther, "There was training up front."

Rose says passionately, "It comes back to believing that this lieutenant is not going to run you into an ambush. You remove frustration by establishing a relationship so that people have faith and trust in each other, that one is not being taken advantage of and that you're respected for your competence."

"Part of the animosity that customer engineering has toward sales is knowing that if they don't do it, we're going to go get Rick Rose," asserts Scaglione. "He is going to come storming in there and get it done. And that's not fair."

Fendrick gets defensive: "I have never walked into Rick Rose's office with something that is a ludicrous proposal and had him make a fuss. The problem comes when engineering says, 'I'm doing this for Alan,' instead of thinking about the customer on the other end."

Katz says, "This company *is* sales driven. People feel like they're always cleaning up after sales because the orders were processed wrong from our end, and that's not true."

Clearly exasperated, Rose stands up and leaning on the marble table says, "Diane, I just sat here and told you that this company spent $15,000 on a system because you went wild."

Katz's mouth flies open and then she sputters, "I didn't tell you how to do it. I just told you what happened and said, 'Fix it.' "

Speaking to the room, Rose gestures toward Katz: "This is exactly what the rest of the company experiences. Instead of her saying, 'I'm sorry. That was never my intent,' she will sit here and argue with me until the cows come home.

"So what is my attitude toward her? You act like a maniac, and I react by trying to correct the problem, which didn't need correcting. I'm a sucker for having done it, and I can't even get, 'I'm sorry.' "

Katz is steadfastly unrepentant, blue eyes wide and flashing. She snaps back, voice drenched with sarcasm, "I don't believe it was too much to ask that they get the software loaded right after the fiftieth time. I'm sorry, I don't agree with you on that point." Rose rolls his eyes heavenward.

Mannix, who has been watching this whole scene with a bemused expression, says, "When we talked about communication, one of the things we talked about was understanding other people's needs; the better you can do that, the further ahead you'll be.

"We also spent several training classes talking about the fact that how you say it is almost as important as what you say.

"Treating people decently is part of 'walking the walk.' The second thing we have going in this company is a high-quality program that states, 'Everything you do, whether or not you like it, every relationship you have is a customer-supplier relationship. Sometimes you're a supplier doing something for a customer, and sometimes these folks are suppliers to you. The hardest thing has been understanding that you have a customer-supplier relationship both inside and outside the company. And you cannot treat the people internally as less important than your outside customers and suppliers.

"If you can ever get that into your heads, then you'd tend to treat them differently. I don't think you treat your customers the way you treat some of the people at Dataflex. To what are you entitled? In a negotiation with your customers, whether it's external or internal, you're entitled to negotiate. Then you have the right to expect them to live up to that commitment. But you have to take the time to negotiate the commitment. Then if they don't do it, you get your manager involved."

"One of the problems when you deal with the rest of the company is that there are ten of you now. Every one of you has a number-one priority item. And your associates have to try to make sure that all ten of you are being served. Everything cannot be a number one priority. It's simply making sure that you do your part in the process."

By this time Rose has vacated his chair and is standing behind Koedding and Mosher. He begins pacing around the arc of the table restlessly with his hands alternately behind his back or gesturing to match his torrent of words. Rose says, "You're either a part of the solution or a part of the problem. My frustration with Diane stems from her lack of suggestions about how to fix it. She just screams about the fact that it's wrong. I don't know if she's had team meetings, I don't know what she does, all I know is I hear someone yelling and screaming that there's a problem."

"I just think it's the difference in the sense of urgency," says Katz, "and we've talked about this issue before. What's urgent to me to get my job done is not necessarily urgent to someone else. There are some times when a customer makes me crazy on the phone, and I'll make somebody else in another department crazy. I know I'm guilty, but it happens."

Katz, who appears nonplussed by Rose's harsh words for her conduct, contrasts the experience she has with one team member who "has the same sense of urgency that I do—he'll call me, just to let me know how things are going"—with the attitude of another person on her team: "I could stand on my head and she would still do the absolute minimum to get the job done."

Says Rose, "For those of you who don't know what Diane described, the term is *withholding*—when someone will not give you all that he or she is capable of giving. What causes it?"

Mosher replies, "Control and anger."

"I agree," says Rose. "The answer isn't to keep on replacing the withholders in the world. The answer is to change the relationship. We have to find a way to do so because we both represent this customer and we're not giving the customer 110 percent because of what goes on between you and me.

"Sales forces have traditionally fought this problem within companies because there is an attitude in the sales department that, 'I'm representing the customer, and that gives me the right to do whatever is necessary.' That is baloney. It gives you the right to present the customer's point of view to the company and then let the company, based on its capability of processes and procedures, take care of it.

"I'm glad that people at Dataflex are willing to express themselves openly because then there's an avenue to correct these bad feelings."

White observes, "We say that the company revolves around sales, but that can lead to the misunderstanding that we have carte blanche to get our priorities met at whatever cost. The objective is not only to take care of the issue at hand, but to foster the relationships that will enable us to accomplish even greater things later on. I don't think you go home and think about the customer at night. It's the Dataflex experience, the people who you work with and enjoy. What we do on a daily basis has a great impact.

"We've got these processes in place, but our communication still isn't what it needs to be. Otherwise, when emergencies arose, it would not be such a big deal. We would have enough deposits in the bank so if there were withdrawals now and then, it wouldn't have the same detrimental effect it seems to be having right now."

One salesperson sees the rampages of others as something he can turn to his advantage and says: " 'Everything reports to sales' is a myth really: We're representing a customer, and everything reports back to the customer. If it could be perceived that way, it would be a different situation. When I'm going around getting things taken care of for my customer, I hope that's what I impart to people.

"And when someone has gone on a rampage through a department before me, the difference in my attitude is going to allow me to get things done quicker."

Rose says, "Let's talk about what goes on internally. Thinking back over my career, I did as much selling internally as I did externally. I've always thought it's extremely important to get people to rally around the things that I want. I never forgot that I was only as good as the people who worked with me, and I always tried to treat them accordingly. I would tell a service engineer, 'It's really nice that I can go over this service call with you because I know that after we're finished with it, I can forget about it. I have confidence that you will always come through for me and get the job done.'

"My goal was to make them feel good and convey my belief in their competence. When the statement, 'Everything in this company reports to the salesperson' is made, it will make everybody in this company react negatively. We have to overcome the idea that sales is incompetent, sales isn't capable of running a company, and sales has no business getting ultimate authority.

"Look at any successful company run by someone who is not from the sales and marketing area, and what you'll find out is that they know good salespeople when they see them. You can have the best company in the world, and if you don't have an incredible sales department, you don't have anything."

Bethann Wapinski, a blonde with brown eyes who has worked at Dataflex for four years since she started as a dispatcher at age seventeen, suddenly speaks up, "It is a salary thing. People are jealous of the commissions, the bonuses, and the attention that Rick gives to the sales force."

"I agree, but that's only part of it," says Mosher. "I came from technical support and I longed to be in the sales department. I would think, 'There are no rocket scientists in this room. I can do what they're doing, and I'm helping them make sales, and I'm not getting a nickel for it.' Plus I hated to be out of the hub. It seemed like all the action was happening here.

"But it also bothered me that everybody always wanted everything right away. I'd say to Alan, 'I'll have the answer in twenty minutes.' And five minutes would go by and Alan would be on the phone again: 'Do you have the answer?' He'd call me three times before twenty minutes passed."

Rose chuckles, "We forget from whence we came, huh? I've been trying to write down business thoughts. One of them is: First-time managers always test their power like little children. We always want to see what we can get away with until someone stops us. It's much more fun being the king than the servant.

"I've never met a technical-support person or a customer engineer who didn't say, 'Here I am, solving all the problems, doing all the selling, designing the network, and those jerks make all the money!' Everyone out there is being driven nuts by the fact that a salesperson can make a lot of money when they feel like they're doing all the work.

"I am trying hard to represent the sales faction of this company to other areas and let them know that what they do is appreciated. But I personally am thanking them. They don't associate it with you because even when you're there, you're not thanking them. There's no sincerity."

Bernstein comments, "On the flip side, it's not exactly easy being a sales rep. At least when they go home at night, they know they have a set income, they have a set job. When you're a sales rep, you don't sleep at night."

Rose says, "if you have product knowledge, if you act as a professional, if you thoroughly research things before you go off half-cocked, people will respect you. They still may be jealous of the fact that you earn a lot of money and they may not like you, but they will respect you. When we do not act professionally, they think: Large paycheck, big jerk."

When the laughter around the table dies down, Mannix points out: "If you took a poll of this company, there would be a much higher percentage of people who do recognize the risks than you think—not unlike the offensive linemen knowing they're never going to be paid what the quarterback gets. But the offensive linemen like it when the quarterback comes back into a huddle after they've saved him from being sacked and says, 'I appreciate what you do.' Yeah, there's jealousy: One guy is making $4 million and the rest of these guys make only $100,000. Not everybody's going to be the star, but the star better do his or her job right."

Rose adds, "I'm not asking you to compromise your attitude toward getting things done for the customer and believing that you are empowered to do the right thing. I'm only asking you to change the way in which you do it."

Banach-Walther says, "I've heard certain people say about their teams, that 'they work *for* me.' Change that to 'they work with me.' Not just in your head, but in your heart. It's a very fundamental thing, but when I hear people say 'they work for me,' it drives me crazy. Everybody works together collectively to make the company a success. I correct people on my team who say, 'I work for Jayne.' "

"The original concept of the team," Rose reminds the group, "was that there was no leader and that the leader could change. If you're smart, you will encourage someone else to be the team leader.

"I have a suggestion. Each of you should spend a day working elbow to elbow with every member of your team. Tell them, 'I want to understand what you want to do; I want to appreciate what you want to do; I want you to talk to me about the good things, the bad things. I want to see the type of interaction you have with the rest of the company.' What do you think?"

"What is the goal?" asks one salesman, cocking an eyebrow. "is it to improve the relationships within the team?"

Rose replies, "You really can't understand what a person does until you walk in his or her shoes. I told you what my son Scott said. He worked in the warehouse for six summers since he was twelve years old, and he came into sales administration for the last couple of months before going off to college. He said, 'I'm a jerk. I always thought those people from sales administration were such a pain, always coming back here and saying 'Change this. Change that.' I thought that they were incompetent. I never realized how hard they work! All the stuff that the customers make us do! Now, if I worked in the warehouse and someone from sales administration came back, I would go out of my way to help him or her because I understand what's causing their sense of urgency.' By the same token, why is Rich Dressler so good at understanding what should and shouldn't be in inventory?"

"He worked in a lot of different departments," Mosher replies.

Rose nods and adds, "To this day, Maurice has an appreciation for the warehouse and prep departments that very few have here. Why? Because when he first came here, we needed him to spend two weeks helping those guys prep stuff. Talk about a guy who can sell what we do for the customer."

Bernstein comments, "I remember all the pizzas that used to be sent every other week from the sales departments to other departments, just to say thank you. It didn't cost very much, but to them it was nice. I haven't seen a pizza in a while."

Banach-Walther adds, "But don't wait for the next guy to do it. Just do it yourself."

White says, "We can try to make this complicated, but it's really not. It's a question of treating someone else like you would like to be treated. And if we've got to get the job done, let's make sure that there's urgency in our voice when we describe what needs to be done. But if you break too much glass, it's going to hurt us!

"I want to challenge you, too, that if there is a relationship between you and another associate that you know isn't right, go make your peace today."

Rose says, "We are nitpicking here. But that's one of the reasons we've been successful. We're willing to nitpick and try to improve. The very thing that you hate that I do to you, you do to your own people. You decide whatever that is, pick out the one thing you don't like, and that's what you do to your team."

Recognition of the truth ignites laughter. Rose grins, wagging his head, "You are some real hypocritical people. The reason you don't like me pointing out when you've screwed up is because you have a tendency to go around pointing the finger at other people. That's why I hate it when Diane does it. And it's very hard for me to say that I screwed up. That's why I talk about it all the time. My nature is to blame someone else. We are blind to our own faults. But you've got to remove the blinders or you have no hope of making a change."

Corcodilos agrees: "If I were working back in the technical-support department, and a salesperson came to me every week and said, 'Oh, sorry. I screwed up. I admit it. Can you bail me out?' I'd eventually say 'No!' Now if that same salesman sat me down one day and said, "Here's why I make so many mistakes. It's because I'm out attempting 50,000 things a week, and every now and then I screw up. And the only reason I'm as successful as I am is because I'm willing to take a risk and possibly make mistakes,' that would put a twist on it for me and my challenge would become, 'How can I be sharper at helping correct problems because of all the challenges he faces?' It's a difference of a few words and approaching people with humility instead of an attitude that implies: 'You owe me.' "

Banach-Walther, a champion of the team concept, says, "Why is it always how can they help you? How can you help them? That's why it was important that we found out what everybody wanted to do on our team, so we could help them get what they want. I've never been a 'glass breaker,' because in this industry in its infancy, there were no companies that had processes in place that worked.

So it was always very difficult wherever I worked to get anything done, and I had to have people behind me.

"I would always want someone to have a little more trust in me. Sometimes I see a lack of trust in people around here; the assumption is made that they don't have the knowledge or creativity to get the problem solved. If you take a little risk by delegating things to people and having them come up with the solution, it may not be the right solution at first. But, after a while, they'll get the problem solved and it'll be better for the whole team."

Rose nods and smiles, adding, "Do we give them that opportunity? There are attitudes in this room that do not promote trust. We're further advanced than most departments in most companies. We're willing to train in areas that most people wouldn't dream of personally, let alone in their business life.

"But there is an attitude problem here. The opening statement that no one from sales even showed up for the human resources meeting means that no one cares enough. How many times have I told you that any event where people get together from another department should be looked at as an opportunity for you to thank them and let them know how much you appreciate what they do."

By this point, Rose is in the football-coach mode, expostulating as though it were halftime in a grueling match.

"Jayne," says Rose admiringly, "has made much further strides in this area than most of us. So we have someone to learn from.

"How about formally taking your entire team to meet a customer? Introduce them and have all the people who are their counterparts meet your team. Print up team T-shirts. How many times have I said it here? You must come up with incentives for your team.

"Have your team's income be dependent on the team's success. Give 10 percent of your commission to the team. Have raises based upon the team's performance. Give days off based upon the team's performance. See that delivery of your customers' systems takes place within eight business hours 95 percent of the time. Get same-day delivery from your team. Are you waiting for the marketing department?" Rose barely takes a breath while he tosses out ideas. He is prowling around the table as he talks.

"Go back to thinking as though you're running a business. At Wal-mart, if we were to talk to a manager of lawn and garden supplies, he could tell you what percentage of the store's business was in that department to the tenth of a percentage point. He could tell you what his objectives for growth were, exactly the plan for getting there, how his store compares to the rest of the nation. He looks at himself as someone who runs a lawn and garden store, not as someone who is a manager of a department within Wal-mart.

"If someone came to me and said, 'We are going to cut two percentage points off the SG & A on our team and save $100,000. I want you to give me half the savings to distribute among the people on the team,' we would make that deal!

"Team-order processing may be the stupidest concept in the world. Then what is it you want to do? Remember how we originally came up with team-order processing? We were going to pick an all-star team and get tremendous production on that team. Now we want to peel that onion one more time. We will take an all-star team from the all-star team. Could that give us an exponential gain again? We're going to take the best sales administrator and we're going to take the best warehouse person, and we're going to see if all by themselves, maybe only two people, could process every one of these orders. And we're going to give them a lot of money to try. Can they do it? I bet the answer is yes. These ideas are off the top of my head, but try something new."

The more Rose talks, the more energy he seems to radiate and the faster his ideas come: "Put a credit person on the team. And what happens? Do you think the credit people will go into a company meeting and start talking about all those jerks in sales if they have been working on a team for a year and a half, contributing to the process? Are you kidding? They'll be the first to stand up and say, 'Don't you talk about *my* sales people like that.'

"So let's start adding vibrancy to this company. And I'm not talking just to salespeople. I'm talking to anybody who took the time to come to this meeting. Do whatever you think needs to be done to make this a better place. You show me a way that we can cut this inside sales force by 30 percent, and we'll pay everybody who's left 25 percent more, and that leaves a 5 percent gain for the bottom line." Rose grins happily at the thought and opens the door to the hallway.

*   *   *

The bell rings furiously a few minutes after the meeting breaks. "What is it?" Rose asks, trotting down the hall, Kerry Mutz at his heels.

"A $200,000 sale," replies Stacey Bender, one of Fendrick's team members.

"Rick," says Mutz, "I wanted to run something by you. For the LAN show, I thought it would be fun to give an aquarium with tiger sharks in it and a plaque that says LAN Shark to the sales rep with the most attendees there."

Rose chuckles and gives his approval. Then he asks, "Are you enjoying the meetings, Kerry?"

"These past seven weeks have been fabulous," answers Mutz, who dates salesperson Elaine Mosher. "I know where we're prospecting and which salespeople are working on what accounts, so I can support them better. The best thing I ever did was start attending those meetings."

Rose looks contemplative and says, "I wish I could get more people from other parts of the company to participate in these meetings. It reminds me of when I was a rookie salesman for Prudential Insurance. We were offered a chance to take a two-day course on selling with techniques developed by Willie Gayle, who was one of the top trainers in the nation for Dale Carnegie at one time. The price was only ninety dollars. Out of forty salespeople, guess how many people signed up for the class? Only two people—me and Travis Young, Prudential's top salesman and one of the best salesmen I've ever known. Whenever I have an opportunity to learn, I'm all over it like a duck on a june bug." Rose still keeps a dog-eared, out-of-print copy of Gayle's book entitled *Power Selling* in his office.

Mutz says, "I'm telling anybody who will listen that they ought to come. But I think it's the idea of having to speak up in front of the class that scares a lot of people."

Rose's attention is on something else. "How is it going with Elaine?" he asks.

Mutz, whose complexion is already ruddy, blushes and replies, "Great, Rick, just great."

Rose laughs. He says, "Kerry, let's have lunch together today. I miss you."

"I'll order Mexican for us," Mutz replies, knowing Rose's love of spicy foods.

After checking the stock prices and his voice mail, Rose calls Tony Hunter, a customer engineer manager who services customers in New York City from Dataflex's office half a block from Wall Street. Hunter, a 6 foot 5 inch forty-year-old black man who grew up in Harlem, just completed a Dale Carnegie course and won the highest honors in his class. The award was voted on by his peers in the class, most of whom had graduated from Ivy League schools, such as Harvard, Columbia, and Princeton. There were traders from the New York Stock Exchange and vice presidents from American Express, Chase Manhattan Bank, and Chubb in the class, but Hunter prevailed.

Every single associate, including Rose, has a personal development path that is a joint effort between the associate and his or her manager. Each associate is required to take a minimum of thirty to seventy hours of courses a year. Some courses are taught on the premises by Mannix, Fasolo, and others. Others are taken at local colleges. Fifty percent of those hours are on company time, and the associate gives 50 percent of the time. The entire bill is footed by the company.

"We want to learn together," says Rose. "In training classes, taught on the premises by both management and outside consultants, you'll see a vice president and the newest associates. It breaks down the barriers of position. Our goal: to have people be able to make their own decisions and think creatively." In addition, every single associate who wants to, goes through a Dale Carnegie course at a cost of $900 per person. In 1991, the company spent $27,000 on Dale Carnegie courses.

"Congratulations, Tony," says Rose. "I just heard the news, and I wanted you to know how proud we are of you."

"I could hardly believe it, Rick," answers Hunter, who manages two customer service engineers. "But I think the reason I won is because it was always on my mind that I was representing Dataflex. We often had to make presentations on how things were going with our companies, and I was full of good news. I'm proud of what goes on here and the role I play in it."

Three years ago, Hunter had quit his job as a customer engineer after getting a review that pegged him as average. "Most people would have been happy with that," Hunter says. "But it hurt me deeply because I knew in my heart that I'd been working really hard and was doing my best. I may not be the smartest, but I'm dedicated and know how to work with customers." He'd gotten the review on a Friday. He spent the weekend contemplating unemployment when he had a mortgage on a nice house in Long Island to pay off and a wife and two teenagers to support. On Monday he went into work and told his manager, "I can't live with myself being around people who think my work is average."

Hunter was cleaning out his desk and checked his voice mail one last time. There was a message from Rose, asking him to call immediately. Hunter returned the call and got Rose's voice mail. He'd scarcely had time to load another box before Rose was on the line. "Tony, I think you are making a mistake," Rose said. "I want to talk to you about your decision."

Rose listened while Hunter described his frustration. Part of the problem was that he had had three managers during the last review period, and the newest one was just looking at the position as a weigh station before his next jump within the company. Hunter loved the hustle-bustle, high-pressure atmosphere of the downtown New York office. He said, "Look, I'm working my behind off. I'm running around making ten calls a day, rain or shine, and I'll come back in the office and hear someone else taking credit for my work. Money isn't an issue. The lack of credit is."

Hunter was impressed that Rose cared enough to call and hung up convinced that he had a future at Dataflex. Indeed, soon afterward, he was instrumental in the sale of a mainsite account to Citicorp. As part of the package, Hunter was on location for a year at the customer's site. "It was a great job," he says. "John Reid, the chairman, was always kind. I was being shuttled around in limos and invited to parties in Connecticut. But after a year I was ready to get back to the New York office." He was promoted to manager. His numbers looked great: Hunter personally was handling an average of ninety calls a month and hadn't had a single recall in a year. But Peter Galati, who manages the department overall, noted that he needed to improve his interpersonal skills. His immediate manager, Charlie Ruvolo, said, "You can't strong-arm people and expect them to perform."

The solution was to send Hunter to Dale Carnegie. "I was cracking the whip, instead of listening to people and asking questions that led them to want to find solutions to the problem," recalls Hunter, who worked as a supervisor in a food-production factory before coming to Dataflex. "I still had the factory boss mentality. Once I started applying the principles I was learning at Dale Carnegie, I saw an immediate improvement. Even though we're operating in a high-stress environment, the atmosphere in our office is much more relaxed. When a problem comes up, I'll grab my slinky and sit and stare out the window for a few moments before I leap."

Rose also leaves a message on Massimo's voice mail, wishing her good luck on her midterm in psychology, a class she has after work on Wednesdays at a local college. Completing her college degree is part of her personal development plan. "It's something I'd always wanted to do," says Massimo, who exudes the same nervous energy that Rose does. "Rick put getting my degree in my development plan last year, and seeing it in black and white gave me the impetus to pursue my education."

Since his days as a rookie salesman, Rose has always put a great deal of faith in training. When a company is growing as fast as Dataflex has in the past several years, management sometimes gets caught putting out fires. However, even though his managers are relatively young and untested, Rose has devoted plenty of time to ensuring that they receive intensive training and support. In 1989 he hired Fasolo, an industrial psychologist from HR Strategies, Inc., in Stamford, Connecticut, to develop a performance-appraisal system that would reinforce the skills that Dataflex needed in its managers.

Fasolo and other consultants were brought in frequently to teach management classes on such topics as how to deal with problem associates, how to give feedback, how to develop performance plans, and how to conduct an effective interview. The first class on a given topic would be on theory and technique, the next session would be workshops, and finally the last session would be case studies of how to implement the new skills. Rose would typically attend all three sessions.

Says Fasolo, "Most important, Rick gave me the charter to talk to the managers on a one-on-one basis and submerge myself in the culture of the company."

The results of the yearly attitude survey are broken down by department, and Fasolo conducts a meeting with every departmental manager to discuss the results. Rose sits in on all those meetings and expects managers to develop action items to address any concerns that are brought out by the survey. "The reaction of many leaders when a company starts to get larger and larger is to withdraw and have less contact with their people on a day-to-day basis," observes Fasolo. "Rick has done the opposite of that. The more Dataflex grows, the more conscious he has become of his responsibility to set the example. He recognizes that the risk is that the norms he has established will break down, unless he continues to train those around him to think the same way he does."

RICK ROSE: In every part of a company, managers readily answer questions, rather than take the time to teach people to think for themselves. Then managers become frustrated when employees come to them with the same questions over and over again. The solution is training. It takes lots of time and doesn't give instant results, but ultimately the investment is worth it. We don't give people a fish, we teach them how to fish at Dataflex.

And we never miss an opportunity to learn from our mistakes. Whenever a salesperson leaves the company, for example, the group discusses at the next sales meeting the reason for that person's failure. We've had several people who are leaving ask to sit in on the meeting where they know they'll be discussed. Even when someone fails here, they still walk away with a wealth of knowledge.

For Elaine Mosher, one of the high points of her career was completing the three-month sales training course, which was initiated in January 1991 and ran through March. "I was in an unusual position because I was selling more than $100,000 worth of business a month during that time," she recalls. "So I had accounts to service, but I was also going through this intense course at the same time. It was like having two jobs."

Mannix taught a three-week course on "How to Make an Effec-tive Presentation." There were eight pond-scummers in the class. They were given daily exercises. One day the assignment was to be so obnoxious that the person on the phone would demand to talk to Rose. The purpose was to demonstrate that most people aren't nearly as aggressive in a sales situation as they think they are. Fendrick, who was participating for the fun of it, was the only one who succeeded in being obnoxious enough to provoke that reaction. Rose laughs, "This woman was practically hysterical, threatening to call the police. I said, 'Ma'am, the last time I checked, there wasn't a law against being a persistent salesper-son.' Finally, she shouted, 'You're just like him!'—meaning Alan—and hung up."

The result for many of the salespeople was more appointments and prospects than they had ever garnered in one day.

"I'm always telling the salespeople that there is a line of confi-dence that I want them to bump up against when they are selling," says Rose. "You can cross that line and become obnoxious, but most of us never even come close. I had salespeople frequently coming into my office that day, their mouths agape in amazement. They couldn't believe the responses they were getting."

Another day, the class was given the task of getting a prospect to "listen to and like you." After talking to a prospect for a few minutes, the salesperson was to ask if the prospect liked the salesperson and if he or she was genuinely listening to what the salesperson was saying. If so, the sales neophyte then explained the exercise and asked if the prospect would mind being transferred to Rose to confirm that the salesperson had successfully completed the exer-cise. "I got so many calls that day," laughs Rose. "And several of them turned into customers."

Glen Koedding edged out Jayne Banach-Walther for top hon-ors at the end of the class. Mosher fondly recalls Rose taking the eight rookies out to dinner to celebrate on April Fool's Day. "He made us feel so good about what we had accomplished," she says.

"A lot of the arrangements are in the works for the sales-recognition event," reports Liz Massimo, standing in the doorway of Rose's office with a yellow legal pad in hand. "Do you have the guest list ready yet, Rick? I need to order the invitations."

Rose motions her inside his office, saying, "I've got it right here. There are about fifty guests." The sales-recognition event is one of the highlights of the year at Dataflex. Rose personally sends invitations to all the associates who have made major contributions to the company for the all-expenses paid, four-day trip. (The cost runs around $100,000.) Rose also chooses the location for the festivities. This year he hasn't made up his mind yet.

In the past, the trips have been held in swanky locations: the Boca Raton Hotel in Boca Raton, Florida; the Boston Marriott Long Wharf in Boston, Massachusetts; the Princess Hotel in Bermuda; and the Phoenician Resort in Scottsdale, Arizona.

At the awards banquet, every guest is given a plaque and a gift, which is usually a piece of Baccarat crystal. This year the gift is a sculpted lead-crystal eagle done by an artist to commemorate the 200th anniversary of the Bill of Rights. Its head is capped in twenty-four-karat gold, and its eyes are sapphire. Its wings are outstretched in flight. Each attendee's name and the date and location of the event are engraved on the brass stand on which the bird is perched. Rose, using no notes, says a few words about each person's contribution.

The finale is the presentation of the Salesperson of the Year award. This year the award will be based on something called the balanced-performance quota (BPQ), rather than purely on sales volume, which will make it more of a horse race. Rose borrowed the notion from IBM. For a new account rep, landing a certain number of new accounts is worth 40 percent of the BPQ, hitting a predetermined profit margin yields another 40 percent, and bringing in revenues above an agreed-upon goal accounts for the remaining 20 percent. For account executives, the ranking differs slightly: making their gross-profit-margin goal is worth 50 percent; making the revenue goal, 25 percent; and selling a healthy mix of hardware and service contracts, 25 percent. The BPQ helps salespeople focus on the many aspects of their job, rather than one or two parts that they think they are especially good at. "The BPQ allows us to underline what is important to our bottom line and ensure that our corporate goals are the same as the salespeople's." (See chart below on how sales goals are met.)

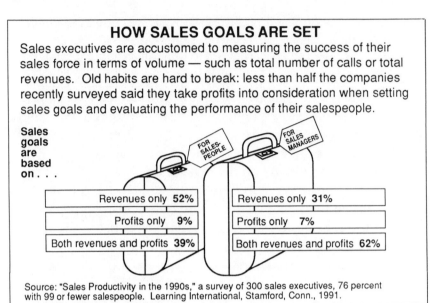

HOW SALES GOALS ARE SET

Sales executives are accustomed to measuring the success of their sales force in terms of volume — such as total number of calls or total revenues. Old habits are hard to break: less than half the companies recently surveyed said they take profits into consideration when setting sales goals and evaluating the performance of their salespeople.

Sales goals are based on . . .

FOR SALES-PEOPLE

Revenues only	52%
Profits only	9%
Both revenues and profits	39%

FOR SALES MANAGERS

Revenues only	31%
Profits only	7%
Both revenues and profits	62%

Source: "Sales Productivity in the 1990s," a survey of 300 sales executives, 76 percent with 99 or fewer salespeople. Learning International, Stamford, Conn., 1991.

Ross Culbert Lavery & Russman, Inc., New York.

At the last sales-recognition event in Scotsdale, the troops went hot-air ballooning one day. Every one had a smooth landing, except for Mannix and the seven people with him. Their balloon landed on its side and was dragged for several yards. A poster depicting a balloon crashing on its side now adds a splash of bright color to his gray office. Another day everyone took a jeep ride up to the red-rock country of Sedona, Arizona, an artists' community near the Grand Canyon. The final day, the company had a Wild West barbecue, complete with a quick-draw shoot-out. Rose boasts that he killed every one of the local area network technicians.

A few minutes after 11 A.M., Diane Katz appears in the doorway of Rose's office. "Rick, I've got to talk to you," she says, running her fingers through her long blonde hair the way she does when she's agitated.

"If it's about the meeting, Diane, I stick by every word I said," Rose retorts, hanging up the phone. His feet are propped casually on his desk. Katz closes the door to his office and the door to the small adjoining conference room.

Katz says, "So we don't see eye to eye on a few things. I can live with that. What I've got to talk about is something I can't live with, and I don't think you're going to like it either. It's about that new account that was just turned over to me."

The company's corporate mission adorns the hallway, and each department also displays its own mission statement.
Photograph by Kevin N. Garrett

Welcome to Dataflex. The first person to greet you is Maria Infusino, the receptionist, shown answering the phones.
Photograph by Kevin N. Garrett

Salesperson Glen Koedding, flanked by Elaine Mosher, listens intently during the morning sales meetings.
Photograph by Kevin N. Garrett

Rick Rose often uses the board to map out strategies while he talks during sales meetings.
Photograph by Kevin N. Garrett

Salespeople Russ Schultz, Maurice Scaglione, Ken Constantino, and new recruit Kevin Coleman join in the playful banter.
Photograph by Kevin N. Garrett

Although his style is the antithesis of Rose's, Joe Rizzo scrawls his thoughts on a board for his marketing staff, too.
Photograph by Kevin N. Garrett

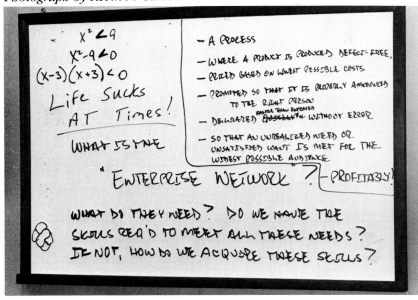

Russ Schultz, at his cubicle, is one of the sales veterans at Dataflex and served a turn as sales manager.
Photograph by Kevin N. Garrett

Maura White, the new sales manager, came from IBM.
Photograph by Kevin N. Garrett

The infamous sales board dominates one wall of the sales department, posting results for all to see.
Photograph by Kevin N. Garrett

		MON.	TUES.	WED.	THUR.	FRI.	WEEK 1	WEEK 2	WEEK 3	WEEK 4	WEEK 5	CURRENT MONTH	LAST MONTH
	3	11,508					311,163						1,255,923
	4	3,771					102,409						1,787,759
	2	5,252					181,053						700,305
	1	21,000					116,363						243,990
	6	73,005					42,851						59,878
	7	62,162					44,449						1,496,579
	11	0					9,132						21,948
	5	275					72,481						147,139
	8	12,677					33,534						80,245
	10	0					2,689						128,585
	9	314					52						137,716
		0					15,112						155,177
		62,478					98,465						132,132
		252,523					1,029,861						6,205,446

Credit manager, Prasad Srinivasan, calls the people at Dataflex his family.
Photograph by Kevin N. Garrett

The measurements in the finance department reflect a glowing record. Each department displays its measurements.
Photograph by Kevin N. Garrett

Veronica Cassiba announced to her peers that her vision of greatness meant she had to lose weight.
Photograph by Kevin N. Garrett

Gerry Soll and the late Jimmy Seccafico standing in the warehouse. Seccafico, who worked with Rose at DJC, accepted the job as warehouse manager at Dataflex before he even knew his title or his salary.
Photograph courtesy of Dataflex

Rick Rose, standing in his office with the walls lined with photos of his children, actually spends little time behind his desk. He prefers to wander around the company.
Photograph by Kevin N. Garrett

Gordon McLenithan oversees the financial end of operations and human resources.
Photograph by Kevin N. Garrett

The three amigos—Tim Mannix, Rick Rose, and Gordon McLenithan—frequently meet in the small conference room adjoining Rose's office. The room is lined with the annual reports of Dataflex's customers.
Photograph by Kevin N. Garrett

Opposites attract: Rich Dressler and Joe Rizzo operate on completely different planes, however, they've become good friends.
Photograph by Kevin N. Garrett

Framed photos line the kitchen walls and tell the tales of Dataflex's special
events.
Photograph by Kevin N. Garrett

The sales department conducts an open house featuring a prize fight (on screen) between Dataflex's contender and one of its competitors.
Photograph by Kevin N. Garrett

Time for a commercial break. The rappers, led by Steve Lamm, take center stage during the sales open house.
Photograph by Kevin N. Garrett

Tim Mannix, senior vice president, meets with associates at his round table.
Photograph by Kevin N. Garrett

Top salesperson, Diane Katz, in the Mercedes she won from Rose.
Photograph by Kevin N. Garrett

The jacket that Rose had designed is now handed out to associates on special occasions.
Photograph by Kevin N. Garrett

Rose participates in target practice during the recognition event in
Scottsdale, Arizona.
Photograph courtesy of Dataflex

McLenithan is forced to walk down the aisle at a shotgun wedding at the
same recognition event.
Photograph courtesy of Dataflex

McLenithan, Ann Marie Bernet, Wayne Isbitski, Elaine Mosher, Jane Banach-Walther, Liz Massimo, and Maurice Scaglione white-water rafting during the 1991 recognition event.
Photograph courtesy of Dataflex

Diane Katz wins diamond
earrings for being Salesperson of
the Year as Rose, his wife, Linda,
and founder Jeff Lamm look on.
Photograph courtesy of Dataflex

Rich Dressler gets a hug from
Rose and a plaque recognizing
his service to the company.
Photograph courtesy of Dataflex

Glen Koedding wins Rookie of
the Year.
Photograph courtesy of Dataflex

Even on vacation, Rose often invites associates. In Beaver Creek, Colorado, Rose (second from the left next to a ski instructor) skied with (from left): his son Johnny, Jim White, Alan Fendrick, Rose's son Charlie, Maura White, and Diane Katz.

Photograph courtesy of Beaver Creek Photography

Fendrick and Constantino always have something up their sleeves. Each year at the recognition event they do a skit. Behind the podium, they appeared perfectly normal in Scottsdale. But when they stepped out, their matching turquoise and fuchsia bike pants almost blinded the crowd.
Photograph courtesy of Dataflex

Liz Massimo and Constantino cut the rug at the Rainbow Room in New York City at the formal highlight of one of the company's Christmas parties.
Photograph courtesy of Dataflex

The Dataflex gang in front of headquarters in Edison, New Jersey.
Photograph by Kevin N. Garrett

Rose's elbows are resting on the arms of his chair, his hands intertwined and brushing his chin. He is motionless as he listens to Katz explain how she's been over and over the records of transactions for one customer and keeps finding services that Dataflex provided the customer for no charge. The salespeople had collectively decided that they wanted the option of giving customers free services on occasion, but they also had agreed that the charge would be applied against the SG&A (sales, general and administrative expenses) of the salesperson who employed that technique. Otherwise the company would take a hit for the costs incurred in providing free services and, on top of that, pay commissions for something for which it received no money.

Yet, in this instance, the sales representative who gave the service gratis did not list the charges on the purchase orders, effectively bypassing the system. He was working in a newly created sales position to bring in new accounts, and part of his responsibility was that he had to bring the account up to a certain margin before he could pass it to another sales representative. Passing the account to Katz would mean commissions in the low six figures for this man.

Rose listens carefully and then blows out his cheeks in a heavy sigh. This young man is a rising star. But if it plays out the way it looks, Rose thinks to himself, the salesman has crossed the line of ethics and lied and committed fraud. And, for the first time, it appears that a star will fall at Dataflex. Katz spreads the purchase orders on Rose's desk for him to examine, and he hunches over them, his eyes narrowing to mere slits.

After a few moments of silence, Rose finishes looking at the evidence and says abruptly, "We'll talk some more this afternoon. You don't have any calls, do you?"

Katz shakes her head no.

"OK, look, I've got a lunch appointment with Kerry, and then I'm in meetings until late in the day," says Rose.

"I'll be around," Katz replies. She opens the door to Rose's office just as the salesman in question rings the bell. Katz and Fendrick are usually the first to ask who made a sale and to whom. This time, the veteran saleswoman stops and looks at the young man for a split second and then walks away without a word.

ACTIONS

☑ Beat "They." In most companies, you hear people complain, "They won't let me do it." Who is "they"? I can't deal with "they." Tim Mannix has a black banner with white type that has those simple words on it framed on his wall. It serves as a constant reminder that "they" statements are unacceptable if you hope to solve problems. When someone says "they," it's usually connected to something negative, and we quickly try to put a face on "they." Otherwise, people start to feel helpless against this faceless organization. Exactly the opposite of what you want to nurture.

I eliminate the excuses. When someone marches into my office to issue a complaint, I don't let him or her get away with placing the blame on "they." Once we've established exactly with whom the problem lies, we can take action to right any wrongs. Action eliminates excuses. It also puts positive pressure on associates to be solution oriented. They know when they bring a problem to light, they had better have thought through some possible solutions.

☑ Define business simply. If it seems complicated, either you messed it up or it is your perception. Either way, fix it. You want to know what's wrong? Ask the people who do the work. Management starts complicating things.

☑ Recognize performance, both good and bad, publicly. A bad example can be used for teaching just as easily as can a good example, but not if you conduct all your business behind closed doors. Some people get offended about that at first, but once they realize it's consistent and that they aren't being singled out, most accept it.

☑ Admit your mistakes at the moment.

☑ Learn from others who do it right.

☑ Be willing to invest time and money in training.

☑ Let the winners win big. Cultivate your star performers. Always make recognition first class and make sure there are a whole bunch of people there. Be specific about the job that was well done. Hold star performers up to others as a role model. Nothing cleans up people's acts faster than seeing those with the right attitude pass them by.

TRAINING, TRAINING, TRAINING

We are like a military organization. We spend a lot of time practicing because we may get only one shot, and when we execute, we must be lethal. Training is the lifeblood of the company, and it gives me a chance to lead the front lines.

We spend an awful lot of time getting ready to do something. We concentrate on learning concepts. The rest of the business world tends to spend time fighting fires. At Dataflex we use training as our fire prevention.

This company is full of young people because I'm more interested in a person's genuine desire for success than mile-long résumés. In some ways I'd rather take someone inexperienced and train him or her from scratch, so I don't have to undo the damage done by uncaring managers at some other company.

Stop trying to make business esoteric. What we do and what almost every other business does is simple. We take stuff in from vendors and then sell it. Almost everything is pretty straightforward, except for rocket science, and those guys just wear white coats and have a lot more formulas.

6

Visions of Greatness

Kerry Mutz arrives for his lunch date with Rose, hands filled with bags of fast-food Mexican fare. Rose doesn't say anything about the crisis he's wrestling with internally, although Mutz senses that something is up. The president fetches a soda for himself and for Mutz from the kitchen and rejoins Mutz in the small conference room connected to his office. Jack Neary, from marketing, happens to walk by and Rose invites him, too. The conversation is light.

Then Rose asks, "Have you guys been working on your visions?"

"Mine's coming along," answers Mutz, who is thirty-three years old and has carrot-red hair worn long. His green eyes study Rose quizzically through gold-rimmed glasses.

Neary, aged twenty-five, thin and fair complexioned, has a pensive expression on his face. He has been with the company for two years. "I'm not too sure about my vision," he says. "It's still fuzzy."

Over the past eight months, Rose has been bothered by the fact that there was a small percentage of the work force that he knew he never would have worked with eight years ago—the result of fast growth and delegating hiring responsibilities to new managers. "I looked around and realized there were people here whom I didn't enjoy working with," Rose says. "But whenever there is a problem, I always assume that I'm 50 percent of it. First, it's true, and second, my 50 percent is the part I can do something about. When I examined myself, I realized there wasn't anything motivating me to get up in the morning, so how could I expect the people around me to be supercharged?"

Throughout his career, Rose had given himself goals that had fired his fierce motivation. His first goal was to become a national sales manager. He achieved that in 1976. Next, he vowed to make himself so important to a company that he'd get a six-figure salary. In 1981 he achieved that goal. That year his father died. Hundreds of people attended Elliot Rose's funeral. Rose's father had many friends. He also had many debts. Rose was saddened to learn that his father had left his mother Phyllis, who was approaching her sixties, in a weak position financially.

His new goal was to earn enough money to provide well for his mother and to secure her future. It took five years to accomplish. Eight months ago Phyllis Rose, an artist, presented her son with a small, marble sculpture she had made entitled "Freedom." She also gave him a note that said that for the first time in her life, she had no financial worries, thanks to him. A few days later Rose, for the first time in his life, realized that he had nothing that he was driving toward. He knew that to breathe new life into his routine, he had to find a new challenge.

Around that time, he was reading a book called *The Empowered Manager* by Peter Block, an organization-development consultant in New Providence, New Jersey. In it the author wrote that the first step toward empowerment is creating a "vision of greatness" as "the deepest expression of what we want." A vision, Block said, goes beyond goals, which merely predict the future: "A vision is the preferred future, a desirable state, an ideal state."

Rose was particularly intrigued by this statement from the book:

> The wish to hedge against the word greatness is to hedge against committing ourselves to something we may not be able to achieve. We fear that greatness is simply not in our story but only in the story of others. Greatness demands that we eliminate caution, that we eliminate our reservations, and that we have hope in the face of the history of our limitations.

Rose agrees with that statement completely: "Most people operate at about 80 percent of their potential. I think the reason is that in the back of their minds, if they fail, then they can excuse it to themselves by saying, 'It wasn't my best effort.' Think about the difference one degree can make: At 211 degrees you have hot water, but at 212 degrees, you have steam that can power locomotives. One of the biggest impediments to associates fulfilling their potential is their inability to turn up the heat on themselves and make a decision in a timely manner. They're afraid of reprisals for a bad decision. They wind up letting their fear of making the wrong move paralyze them."

The book discussed visions of greatness related to the workplace. Rose was intrigued and spent the next eight months tinkering with his own vision of greatness, before finally presenting it to the executive committee, which is comprised of ten people, including Rose.

During his presentation, which had overheads and full-color graphics, he first explained how he arrived at his personal vision. He also told the executives he expected them to make a commitment to pursue a vision of greatness on their own terms. Next he gave the key beliefs upon which he based his vision:

- Most of us will spend the remainder of our lives working.
- Organizations are the primary meeting places for people. We spend more time with people at work than we do with our families.
- Therefore, work ought to be more than just a job.
- All of us should push the limits, regardless of our positions.
- No system is going to work for all people.
- I want to create a culture that supports the best of what people want.
- I will not cater to those who would not respond under any circumstance.

"I want to establish our corporate culture for people who want to be top performers and who are seeking more authority, more self-expression, and more freedom," Rose said. "I am not working to make things easier on those who are unable and unwilling to contribute their best. Those people will find themselves unemployed."

Rose continued the presentation, saying that many businesses are set up like families in which children aren't expected to do much and, therefore, they don't. "We expect less of average performers, and we get less," Rose stated. "We must demand to break the paradigm of average performance."

At Dataflex, however, he wants each associate to take total responsibility for the success of the business. "Over time we will create top performers," Rose noted. "People who do not wish to take responsibility will find ways to avoid it. Let them find those ways somewhere else.

"My preferred future is based on making decisions that are good for me as an individual and good for Dataflex. I'm not sure what a company president is supposed to do. I feel like I'm inventing the position. But I believe that expressing my vision to you is an essential act of leadership.

"It's different from goals and objectives. Those are predictions of the future. I'm talking about what you'd like to find at the end of the rainbow.

"The end of the rainbow for me would be working with a group of people who feel responsible for creating a workplace they personally believe in and whose work is an expression of their deepest values.

"I can't give you a definition of greatness, but I know what it tastes like. It doesn't mean being the absolute best. Greatness means living up to your own maximum potential. Many people can be great at something, but they may not be the number one person in the field.

"Stating our vision:

- signifies our disappointment with what now exists,
- questions the way we operate,
- questions the way we serve our customers,
- questions the way we deal with each other,
- opens potential conflict with the visions of others, and
- forces us to hold ourselves accountable for acting in a way that is congruent with that vision."

Rose explained that he was stating his vision of greatness publicly for the same reason people get married publicly: "For many of us our wedding vows are the first thing we've publicly declared. Your friends are there to help you act appropriately later on and stick to your promise.

"My vision of greatness is simply this: To seek greatness for myself and surround myself with and contribute to others who are pursuing that ideal. And I will do anything to support you in reaching your own vision.

"What does greatness mean to me?

- Recognition of world-class customer service for Dataflex.
- Peer and industry recognition as a great sales-team leader.
- Peer and industry recognition for creating a great working environment."

In his explanation, Rose echoed Abraham Maslow's theory of self-actualization, which means improving self-esteem by decreasing the difference between self-image and self-ideal.

"I am looking for people who are willing to take the risk to climb mountains. If you are caught in the survival mode and all you care about is the basic comforts, go work somewhere else. It doesn't mean you're a bad person. It just means that I don't want to work with you. If you are new here and are still trying to get the basics of survival, security, and social acceptance together, that's ok. It took me eight months to figure out what my vision is.

"As you are formulating your vision, though, don't look for something that I will approve. For example, greatness to you may mean graduating from college. If you come from a family in which no one has ever achieved that dream before, then that would be a great achievement. And don't make achieving your vision depend on

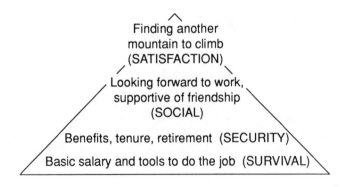

Finding another
mountain to climb
(SATISFACTION)

Looking forward to work,
supportive of friendship
(SOCIAL)

Benefits, tenure, retirement (SECURITY)

Basic salary and tools to do the job (SURVIVAL)

someone else. You also must be able to measure whether you are making progress in the quest for your vision."

"Who do I think is seeking greatness in this company right now? Charlie Milo. Charlie has been offered jobs at more than twice what he makes here, but money is not his primary reason for doing what he does. He wants to be the technical expert in his field and believes he has the platform here at Dataflex to achieve that level of greatness.

"Deron Illarraza. Deron has three kids and works three jobs, and his vision is to be a great policeman. But he does an incredible job wherever he is. Friday is his last day at Dataflex because he just got a position with the Monmouth County Police. He is seeking greatness in the form of being a decent human being.

"Finally, Gordon McLenithan is a man who seeks greatness. Gordon is one of the most motivating men I've ever met. From the time he graduated number one in his class at Bentley College, he has sought greatness."

After Rose finished his presentation, the executive committee broke into applause. Mannix said, "Rick, every one in the company needs to see you do this. It will help us all start thinking in the right direction." The other directors agreed. They also decided that developing a vision of greatness should be required of every associate. The individuals on the executive committee were given two weeks to formulate their visions. "You don't have to use overheads or anything fancy, just make it from your heart," Rose exhorted.

Two weeks later on a Wednesday morning, Rich Dressler walks to the front of the conference room. Typed on the sheet of paper he carefully lays on the overhead is the following:

My Vision of Greatness
1. A house
2. A wife
3. A family

Dressler, tall, muscular, and handsome, shifts his weight uneasily and says, "Before I tell you about my vision, there are some things I need to tell you about me that will help you understand why these things would be the greatest thing to me."

His voice grows husky with emotion as he continues. The only light in the room is coming from the projector. "I grew up in a home where not a lot of love was shown. I spent countless nights sleeping on the porch or over at friends' houses just to get away from the noise of my sisters' crying and the sounds of my parents' fighting. I got out on my own as quickly as I could and put my energy into not depending on anybody. I've rented all these years because I didn't want any ties.

"For a long time I've lived in fear of repeating the pattern I grew up with, but from being here I am starting to realize that I can have a normal life. Every day I see people leave early to be with their families. I think that must be the greatest thing—to have people you want to see at home and people who want to see you. Without that foundation, I don't think I can build what I want to build."

When he sits down, tears are glistening in the eyes of many around the table. Rose says quietly, "Thank you. That is very much a vision of greatness. I want to support you in this and be your friend by telling you when you're not working toward achieving these goals." He leans over and whispers, "I love you" in Dressler's ear.

Ann Marie Bernet, the thirty-four-year old director of finance, is next. Simply dressed, she has brown hair flecked with gray and large blue eyes. "My vision of greatness would be to make Rick crazy," she cracks. "Like Rich, I need to give you a little background. When I was very young, my parents separated, and my mother had the primary responsibility of supporting the three of us. Even though she worked hard, things were often tight financially. I vowed never to be dependent on a man again. Later, when my male friends were offended by that statement, I amended it to never being dependent on anyone.

"My moments of greatness were finishing the Dale Carnegie course, paying off my student loans, and taking the CPA exam. My vision is to develop my skill level to the point where people are banging my door down, begging me to work for them. I don't want to depend on the economy or on a job with any one company. I want to be well-enough known in my field, so headhunters will call and ask about *me*." She pauses, then grins mischieviously and adds, "*Not* Joe Rizzo."

Mannix says, "Hmmm. That's an interesting juxtaposition. Rich wants to depend on someone. Ann Marie wants to build a moat around herself."

Rose says gently, "I know things that happen in your childhood can be a powerful motivator. I always recognized that my father didn't achieve greatness, and that fact made me all the more determined."

Peter Galati, vice president of customer engineering, stands before the group. His vision fills an entire page, single spaced. He has divided it into work and family. What is important to him is being respected and being known for cultivating teamwork. He wants to be known as a good listener at work and at home. Galati, of medium build with brown hair on the long side, concludes in a heavy Brooklyn accent that "my home will be filled with love, laughter, happiness, and encouragement."

When he is finished, Rose is leaning back in his chair and says, "What is it you want to be great at? If your child becomes a drug addict, have you failed? How will you measure it?"

Galati says, "If I know I've done my best, no, I wouldn't consider myself a failure if my child became a drug addict, no more than I would be a success if he became a doctor—that's my child's choice. But being a good dad and a good listener are important to me. Tim Mannix is great at both, and I admire him for it."

McLenithan offers, "I think he's trying to establish a style of living."

Rose still looks quizzical, so Galati adds, "Okay. Maybe I need to give a little history, too. Ten years ago, I was working at a company in New York, and after twelve months there, at review time, I was told I wasn't cutting it. I was totally shocked. There was no warning, and I thought it was totally unfair. That's part of the reason fairness in dealing with my associates is so important to me. I know what it feels like to be blindsided when you are honestly doing your best.

"The other reason is that my father and my mother did not communicate well at all. And my father has always had a difficult time expressing his love and support for me as well. I want my marriage and the way I talk to my children to be different."

Wayne Isbitski asks, "How would one know if you'd achieved this?"

"We've been married over twelve years," says Galati, "and we're making a real effort to understand each other as individuals."

Mannix says, "The most important measurement is being able to look in the mirror and answer affirmatively that you are living the life you've laid out before us today."

"When your children get married, if they say, 'I want to have a marriage just like Mom and Dad,' you will know you have accomplished greatness," says White.

Nick Nicholson, Mannix's former partner and the consultant Rose has brought in to run the meeting, adds, "If he did the things up there on his list, he'd be not just a good manager, he'd be a phenomenal manager."

Tim Mannix ambles up to the front of the room and takes a rumpled piece of paper out of his pocket. In his booming voice, he announces, "I've been working on some semblance of this vision since 1972. I was at a marriage-encounter weekend, and a question we were asked was, 'If this were the last day of your life, how would you spend it and who would you talk to?' I realized I hadn't been giving the best to my family.

"My father died when I was thirteen years old. I was the third oldest of seven children, and I learned to be very independent from that time on. I'd also become driven to succeed. However, during that weekend, I caught a glimpse of how far I'd let my marriage and my family slide down in the ranking of my priorities. I realized that if I only had twenty-four hours left, I sure wouldn't be concerned about closing the next sale. I'd want to spend it with my family.

"The next jolt I got was in 1975. The year before I'd been praised as the number one branch manager in the nation for IBM, but in 1975 my boss gave me a six out of a possible ten. I went from being a genius to a jerk in the space of a year. It made me stop and think about what I really wanted—being good at what I do or desiring fame and recognition.

"So I will have achieved greatness if I have done the things I have written on this little piece of paper that I carry around with me all the time:

- Living my life as I believe my God wants me to.
- Liking the man in the glass.
- Looking forward to getting up each day.
- Loving and being loved by my family.
- Being true to and there for my friends.

- Using my talents and skills to their fullest.
- Giving more than I got.
- Creating a climate that allows others to be the best they can be.
- Knowing that greatness consists of the combined total of the outward things I do, coupled with the inner being I am.

For my epitaph, I hope it will say: 'He could be trusted and relied upon by God, his family, his friends, and those he dealt with.' "

Maura White has been with the company only seven months. She starts by saying that her vision isn't clear to her yet, but she has two main desires:

- To use the gifts that God has given me.
- To leave things better off than the way I found them.

"I grew up in a well-to-do community," she says, "but my family was not well off. For many years I was motivated by money. I didn't want to have to buy my clothes at K-mart anymore. But a few years ago, driving back from the beach, I realized that I had to derive satisfaction from something beyond material goals. That's when I came up with these desires.

"As for goals, security is still important to me, so I have set as a goal to save $100,000 in the next five years for my son Casey's education. My method for achieving success in the past has been to be a counterpuncher. In other words, I waited for someone else to take the first step and then I analyzed that step like crazy and figured out how to improve upon it. I think I'm like Martina Navratilova in that she had to work hard to learn to rush the net and be aggressive. I am going through a maturing process: I no longer live for the applause from others. Pleasing myself is more important, and if others like what I do, then that's great."

Finally, she says, she wants to be considered a leader versus a good manager. She points to a pyramid that she has projected on the overhead. At the bottom is chemistry, in the middle is sales and personnel management, and at the top is "thumbprint." "Right now I'm still working on helping make the sales force better and honing my personnel management skills," White explains. "I'm not in a position to be a leader because I'm still working on the basics. A leader is a person who has the vision and the ability to make that vision a reality. I'll know I've accomplished my vision when I get a standing ovation from the sales force at the recognition event. I want my hallmark to be helping make the best better."

Joe Rizzo, director of marketing, stalks up to the front when White concludes. He starts off by saying, "I'm not too crazy about putting these up here." Rizzo, who spends a good deal of time weight lifting, is known for his innovative marketing ideas and his intensity. His vision of greatness reflects his tremendous desire to make his mark:

- to own intellectual property
- to be named Person of the Year by a professional association or business publication
- to gain national notoriety resulting from a contribution to our society (in excess of fifteen minutes' worth)
- to contribute to the political process
- to own a sports franchise

When he is finished, McLenithan notes that the "common theme is personal recognition."

White asks, "Have you wanted these things a long time?"

Rizzo, who has short dark hair and hazel eyes and who usually wears suspenders with his suit, nods yes.

Someone asks why a sports team. Rizzo shrugs and says, "I can't play, so I gotta own."

"Do you know somebody who's done all this?" asks Rose.

Somebody names George Steinbrenner, but Rizzo quickly shoots him down as a role model. Rose says, "Ah. So part of the formula for your vision is that you must be a decent human being. Greatness doesn't necessarily mean fame. For instance, Ted Kennedy has accomplished some of the things on your list, but he hasn't achieved greatness by your definition. Correct?"

There is agreement around the table. "Then," Rose continues, "what all of you have mentioned so far really boils down to having a balance in your life. It means doing the right thing, not just in business, but for your family and in every facet of your personal life. I've always tried to make my decisions based on whether the person sitting across the table would do the same for me if the situation were reversed."

Greg Coccetti, director of information systems, keeps his vision short and sweet. He's entitled it "Greg's Rules for the Road," and it says:

- Integrity
- Knowledge
- Leadership
- Sense of humor
- Doing whatever it takes (without breaking any of the previous rules)
- Living on the edge

Rose, his arms crossed and resting on his chest, says, "Yeah, that's greatness. Although I don't know that you have to have leadership in there. Ken Constantino has all those other ingredients, and I believe he has achieved greatness. You absolutely can't get by without integrity, though."

Wayne Isbitski, blonde with blue eyes, takes the floor. "I have two visions," he says.

Rose interjects, "You're schizophrenic!"

Isbitski casts Rose a sidelong glance, grins, and continues: "I have an internal vision that is judged by a higher entity that I don't wish to be judged on here. But that vision directs me to give back more than I get. My external vision is to be the absolute best at whatever I choose to do. I've been at Dataflex four years, eleven months, and twenty-eight days, and I've had six different positions. In each of them I was the absolute best. When Dataflex does not allow me the opportunity to be the best, I'll leave. To me, if you can't set your sights at the pinnacle, there's no reason to go after it."

McLenithan stands up slowly and walks to the front of the room for his turn. "When Rick made his presentation, he paid me the compliment of calling me great," he says. "I was genuinely surprised, but honored. I first developed a vision at age twenty-one. My early years were really tough. I was the oldest child, and I lived in a home where I was emotionally deprived. Nobody ever told me they loved me. Nobody ever hugged me. Then when I became a teenager, I couldn't cope because I was never a child. After my sophomore year in high school, I started to drink excessively and pretty much muddled my way through the rest of high school and three years thereafter.

"I don't know what stopped me, but when I was twenty-one years old, I wrote this statement: 'There is not a challenge I would give myself to which I will not succeed.' The negative way I stated it gives you an indication of my mind-set at that point. The process of carrying out my vision is to be the best I can be in whatever endeavor I undertake. I then took all my problems and put them in boxes without resolving them so I could address my vision."

On the overhead projector he lays down a page that looks like this:

Objectives
Accomplished

- To be a partner at Price Waterhouse (unfulfilled)
- CPA
- Graduate number one from Bentley College
- Become a CFO of a company
- Provide well for my family
- Own the business I work for
- Become a millionaire

Halfway:

- Travel around the world
- Have nationwide recognition

At some point:

- Write at least two novels
- Build my own home
- Understand who I am

"All my life I've suffered from low self-esteem," says McLenithan in a low, gravelly voice. "I'm a very logical person, but I have a lot of emotions locked up inside, which have caused an imbalance in my life. About two years ago, I started opening up the emotional boxes that I had sealed as a teenager. And I've got to tell you, it's the most challenging thing yet. I write poetry and that has proved an outlet for some time now, but I want more. I'm continuing to work on understanding who I am and how I can balance my emotions with my logic."

When McLenithan has taken his seat again, Rose says, "I want to take responsibility for being supportive of helping you achieve each of your visions. I said I wanted to surround myself with people who seek greatness, and I'm so encouraged by what you said here today."

The consultant, Nick Nicholson, adds, "The courage and willingness of your people to take risks is outstanding. And the desire for principle-based living is also inspiring."

The rest of this afternoon, Rose sits in on a session with about forty associates, all of whom will be sharing their vision of greatness. Rose has been amazed at what has come out since he challenged everyone in the company to develop a personal vision. Some people have expressed dreams of wanting to open schools for underprivileged children. One woman said greatness to her would mean never having to stand in the unemployment line again. Another woman said it would be achieving a balance among family, work, and friends.

Rose made it clear that the style of the presentation was not important; the substance was the important thing. One person came in the room and punched a button on a tape recorder and played a prerecorded recitation of her vision.

Not everyone has embraced the idea. The day after Rose announced that everyone in the company would be required to give his or her vision of greatness, one salesman left. "He knew he couldn't stand up in front of his peers and mouth a bunch of words he didn't mean," says Rose. "In the past year, he had continually made empty promises about how he was going to change this or that. This time the stakes were too high."

This afternoon, most of the people in the room are from the finance department. Several people make their presentations. Then one young woman comes to the front of the room. She is five feet seven inches and has brown, curly hair that brushes her shoulders. She is almost as white as a ghost, and her hands are trembling as she reads her vision from a printout:

"My vision is divided into three parts, meaning, I have a personal, professional, and a combination of both personal and professional visions.

On the personal side, greatness for me can be achieved only

when I am truly happy with my appearance. I am tired of hearing what I call the classic lines: You have such a pretty face and you're such a nice girl. Not that those are bad things to hear, but when they are nice ways of saying you should lose weight, they are.

I know I am the only person who can change all that. Therefore, during the next six months, I *will* lose a certain amount of weight. Anyone who has ever dieted before knows that this is not an easy task. You need to want it more than anything; you must become almost obsessed with it. To achieve the weight loss I want, I have taken several steps. First, I have lowered my daily caloric intake to between 1,000 and 1,200 calories. And second, I have begun an exercise program that includes, to start, fifty sit-ups and sets of other various exercises each morning. As I go along, I will have to add more sets of each exercise to maintain the loss. I want to become a woman who turns heads, and I don't mean away. I will know I have achieved this vision, not only when I have lost the number of pounds I intend to lose, but when I can look in the mirror and say 'I look and feel good!' This will give me added confidence to strive for success in all my future endeavors.

"Professionally, I see myself achieving management status within three year's time here at Dataflex, assuming the opportunity arises, hopefully within the credit department. Perhaps the expected growth in Connecticut will make it necessary for there to be a credit manager in the Connecticut office, or perhaps Prasad will be promoted, which could open a position for me. I want to be recognized and respected for my work, not only by my peers, but by other departments and by the management team at Dataflex. I want to be as good, if not better, than Prasad; to be able to manage a credit department better; and to beat all his goals, which seemed unsurpassable to me two years ago. I want to be able to analyze an account at a glance, with complete accuracy—to become a well of knowledge and information for the sales team, my department, and the entire management team. To accomplish this, I am attending college to obtain my associate degree in credit and financial management. Later I plan on pursuing my bachelor's degree. I am also attending seminars and, most important, I am constantly working with Prasad and observing him to learn how he handles the department and his job.

Last, incorporating the first two parts of my vision, I want to be married within the next three years. But it will not be enough for me just to be married; I want to be the epitome of the nineties woman: to be able to manage a family and a career at the same time. I see myself being successful at my job, while still being able to go home; cook a full meal; spend quality time with my husband and, hopefully, my children; and be the best wife and mother I know I can be. My first goal, being the toughest to achieve, will make me find the inner strength necessary for me to achieve all my visions of greatness."

Immediately after Veronica Cassiba, aged twenty-six, the credit analyst, finishes her speech, she is clearly taken aback when the forty associates in the room give her a rousing standing ovation. Tears well her blue eyes, but she is beaming with joy. Two days before she read her vision to the group, she had read it to her manager Prasad Srinivasan; Mary Sheehan, who is McLenithan's executive secretary; and Colette Durkin, a financial analyst, but until the moment she stood up, she was unsure that she could follow through on her vow to herself to read it.

After the applause dies down, Rose says, "Veronica, I think perhaps more than anyone I've heard give their vision of greatness, I can relate to what you are saying. I've struggled with a weight problem all my life. My weight is the one area that I absolutely have no control over. I know exactly what I can do to help you achieve your vision. Every day that I'm in my office, I'll eat lunch with you, and we can diet together."

Then Rose turns to the associates and tells them that he will meet with them again for a follow-up meeting in two weeks to learn their progress.

Although the visions of greatness have driven the point home to Rose, he has long understood the importance of dealing with individual associates as whole people, rather than trying to separate their business personas from their personal lives. Associates often seek his advice on personal matters, and he takes the time to listen. For instance, when Prasad Srinivasan came home on Friday, July 19, 1991, after spending the day at Dataflex's annual picnic, he found that his wife and four-year-old son had moved out, leaving hardly anything behind. The twenty-eight-year-old Indian turned to Rose for support. After a torturous weekend, Srinivasan was Rose's first appointment the following Monday morning. Rose was quiet as Srinivasan poured out his anguished story. Distraught, he asked for some time off to visit his investment banker father, whom he hadn't seen in eight years, in Saudi Arabia.

"As I was leaving his office, I asked Rick if I could do anything for him," Srinivasan recalls. "The Gulf War had just ended, and he asked for some sand from the beaches of Kuwait where the marines had landed. It's a small thing, but I knew it was his way of letting me know he wanted me to come back. He still has that bottle of sand in his office. I will remember his kindness until the day I die.

"I stayed over in the Middle East for a few weeks, and my father tried to persuade me to stay there. He said, 'You don't have anything back in the United States.' And I said, 'Oh yes I do. I've got my family at Dataflex.' At that moment, I realized how much I'd grown to care about the people at the company. A few months passed, and on Christmas Eve, my phone rang. It was Rick. He extended an invitation for me to join his family on Christmas Day for dinner because he didn't want me to spend it alone. In my eyes, Rick Rose stands on equal ground with my father."

Rose has a tremendous capacity for remembering details. Very little escapes him. Each year at Thanksgiving he buys turkeys for every associate. Rich Dressler caught a ride home with one associate on Tuesday before the holiday. On the way, Dressler dropped his turkey off at a church that was sponsoring a drive for the poor. Wednesday evening, around 6 P.M., there was a knock at his front door. A man from the warehouse was standing on his doorstep holding a twelve-pound turkey. "Rick was sitting in the lunchroom when he heard that you gave your turkey away," the young man explained. "He gave me money and sent me out to buy this one for you."

Says Dressler, "I can tell you a million stories like that because Rick really cares about people."

At four-thirty, Rose and McLenithan meet in Rose's office.

Doors at Dataflex are rarely closed. But after McLenithan strides in the room, Rose swings the door shut behind him and then begins to tell him what Katz has brought to his attention. The salesman in question has been at the bottom of the rankings lately, but was on the verge of bringing on a huge account, which would have bumped him up considerably. Besides, at Dataflex each salesperson represents a good portion of business, and there will be some fallout. Rose is set on a course of action, but he wants to get input from his partner. He also speed dials Dataflex's lawyer and puts him on the speakerphone. After an hour of discussion, Katz and Fendrick are summoned to the meeting as well.

"You know what I think Rick," says Katz bluntly. "I told him the first day he came on board here that I didn't like the way he did things."

Rose says with a sigh, "I remember, Diane. I remember."

ACTIONS

☑ Figure out what greatness means for you. Then tell someone your vision.

☑ Cite heroes so that associates will have a picture of what greatness looks like. Try to find heroes in your own company.

☑ You can't want things for people. They have to want them for themselves. Management from any other perspective is short term. But you can motivate people to want what you want.

☑ Don't pass judgment on others' dreams.

☑ Make sure newcomers don't feel pressured to whip something up. A vision grows out of passion.

☑ Know the difference between enthusiasm and animation. Enthusiasm isn't jumping up and down and waving your arms all around. That's animation. Enthusiasm is that glow that results from an inner belief in convictions. It's believing that what you do truly makes a difference. And for everybody, the source of enthusiasm is different.

TRANSFORMING A VISION INTO REALITY

Over a four-week period, I presented my vision of greatness and challenged all 210 associates in this company to develop one of their own. During that time, I tried and could not document a case of another company that had more than a few people in the stage of self-actualization that would allow them to pursue greatness for themselves. At Dataflex, before we made it a goal to do so, I'd say only a few people, including Gordon and myself, were truly pursuing greatness. That means we were dragging the other 200 people with us. At IBM, which has more than 300,000 employees, there are probably only about two dozen seeking greatness by the definition we've discussed in these pages. Can you image the results that a company comprised entirely of associates who are seeking greatness as individuals could achieve?

What we told people was that if they want a company that is parental in nature and doesn't require initiative or want associates to share in responsibility for the business, that's fine. You just can't have it here. That's the way 99 percent of the companies out there operate, but not Dataflex. The whole point of my personal vision is to pursue greatness myself by surrounding myself with people who are pursuing the same ideal.

Over the next six weeks, I listened to almost 200 associates present their visions of greatness. That experience was the most privileged thing I've ever done in business. I can't tell you how many times I was moved to tears. I didn't care about the eloquence of their presentations: It was the content. I always thought I worked with wonderful people, but I had no idea. They talked about wanting to become religious leaders in their communities and help people find their way, giving underprivileged children a place to go and role models, wanting to be part of the executive management of this company, achieving balance in their lives, improving themselves physically, wanting to be experts in their fields, and providing an atmosphere for their children in which the children could achieve their dreams. One associate, Don Lorenzetti, a senior customer engineer, even talked about his vision of winning an Olympic gold medal in archery for the United States.

I've always tried to be sensitive and compassionate to other people's dreams that are different from mine. But the experience of listening to our associates talk about their innermost desires has made me look at the associates in a whole new way. It is not important what vision of greatness you seek. The key is to seek something. The journey itself is gratifying. To think we have an atmosphere around here in which people would be willing to express their deepest convictions about what they want out of life is to me the success of Dataflex. If we divided up the equipment and went home tomorrow, I will have been part of something that has never been done on such a grand scale in the anals of business. Of course, when people work in a small-business environment where there are ten or twenty employees, over the course of many years they get to know the personal endeavors of individuals. But we are not ten people; we are close to 200.

The main comment I've heard is: "I never really thought about my dreams much before, but I don't look at this vision as an exercise. I will revisit my commitment to this vision often, and I hope we will revisit it together next year." Our visions of greatness are a living document that reminds us of the power of one to change things around him or her. We will use these visions to guide us in the coming years.

After each person gave his or her vision of greatness, I expressed my support and asked how I could help him or her achieve it. We are already working to make visions reality. Many people mentioned wanting to give their families an opportunity for higher education because no one in their family had ever gone to college. I am looking into extending our educational benefits to include the children of associates. The expense could be overwhelming, but what a tremendous benefit! We are working to put together several of the people who expressed wanting to help underprivileged children. We are checking into renting a church basement in Edison, New Jersey, where after-school care could be provided. I want to help people get what they want, and the things that they want are not necessarily related to what they do here at Dataflex. But working here gives them the security and position as a means of influence to accomplish the vision of greatness that they have.

When I see people now, I view them entirely differently based upon the things that I heard. I don't recommend that someone try to implement this program in his or her company. For it to work, you must have a company with a high level of trust among your associates. The proper work environment must encourage openness and honesty by proving that people will be treated fairly before you can expect people to demonstrate this depth of vulnerability.

I am now starting to believe that there are absolutely no limits on the personal interactions of the associates who work here. I'm always concerned when we take a step like this one because there is an opportunity for those whose minds are turned that way to exploit others' vulnerability. There is a chance that someone could use information in a way that would be destructive to this type of process. However, the reason I chose to move ahead with this vision goes back to my basic business philosophy. I'd rather take the shot for all the goodness that will come out of doing the right thing, instead of missing out because I'm controlled by the fear that a few may take advantage of the situation.

If putting something together like visions of greatness and installing it in your own company is difficult for you to imagine and so scary that you wouldn't even know how to go about it, you need to take a serious look at whether your company is even remotely close to being the best it can be.

7

When Push Comes to Shove

Rose has been in his office since 6 A.M. That's early even for him. He didn't sleep well last night. He woke up at 4 A.M., wide awake.

Yesterday was a roller coaster emotionally—from plumbing the depths to which one salesman would stoop for the sake of extra commissions to the mountaintop experience of listening to people talk about their dreams.

The former incident was so stupid, Rose thought. If the salesman had claimed the charges against his team's profits as the staff had agreed, he would have made about $10,000 less in commissions, hardly a dent in the tens of thousands in commissions he stood to make on the deal. Yet greed had raised its hoary head. Rather than being repulsed by *Wall Street*'s reptilian Gordon Gekko's "greed is good" speech, this salesman apparently had embraced it as his credo.

When he awoke before sunrise, Rose tried playing his guitar in the quiet of the living room to ease the stress that was coiled in his neck and shoulders. He learned to play the instrument when he was twelve years old. His grandmother, a saleswoman at Sears & Roebuck, had given him a fifteen-dollar guitar and six months worth of lessons, along with a songbook of her favorite songs from her girlhood. But even strumming those simple tunes failed to soothe him this morning.

Almost before he knew it he was in his car, tooling up the Garden

State Parkway, his favorite James Taylor CD playing loud in wrap-around sound. He turned into Dataflex's empty parking lot about the time the sun came up, a pale yellow haze through the dense cloud cover. He pulled into the empty spot next to the one reserved for the Performer of the Month. There are no reserved spots in the parking lot at Dataflex except for that one and one for Salesperson of the Month.

He hasn't stopped thinking about the bombshell Diane Katz dropped on him yesterday. Not that he had much of a chance to forget it: The young man whose future at Dataflex was suddenly shaky called him four times at home last night, asking for forgiveness and another chance. But Rose has made up his mind. He cannot justify keeping someone on staff who has shown a basic lack of integrity. "I place a great deal of trust in the people I work with," Rose often says. Knowing that one of those he'd taken into that fold violated that trust weighed heavily on him.

Finally, Rose hears noises in the building signaling early arrivals. And soon enough the repentant salesman is standing at the threshold. "Please don't shoot me," he says, almost cavalierly, holding up his hands, fingers splayed.

"You shot yourself," replies the president, gaze unwavering. "We have a basic philosophical difference here. You are the kind of guy who would roll through a red light at 2 A.M. When you got pulled over for a ticket, you'd argue that there was no traffic and no one got hurt. So running a red light didn't matter. But no matter what you say, running a red light is against the law." Rose dials Gordon McLenithan's number and asks him to come in to Rose's small conference room.

Rose, McLenithan, and the salesman take seats in the small room, which is decorated with the annual reports of Dataflex's blue-chip customers. For a few minutes, the salesman continues to defend what he did, saying that he doesn't understand what the big deal is. When he sees he isn't gaining any ground with that argument, he shifts tactics and says, "I do know what I did was wrong. But please don't fire me. This company is like my family."

McLenithan, fiddling with a gold ring on his right hand, says quietly, "We are disappointed because you have tremendous potential, but it's a question of ethics."

Rose agrees, "I have to fire you. We have a basic disconnect here.

You do not share the ethics of the management of this company. We've written you a check for earned commissions—even though you don't deserve them— for the work you've done in the past few months. I don't want you to have to start scrambling for work right away. But I do expect you to honor your noncompete contract."

"I could never compete against you. Dataflex is a part of me," the young man protests. "You have my word that I will never say anything against Dataflex or the people. All my friends are here. Can I at least go around and say good-bye to everybody?"

"Sure," Rose says softly.

In fifteen minutes the young salesman has said his good-byes and cleared out his desk.

Within another fifteen minutes, Rose has gathered the entire sales force into the conference room to discuss the salesman's sudden departure. There usually isn't a sales meeting on Thursday, but Rose always conducts a meeting immediately after a salesperson has resigned or, as is rarely the case, has been fired.

During these meetings, which the departing salesperson is given the option of attending, the staff talks frankly about what went wrong and what they might have done to help the person succeed at Dataflex. One sales rep who resigned was very argumentative, for instance, and the staff thought they were remiss in not pointing out that unpleasant trait more frequently. In the past, they've come up with ideas like partnering the successful reps with newcomers and taking turns inviting the new person to lunch. Most of the time, the salesperson who is leaving chooses to sit in on these meetings.

The staff immediately senses that something is different this time. Rose, clearly saddened, initially doesn't have much to say, beyond the fact that the salesman conducted himself in a manner that the group had agreed was unethical. "This salesperson," says Rose, "had rationalized in his own mind that as long as the end gain was to make a sale, it didn't matter how you pushed and pulled. He thought that ethics are a set of rules that apply only in certain situations." There is shocked silence for the first several moments. A few people aren't so surprised, citing the man's barely controlled temper that had boiled over in the past. The hour-long discussion revolves around ethics.

The locksmith is already changing the combinations, and the salesman's name has been removed from the sales board. His sales have been relegated to the slot labeled HOUSE on the board by the time the salespeople return to their cubicles just before 9 A.M.

Glen Koedding, the youngest salesman on the team, takes the dismissal hard. He describes himself as a loner, but he admired the smooth selling style of the man who was fired. Koedding says, "When someone leaves, you feel it a lot at first because we work so closely together and spend so much time training together. But then after just a little while, the person loses his or her face and name and becomes salesperson X in our discussions."

Rose goes back to his office for a few minutes to take a scheduled call from the company's IBM representative, Gerry Zagorski. The two men talk about some business they are working on and about the success of this year's Top Gun event. After he hangs up, Rose thinks about another painful decision he faced the year before. When Tim Mannix was still working as a consultant for the company, he confronted Rose and McLenithan with a hard piece of reality one day in Rose's conference room. Pointing to the plaques awarded by IBM for sales volume, Mannix said, "If you aren't careful, they're going to line your coffin with all those plaques some day." He then proceeded to tell the two men that one of the biggest myths in business was that large-volume orders don't cost as much to service as the smaller ones. "Don't be fooled," he said. "Overhead is overhead."

IBM had been giving Dataflex huge incentives to go after large accounts, but when those incentives were removed, the company was left carrying business that was unprofitable. Rose and McLenithan decided that they wouldn't accept any business that would leave them with less than a 5 percent net after-tax profit. That meant walking away from $16 million worth of their business. The knowledge that any competitor who took on the business would be taking a loss gave Rose small comfort. For the salesman's soul that was imbedded in Rose saying, "Thanks, but no thanks" to major customers and, thus, giving away business was the most gut-wrenching moment in his career.

Until today.

Rose had high hopes for the young salesman, and he cared for him on a personal level, despite his volatile nature. When he first came to Dataflex, he would explode in rage over the slightest mixup on one of his accounts, but he had successfully harnessed his biting sarcasm and had become a role model in recent months for his treatment of the members of his team. Unfortunately, he had a hole where his conscience should have been.

RICK ROSE: If I had wavered on firing that salesman, he might have done much more damage down the road. He believed that ethics aren't binary, but a gray area. He was influenced greatly by the pressure, which can be interpreted as the rewards. In other words, to him, the bigger the reward, the more one can compromise the formula of ethics. The sales staff had specifically conducted a meeting on the topic that became the issue in this case. If a salesperson did not want to charge the customer for a particular service, we decided that the cost would still be deducted from the salesperson's gross profit. If the company performs a service, we have to have a record of it. There was no gray area here.

"It is a tangled web we weave. . . ." You must have an excellent memory to be a good liar because you have to remember what you said to everybody. The integrity was never there. After Diane Katz said, "There is absolutely something wrong in this situation" and the salesperson was challenged with that situation, he said, "There's nothing wrong here at all."

Then after he was shown the evidence, he went through the whole process of rationalization, ultimately admitting that he had done something unethical. If he had to pay for the services himself, he still would have made a fortune. Either you can trust someone or you can't.

In the course of business, we are often called upon to make tough decisions quickly. For example, if we had delayed in turning away from the $16 million worth of business, Dataflex probably wouldn't be profitable right now. (Incidentally, about 25 percent of that business returned to us, and the customers agreed to pay higher prices.)

We encourage people to make timely decisions. I constantly tell my managers, "If you aren't making mistakes, that means you aren't making decisions fast enough. At times tough decisions have to be made without having all the information at hand." We don't punish mistakes. When one makes mistakes, it signifies that they're trying.

The other weakness in the decision-making process that I've noticed through the years is that people often fail to honor their word once they've given it. Back in 1984, Gordon and I made a strategic decision to partner ourselves with IBM. To us, that meant sticking by that company through good times and bad. Loyalty is rare in business, and sometimes that decision has been hard to live with. But I believe our enthusiasm in making the decision to base a good portion of our business on IBM products has been rewarded. Once you make a decision, follow through with it wholeheartedly.

The art of leadership means making tough decisions. The heart of the difference between management and leadership is being able to make the tough calls. I've made my share of good ones, and I've made my share of bad ones. But I've never regretted making the calls. I wish the outcome could have been different on some of them, but I'm still satisfied with what happened. And more than any other trait, making tough decisions marks a leader. Management and leadership are like oil and water to me. I never claimed to be a good manager, but I think I'm a good leader because I don't pass the buck.

Rose and Koedding have a 10 A.M. appointment with a potential customer. It's Koedding's first sales call with Rose. He waits at the door of Rose's office while the president finishes a phone call. Koedding, a twenty-four year old whom Rose playfully calls Vito because of his predilection for gel to slick back his black hair, has worked for months to make sure Dataflex is among the finalists competing to supply hardware and services worth about $1 million to a major pharmaceutical company.

At last, Rose hangs up and snatches his jacket off a chair where he tossed it. "You ready, Vito?" he asks grinning as he slides past Koedding, who practically snaps to attention whenever Rose addresses him.

"I was born ready and never got over it," replies Koedding, keeping up with Rose's brisk pace. He follows on Rose's heels, and almost smashes into him when Rose suddenly turns into the men's room.

Koedding goes into the bathroom, too. "Rick, there's something I've wanted to ask you for a while."

"What is it?" asks Rose. He washes his hands and then impatiently tugs at his tie and mumbles, "I hate these things."

"How come you hung that framed picture of you and Gordon and Tim from the annual report on the back of the door in here?" Koedding asks. "I want to have an answer ready because I know some client's going to ask me."

Rose laughs and shrugs, "I don't know, Vito. It just seemed like a good place for it." Rose turns right and continues down the hall toward the associates' entrance and the parking lot.

As they climb into his Lexus, Rose says, "I'll lead the meeting."

Koedding, broad shouldered and a snappy dresser with a penchant for suspenders, watches admiringly as Rose makes the sales presentation. All goes smoothly until the young man starts to answer a question. He feels a crushing pressure across the top of his foot under the table. Rose is staring straight at him and expertly fields the prospect's question. The next time the salesman tries to speak, he feels a sharp pain in the same foot. Rose answers again with nary a glance in Koedding's direction. The young salesman gets the message this time.

When Rose starts to talk about the hotline phone support Dataflex offers, the decision maker says, "Don't even talk to me about 800 numbers for service. We've been trying to get help from our two present vendors over the phone for three months on a basic problem. The phone just isn't an efficient way to deal with these technical snafus."

"May I use the speaker phone in your office?" Rose inquires of the man.

"Of course," he replies.

Rose says, "Let's all go in there right now. I want to call our technical support people, and if they can't answer this question without hanging up the phone, we don't deserve your business."

Koedding shoots a quick look at his boss, his brown eyes widening almost imperceptibly, but he doesn't flinch. Inside, he is dying. He can't believe that all his hard work is going to be made or broken by a single telephone call.

With the director of management information systems and three of his staff people gathered around the phone, Rose dials the number. Charlie Milo, who specializes in local area networks, answers on the second ring. "Hello, Charlie," says Rose jocularly.

"Where are you calling from, Rick, the bathroom?" asks Milo, a dark-haired, cheery fellow in his midtwenties, who sports a buzz haircut.

Rose replies, "I've got you on a speaker phone. There's a potential customer here with a question, and I want you to help them out as if they had a contract with us."

The man explains the problem in about two to three minutes. Milo asks a few questions and then proceeds to answer the question correctly. After four or five minutes, the man stops him and says, "Thank you."

"But wait," says Milo, warming to his topic, "there are some other factors that may affect you with this problem." He proceeds to give the man another fifteen minutes worth of information.

When the man hangs up, he turns to Rose and Koedding: "Dataflex has raised the bar again." He tells Rose and Koedding that he'll schedule a contract signing in two weeks.

During his career at Hazeltine, Rose learned the value of knowing when to lay it all on the line. At one point, Rose left the company for a few months. In his absence one of his best clients had been given to another salesperson. The client represented $1 million worth of business. On a Friday morning over breakfast, Rose, who had just returned to Hazeltine, read in *Computerworld* that the client had just signed a contract with the competition. He promptly called his contact at the client and said, "Why are you going with someone else?"

The man answered, "We haven't been happy with the attention we've been getting from your replacement, and besides, this deal is practically done. We're signing the contracts on Monday."

"Wait a minute," Rose said. "You mean the contracts aren't actually signed yet?"

"Well, no, but. . . ." the man replied.

Rose interrupted, "Please get together the people I'd need to see Saturday afternoon and give me a shot. I'll only take an hour of your time, and I'll get on a plane tonight." The man agreed to his request. And Rose retained the business for his company.

"I learned early on that you have to be willing to gamble," Rose reflects, sitting in his office. "I had one client who told me we weren't in contention for his business because we refused to compete solely on the basis of price. I showed him his own advertising that said, 'You can do it right, or you can do it for less.' In his company's annual report, I pointed out that in black and white its own philosophy was that they charged more and gave more value. The director sat back in his chair and said, 'You know that's true. I can see where we're being hypocritical on this.' Now it was risky to challenge that man like that, but I knew the potential far outweighed the risk, and we ultimately won the business."

Rose's willingness to gamble on future success enabled him and McLenithan to bring Mannix into the company. Rose and McLenithan did not want to make Dataflex pay any more in executive salaries. They believed that if Mannix was to be a partner, his compensation should come out of their piece of the pie. "That was a painful decision to make because we knew it would mean that for the next two years at least Gordon and I would make less money than we had been making," says Rose. "But we were willing to bite the bullet because we think eventually we'll have a bigger pie thanks to Tim's contributions."

Word spreads quickly about Koedding's morning adventure with Rose. One of those who listens is sales rookie Elaine Mosher. Shortly before lunch, she and White drive to an 11:20 A.M. appointment with a potential client. "Tell me your toughest problem," Mosher coaxes after she sets down her briefcase.

The director of management information systems describes a problem with a software package on a network that Dataflex doesn't support. Mosher listens and then says, "I think we can help you." She and White make a ten-minute presentation on Dataflex and leave. As soon as they reach White's car, Mosher dials technical support. Charlie Milo answers on the first ring. Mosher explains the problem to him.

When she arrives at her cubicle fifteen minutes later, there's a message waiting for her. It's from the potential customer, thanking her for having Milo call with a solution so quickly. She gets the man on the phone. After she hangs up, Mosher gives a yelp for joy and sprints to ring the brass bell. Dataflex has another new customer and new business worth $100,000.

ACTIONS

- ☑ You must stick to your code of ethics even when that means making a painful decision.
- ☑ Teach your sales staff the art of making a good bet by

instilling in them the fact that the potential often outweighs the risk. They must learn to discern when to bet it all.

MAKING THE TOUGH DECISIONS

Shortly after the terrible day when I had to fire that salesman, I came up with an idea that would serve as a constant reminder of the stuff Dataflex is made of. We printed laminated cards for our associates that have our mission statement on one side, along with the following list of goals:

- Delighted customers.
- Enabled employees.
- Industry respect.

The flip side reads: EMPOWERMENT TEST.

1. Is it the right thing for the customer?
2. Is it the right thing for Dataflex?
3. Is it ethical?
4. Is it something for which you are willing to be accountable?
5. Is it consistent with Dataflex's basic beliefs?

If the answer is YES to all these questions . . . Don't Ask, Just Do It!

Once you uncover the lack of integrity, don't accept the assertion that it is a mistake: Lack of integrity is an inherent disease that people get from their upbringing. People who are unethical have a rationalization process that helps them feel OK about themselves. The point is that the moment you find a person on your staff who does something unethical, get rid of him or her. Don't waste your breath talking about it. There is a big difference between a mistake and a question of ethics. I wish someone would develop an ethics test like the home pregnancy tests that are available. The lack of ethics is just as destructive as is drug abuse.

One way you can spot-check the ethics of your people is to answer their telephones when they are on vacation. You'll find out whether your associates are ethical. Associates know that I will randomly fill in for them when they are on vacation. Ethical people are thrilled to death that the president of the company is going to be talking to their customers. Those who are dishonest will be terrified that you'll uncover their questionable dealings in their absence.

Quit fooling yourself. The lack of ethics will destroy the fiber of your company. It has to be eradicated as surely as if it were cancer.

8

Get the Rust Off the Wheel

True to his word, Rose keeps his lunch date with Veronica Cassiba. At noon they eat together in the small conference room adjoining Rose's office. Both of them eat thin slices of turkey meat—with no bread and no mayonnaise. Says Cassiba, "I was so sore and tired this morning when I woke up to do my exercises, but then I thought about that standing ovation yesterday, and it got me right up out of bed."

Rose looks forlornly at the turkey and says, "I know I couldn't stick with this diet if I weren't doing it with you. You are a real inspiration for me, Veronica. Hey, by the way, what did your family have to say about your vision?"

"I didn't show it to them," Cassiba replies. Her family is Sicilian, and meals at the Cassiba household are typically high in calories.

"What!" exclaims Rose. "I can't believe you haven't shown it to them. You've got to enlist their help in it."

"OK, OK," says the young woman. "I'll let them read it tonight. I've got copies plastered all over the place at home and at the office. It won't be a problem getting them a copy."

After a few moments of silence, she asks, "Are you coming to the open house today? We've been rehearsing all week. But after yesterday, talking about what I do will be a piece of cake."

Rose rolls his eyes and exclaims, "Veronica, did you have to say 'cake'? Here. Have another slice of turkey." She laughs.

170

A sales representative from Epson America walks by the conference room and spies Rose eating his lunch. Tall, blond, and athletic looking, the rep spends a few moments chatting about college football with Rose and then asks for a minute to demonstrate his company's new laptop computer to the president. Rose asks Cassiba, "Is it alright with you?"

"No problem, Rick," she says.

The salesman deftly sets up his product. The small computer appears well-designed and has a nifty feature that Rose likes: a hard drive that easily pops out. "This way if you are having a problem with your machine, we'll send you a replacement machine within twenty-four hours anywhere in the United States, and you can just plug your hard drive back in," says the salesman. He also points out that it can use two different kinds of batteries.

The presentation takes about fifteen minutes, which is the entire time Rose has allotted for lunch. "These are going to be hot sellers for us," the young man concludes. "We've got a new printer, too, that rivals Hewlett-Packard's. Do you have a few minutes to check it out? I have it set up back by Kevin Denecour."

"Sure," Rose shrugs. "Veronica, it's been lovely. I'll be slinging burgers tomorrow, and I'll be out of the office Monday on an appointment in New York. But we'll eat together on Tuesday, OK?"

"That'll be great," says Cassiba, gathering up the trash. Rose follows the man back to the technical-support department where Kevin Denecour and Ken Cavanagh are checking over the printer to see how it stacks up.

Rose stops and watches for a minute. Then he asks, "So whaddya think?"

"Looks pretty good, Chief," says Denecour, straightening up from his bent position. Cavanagh, dressed in a coat and tie reflective of his corporate background, asks the salesman a few questions about the products Epson America is introducing. Rose bids the man good-bye and walks back to the other side of the building, using the hallway that passes by the kitchen, where the last of the lunch crowd is lingering over pizza.

Dressler calls out, "Hey, Rick, you want a slice?"

Rose walks back to the doorway and pats his stomach. "Nope, I want to get rid of this," he says. "But thanks anyway."

*   *   *

It's 1 P.M., and Rose swings by the finance department to see how the open house is going. Each area within the finance department has prepared and carefully rehearsed a presentation on exactly what its function is within Dataflex. The open house is organized so that different departments go as a group to visit the finance department. The presentation starts with the credit check and ends with invoicing. When a group arrives, all are handed pens that say, "Finance works their assets off"—a line that Donna DeVito suggested. The twenty-person department is also serving cheese, crackers, and wine.

At 1:30 P.M. the entire sales force is meeting in the large conference room. Rose, at White's suggestion, has hired two consultants to come in and work with the group. Instead of taking his usual seat at the front of the table nearest the door, Rose selects a seat at the opposite end of the table, and the salespeople gravitate in that direction, following his lead. The first consultant is Marilyn Nyman, president of Communication and Speech, Inc., in Horsham, Pennsylvania. Nyman is an attractive woman who strides into the conference room in a fire-engine-red power suit. One of the first points she makes is that, according to a book called *The Intuitive Manager,* people judge you 38 percent on the tone of your voice, 55 percent on your nonverbal presentation, and only 7 percent on the content of what you say. And they decide whether they like you or not in the first five seconds.

Nyman uses strong hand gestures to punctuate every sentence and, as you may expect, has excellent diction. She pulls out a beach ball and begins tossing it to different people around the table as she talks, explaining that her purpose is to do an exercise that will demonstrate how the power shifts when you're having a meeting. The ball represents the focus of the room. Rose is slouched in his chair and slings a few one-liners her way. It's almost as if he's testing her the way he would a potential salesperson in an interview. They pitch the ball back and forth at one another. Suddenly he bristles when she refers to making a "sales pitch."

"One thing you should know right now," he says sternly, "is that we never use that term. It sounds completely unprofessional, and it is not part of our jargon. We make sales presentations."

She stops her presentation and says, "Thanks for letting me know that. I would have hated to go on saying it only to find out later that it wasn't acceptable in your corporate culture. And that's an important point, because every company creates its own language."

She pauses and says, "Boy, oh boy, is this going to be a tough one because I've got the president in the back of the room and everybody's attention is going toward him."

It serves to break the tension that was palpably building up in the room. Next, she talks about nonverbal clues, in order of their importance:

eye contact
posture
facial expression
gestures
appearance
space
movement
handshake

After she finishes scrawling those clues on a white flip chart, she says, "Men don't smile enough, and women tend to smile too much."

She continues moving around the room, until she reaches Rose and touches him lightly on the shoulder. "Here we have a perfect example of a power gesture in corporate America," she says. "Look at what Rick is doing with his hands. He is doing what we call steepling, elbows resting on the table and fingertips touching lightly.

"I'll bet you've also seen him do this." She begins drumming her manicured nails on the table. She pulls laughter out of that one. "That's a sign of aggressiveness that means 'Get to the point.' "

She puts her hands behind her back, resting one hand in the other. "This posture is relaxed aggressiveness.

"What about nervous gestures? Do you ever fiddle with a rubber band or a pen? Take a paper clip apart? Or, for the women, play with your hair? All these gestures betray a lack of confidence."

She asks several salespeople to stand up and has them demonstrate different gestures and postures. Those who are seated are asked to guess who the decision maker and the salesperson are in several scenarios through their body language. Then Nyman asks each person in the class to strike a stance he or she is comfortable with. She quickly assesses the participants and critiques them, offering advice to help them appear more "powerful and confident."

After an hour with the group, she comments, "What goes on here is family. It's very warm. The only danger in that is making sure you don't try to take that with you when you're on a call to a corporate customer." She singles out Diane Katz and advises her not to be so touchy-feely.

Nyman talks at length about voice quality, noting that James Earl Jones was a stutterer before he developed his deep, resonant voice. The ten components of the voice, she says, are resonance, rate, volume, diction, intonation, pause, pitch, clarity, vocabulary, and speech mannerisms. Then she states that people in business situations tend to fall into five categories in their speech patterns: the Placater, the Blamer (who whines like a child), the Computer (who states the facts), the Distracter (who rambles), and the Leveler (who lets you in on exactly what he or she is thinking at all times).

She winds up her portion of the afternoon by handing out a sheet and asking everyone to check off ten characteristics that describe him or her and then asking everyone to exchange papers. The person's answers are covered, and the person who gets the paper checks off ten characteristics he or she thinks best describe the person whose paper he or she has gotten. It is another version of the self-actualization exercise the class has recently undertaken. The person who comes closest is Fendrick, in his assessment of Rose: Fendrick checked off seven of the same characteristics that Rose checked for himself.

The next consultant is Nicholas Pagano, a leadership-development instructor who has been with IBM since April 1966. A dynamic speaker, he launches into a discussion about what he calls "transformational leadership." "It's the creative destruction and simultaneous building up of your company," he asserts. "First, I want to take you through some exercises that will let us see how you work together."

Pagano spreads out a huge jigsaw puzzle and informs the group that they have seven minutes to complete the puzzle. Rose, Mannix,

Corcodilos, and Fendrick emerge almost immediately as leaders, organizing the others by asking them to hand them certain parts of the puzzle. For instance, any piece with white lines on it goes to Corcodilos. Some people hang back on the fringes, while most are in the fray. Although many directions are being shouted, no one is rude. Rose clearly leads the effort overall, but once the framework of the puzzle has taken shape, he steps back and lets others take over the details.

They complete the puzzle, which is the IBM logo, in $4\frac{1}{2}$ minutes. Pagano asks, "What did you learn?"

Someone answers, "Unless you take the initiative, nothing gets done."

Rose offers, "All of us are holding a piece of the puzzle."

Another says, "All people weren't willing to accept a piece of the puzzle."

"Good," Pagano comments. "Now let me tell you what I observed. I saw a lot of celebrations, impromptu parties all over the place, as you were progressing with the puzzle. You don't see that in many places. At a larger company, I usually see less participation from the top."

For the next exercise, he lays a mat out on the floor. The mat has a maze of squares marked on it. "Now we're going to see how you work together to get through the electronic maze," he says. "You can discuss strategy up front for as long as you want, but once someone lays a foot on the mat, there can be no talking, only hand signals. The object is to get everyone safely through the maze without setting off the alarms. Each time someone sets off the alarm, everyone who has passed through safely has to backtrack through the maze. You have seven minutes once I start the timer. Go!"

This type of exercise is the sort of thing Rose thrives on. His mathematical mind kicks in, and he assigns people around the mat to take a row of squares and to be responsible for remembering where the alarms are hidden. Then the person at that row will direct the person trying to cross the mat to the safe squares. He organizes it quickly, although Fendrick and White are arguing that they should take a few more minutes to be sure that's the best strategy. Elaine Mosher is the first to step out, and the room falls silent. After a few false starts, the team quickly establishes the safe path. Again there is plenty of celebrating with each person who passes through safely. The last person is Constantino, and he dances over the pattern with lightning speed.

"Now we're going to do it again," Pagano says. "But just remember there are changes in business." This time the team talks about strategy only briefly, and then the first member jumps out on the rug. So far so good. About half the sales staff has made it through, when the pattern changes. Alarms start going off all over the place. Several frustrating minutes pass before they reestablish a safe route. Just as the buzzer sounds, signaling that they're out of time, Russ Schultz takes his last step.

Pagano smiles, "That's a common mistake in business. Something works once, so you stick with it and fail to get an alternate plan organized before you jump out there. What are some responses to change?"

Fendrick says, "I found myself resisting."

White says, "I was just trying to cope."

"I wanted to innovate," says Scaglione, "but I couldn't get anyone to listen to me."

Mosher says, "I tried to adapt."

"Good," says Pagano. "Write in your books what you noticed about yourself as you're going through these exercises. Note your observations of the group, too. Take a few minutes to do it."

There is silence while everyone writes.

Finally, he says, "What I saw here was a high level of excitement, people who care and who work well together. I hope today has made you think about your own style and where you are in terms of your leadership skills."

It is a few minutes past 5 P.M. when the seminar concludes. Rose stands and says, "Thanks to both of you for coming. I'm sure we all learned a lot about ourselves, and you gave us some food for thought."

Outside the conference room, Nyman says of Rose, "What you see in there is a true leader. He is encouraging people to take risk, and he himself risks losing his credibility among his associates. He's not afraid to get his feet dirty."

Today is a big day for Ken Constantino. Last week he was named Salesperson of the Month for the first time in his five years at Dataflex. The first time a salesperson achieves that honor, he or she gets to select a place for dinner, and the company pays for the entire sales staff to go out to dinner to celebrate. For several years, Fendrick's and Katz's names were the only ones on the plaques recognizing the Salesperson of the Month, except for the few months when Tom Beer won. However, since White and Rose instituted the balanced-performance quota (BPQ) to measure and compensate the sales staff, there have been some new inductees into the elite group: Jane Banach-Walther; Glenn Koedding; and, now, Constantino. Beer also won for his second time.

Rose wanders through the maze of cubicles at 5:30 P.M. calling out, "Is everybody ready? This train is pulling out." Koedding, Mosher, and Katz are still on the phone with clients. Russ Schultz; Bethann Wapinski, who is the only one on Constantino's team who is able to make tonight's event; Ralph Hrovat, a sales specialist in maintenance; and Tom Beer, who is rarely in the Dataflex office because he works at a customer's site, are all clustered next to Constantino's cubicle, laughing and talking. Constantino is sitting, cowboy style, his chair turned backward, in the middle of the action.

The phones are still ringing, and it seems to be one of those days when many people are staying late.

"So, Ken, exactly what is this place we're going to?" asks Schultz.

"You kind of just have to experience it," Constantino replies. "I didn't want to have a normal 'Let's eat and get fat' dinner."

Hrovat cracks, "I don't think anyone would expect you to do anything normal, Ken."

"We're going to have a great time tonight," Rose says when he reaches Constantino's cubicle. "Has anybody seen Tim? Is he back from his meeting at IBM?"

Constantino answers, looking up at Rose, "Yeah, he's back, and he said he wanted to change into casual clothes for tonight, which isn't a bad idea." Constantino has changed into blue jeans and a simple button-down shirt. For the site of his honor dinner, the salesman has chosen the Medieval Times in Lyndhurst, New Jersey. By 5:45 P.M., Rose has marshaled the group of twelve together, and everyone has settled who is riding with whom. Mosher and Heidi Gray, the quality coordinator, climb in Rose's car for the forty-five-minute drive.

Medieval Times is exactly what its name suggests. It is a compound that holds 2,000 people and is sort of a mixture of Monty Python, All-Star Wrestling, and Williamsburg. On their arrival, visitors are greeted by wandering minstrels, knaves, knights, serfs, and maidens.

Guests are eventually shuffled into six different sections and handed a colored paper crown according to which section they are assigned. Ralph Hrovat's crown looks too small for his head, and Fendrick says, "Hey, Ralph, you look like Jughead from the Archie comics."

The crew from Dataflex is assigned to the green section, where their job is to root for the dreaded Green Knight. On their way into the torture room, Rose notices a teenage couple wearing elaborate court jester caps, red with tiny bells sewn to the spiked ends. "Hey," he signals them over, "what would you take for that hat?" He points to the one the boy is wearing.

The teenager, shakes his head, "No way, man. I can't sell you this hat. One of my mom's friends made it for me, and I wear it skiing."

Rose isn't easily dissuaded when he's set his heart on something, and hats are one of the only things he collects. Besides his cherished fireman's hat, which he used to don whenever he was in the midst of handling a company crisis, he has a Top Gun hat, a Union College football cap, and a U.S. Navy cap lining the top shelf behind his desk in his office. "Well, if you were going to sell it, how much would you take?" he asks.

"No can do," the youngster says firmly.

"How about fifty dollars?" Rose says, taking out his wallet.

Still, the boy shakes his head, although his eyes grow round. His girlfriend elbows him sharply, but to no avail. He walks away.

The Dataflex troupe wanders through the torture room, which features racks and other instruments of agony from the Dark Ages. Constantino convinces Mannix, who is constantly reminding the sales force to sell "by the Dataflex wheel," to pose for a picture by the wheel, a torture instrument that was used systematically to tear a victim limb from limb. "This is fitting," teases Constantino, "since the wheel is Tim's favorite tool of torture for us sales reps." They all, including Mannix, enjoy a hearty laugh over the crack and then make their way to their seats next to long narrow tables in tiers around the arena.

In the middle of the arena is a 75 foot by 100 foot dirt courtyard.

At the beginning of the evening the king, who is seated on a throne, calls Constantino and Rose from the crowd. He informs the two men that he has decided to knight them and regally performs the ceremony on the spot. The next spectacle is a horse show starring thirty-five Appaloosas, who dance and do an assortment of tricks. Meanwhile, in the stands, the first course is served by wenches and knaves: soup out of a pewter tureen with no utensils, although there are a few napkins. Mead is the drink of the evening.

Vendors move through the crowd hawking souvenirs. Rose buys a three-foot-tall pointy hat with a lengthy scarf attached and gives it to Heidi Gray, who stands six feet tall without heels. Meanwhile, the teenager with the jester's hat has picked Rose out of the crowd and comes over, girlfriend in tow. "I've thought about it some more, and I'll meet you in the torture room after the show to sell you the hat," he says. "I just want to wear it tonight."

Rose answers, "You've got a deal. I'll wait for you for ten minutes after it's over."

Next, the knights, each sporting full armor and mounted on horseback with their squires alongside, are introduced to wild cheering from the crowd. Then the real action starts as the knights compete in jousting, throwing spears from horseback, sword fighting, and other events. Meanwhile, everyone is served dinner—whole small baked chickens and vegetables. Even the main course is eaten with fingers.

Finally, the Green Knight and the Red Knight are the only two left in the ring. During the final jousting match, the Green Knight knocks the Red Knight from his horse and springs on him. They battle with an array of weapons—an axe, a mace, and swords—before the Red Knight prevails. With much pomp and circumstance, the king announces that the victorious Red Knight can choose a princess to reign over the remaining festivities.

Normally, the Red Knight plucks a damsel from the crowd in his section. But tonight he goes into the stands of the green section and grabs Bethann Wapinski's hand. A good sport, she allows him to lead her to the balcony where the king is seated, and she takes the throne beside him. Suddenly, the Black Knight from a neighboring castle gallops into the ring, shouting his intention to take over the castle. The wenches and knaves move through the crowd, serving coffee and pastries. The Black Knight reigns in his horse in front of the king's platform and eyes Princess Wapinski as he repeats his intention.

The six knights and their squires unite forces to expel the interloper, and, after a lengthy battle, the castle is saved from the Black Knight's threat. By 10 P.M. the excitement is over, and the crowd disperses. Rose walks to the torture room. The teenager is already there waiting for him and eagerly hands over the hat in exchange for the crisp fifty-dollar bill Rose extends. "Thanks," Rose says. "I've got plans for this hat."

ACTIONS

- ☑ Put your lunch hour to good use. Keep it free occasionally and encourage people to drop in. You may be surprised at what you can find out over a slice of turkey.
- ☑ If you want to be treated courteously, treat others the same way. How often do we complain about how we are treated as vendors, but then turn around and show a lack of regard for our own vendors. Don't be a hypocrite.
- ☑ Use consultants. Consultants are preventive medicine against the inbreeding that can result from promoting from within the company.
- ☑ Even if you don't agree with everything a consultant is teaching, expose yourself and your staff to new ideas.
- ☑ Participate in everything.

KEEPING THE WHEELS OF CREATIVITY TURNING

To accomplish greatness and to achieve the radical improvements we have made at Dataflex, you must encourage people to experiment. Don't get stuck in "This-is-the-way-it's-done-in-my- [industry, company, division]" thinking. We've asked our purchasing people to join us at sales meetings. We've asked our customers to come and tell us why they chose us.

Whenever a new manager joins the company, a complete biography is written on the person and circulated throughout the company. Salespeople often include these biographies in proposals to their customers, so the customers see the kind of management muscle that Dataflex has. Let your imagination run wild. Do you want to get across to your staff how serious you are about an open-door policy? Take your door off its hinges. Don't have doors.

When I think about creativity, I picture this creative wheel inside our brains. Unfortunately, most of us have allowed that wheel to get rust locked. Thinking creatively is like doing anything else: The more you work at it, the better you get. The key is to do exercises continually that help you find a better solution to the problem at hand. If you were to go into a room of comedy writers for Arsenio Hall, you would see a bunch of people sitting around trying to take a different point of view and find humor in everyday events. That is why the sales meetings are so important. During those two hours, we are practicing creative thinking.

In our sales-training class, we've been reviewing a book called *A Whack On the Side of the Head.* The first chapter is entitled "The Meaning of Life." It's an exercise that instructs you to define life in terms of food. It starts out, "Life is like a grapefruit. First you have to break through the skin. Then you have to take a few bites to get used to the taste, and just as you begin to enjoy it, it squirts you in the eye." These are the kind of exercises we go through in class. As we mentioned earlier, Alan frequently teaches classes to the sales staff on exercises he used to do as a stand-up comedian in which we do wacky word associations. Alan acts as a sales prospect and gives an objection, and the class has to respond to that objection. We've come up with some great responses. For example, when a potential customer says, "I'm happy with my current vendor." The salesperson replies, "So?" No one ever says that. The prospect is so stunned that then you can talk about why the person should use your company's products and services.

What's the point of emphasizing creativity? It helps us sharpen our skills in dealing with customers.

Let's say a customer asks you for something. If you simply give the customer what he or she asked you for, you're doing the customer a disservice. Instead you should try to understand what the purpose of the question is. For instance, if a customer asks, "When can I get the equipment?" You could just answer, "Tuesday," but the customer may be thinking, "If I could get this tomorrow, I'd be a hero to my boss." Or the customer may not need the equipment for two weeks. Go beyond the surface.

We are drilled with right answers in school. We go through life looking for the right answer, but there are so many potential answers.

What we do well here is look at all the answers and then pick the best one.

Through our upbringing, we are constantly struggling to distinguish between right and wrong. But thinking in those terms can throw a wrench in the wheels of creative thinking. One of the most interesting mathematic proofs I ever did was to prove that $1 + 1 = 2$. You may say, "Now wait a minute. I know that $1 + 1 = 2$." But how do you prove it? The way you prove it is by making the assumption that $1 + 1$ equals something other than 2 and coming up with the fact that it can't equal something other than 2. Therefore, $1 + 1$ must equal 2. What it demonstrates is that you can't look at things the way they are. There are always alternatives.

Once I placed a dried-flower arrangement in the middle of the conference table and said, "The answer to increasing revenues is somewhere in the flower pod." Someone said, "It seems organized. You have to be more organized to sell more."

Another person said, "You have to give it the proper nurturing for growth."

Somebody else commented, "You want it to grow thick and lush, so you don't see all the dirt underneath." That exercise was using the plant as an oracle, which was suggested in the book on creativity. We study how to be more creative. I'll say, "Name all the different kinds of ships, and one person will respond, 'The Titanic, tugboats.' "

"No, no. Be more creative. I'll help the group with a clue like 'friendship.' "

Then all of a sudden the creative juices start flowing. We do exercises. We read books on the subject. We try to do the most bizarre things we can think of. You can't say you want a creative atmosphere, but have a very conservative management team. A creative atmosphere must come from leadership, which is another kind of ship. That's why I try hard to be creative.

Sadly, we tend to try new and creative thinking only when we are failing, rather than when things are going well. If business is good, the last thing you are going to do is experiment. Our nature is to stick with the tried and true that got us to a certain level of success. We get creative when we're failing because we figure that taking a risk can't hurt. What I'm trying to foster at Dataflex is creative thinking even in boom times.

The first time I went skiing, at age forty-three, when the ski instructor said, 'Put all your weight on the downhill ski,' everything in my body rebelled. All the information that my eyes and my brain had gathered over the years was screaming, 'Don't do it. Don't put your weight on that downhill ski. If you do, you will tumble over and break your body.' The ski instructor kept saying, 'You must put your weight on the downhill ski.' You get that same feeling when you try to implement a new technique when you've been doing fine using a tried-and-true method. Everything you've ever learned as a salesperson, as a manager, as a CEO is 'Don't rock the boat! It's going great.'

Momentum is powerful. When you do things right, you create momentum. When you need to change, it's never readily apparent because the momentum keeps things heading in the right direction. Momentum can also be a tremendously negative force. When you are in a turnaround situation, you can be making all the right moves and yet your company will still be caught in a downward spiral because of momentum. If you are constantly trying innovations, you will make the best better and you will limit the impact that bad decisions have on your business. When you refuse to poke the lying dog because things are chugging along nicely, you get into long periods that you can't control because of the momentum. That momentum can give you a false sense of security, or, if it's momentum in the wrong direction, it can imbue you with a sense of hopelessness that is just as inaccurate.

We must force ourselves to put our weight on the downhill ski even though everything tells us that's dumb. My five-year-old son trusts the ski instructor and flies down the mountain, while I'm still struggling and falling backward because I'm leaning into the mountain, rather than down it. Little kids are creative. They love new experiences. If they try a new game and it goes well, they are all the more eager to seize another challenge. Along the way, we start to listen to the chorus of voices that say: "Don't rock the boat. Don't disturb things at rest. Be seen and not heard." The common wisdom that is foisted upon us tells us to leave well enough alone.

To get the most out of consultants, you have to set up the situation right. Most consultants say what they think you want to hear, and you pay a tremendous amount for them to do so. Indeed, that's exactly what many companies expect from consultants. But when a consultant comes to Dataflex, we explain that their job is to challenge the beliefs of this company. Just because we've done something a certain way doesn't mean it's going to get us to where we want to be in the future, so I encourage our consultants to speak up on any topic. Nothing is off-limits. You've got to challenge the system. I judge a consultant's effectiveness by how many changes the person suggests—not by how many things he or she finds that we're doing right.

Most companies wait and bring in consultants when business has gotten out of control. Consultants look like heroes because the business is so screwed up that any suggestion is positive. We don't ask them to work on the areas of our business that are messed up. That's our job. We solicit their help in improving the things we do the best. All you have to do to change what's wrong is to ask the people who are doing the work and then change it. Companies have that resource, but they often bring in consultants to talk to their own people instead of kicking management out of their executive offices and into the ranks to find the answers. That is an extremely expensive form of communication with your associates.

On the other hand, we use consultants to help make the best better and to get the creative juices flowing. Another way we differ from most companies in their use of consultants is that we want our consultants to spend time soaking up the culture here. We don't bring consultants in for three days and expect them to work miracles. We look at consultants as long-term partners.

Consultants also keep you honest. They bring objectivity to your day-to-day operations and aid your business by barraging people with questions that you may not have had time or the inclination to ask. If someone on your staff becomes prickly when asked questions, you should ask yourself, "Why? Is there something to hide?" People who don't have integrity hate having to answer to outsiders because they're afraid they'll be found out.

Let's get the creative juices flowing. I want to hear from you. The same offer that I made to associates and friends at Dataflex—to answer any business question for a dollar—stands for the readers of this book. If you are motivated by what you've read and have a good question, send me your business card, and I'll send you my answer to your question. Write me at the following address:

Richard C. Rose
Dataflex
3920 Park Avenue
Edison, NJ 08820

9

How to Separate the Orchids from the Onions

Maura White arrives at Dataflex early. Fridays are dress-down day. Everyone dresses casually and the atmosphere typically matches the dress code. However, White feels anything but relaxed today. Yesterday's scene with the firing of the salesman capped the last few weeks for her. Sales haven't been going as well as she would like, and her nerves are wound tight. She punches the combination on the side door. On the first try, she presses the wrong numbers. Then she remembers that the combination was changed after the dismissal. She stands at the door for a minute, looking up at the sky and struggling to remember the new combination. Gray clouds hang low overhead, threatening rain. "They match my mood," she thinks to herself.

White knows it won't do any good to bang on the door. Rose's and McLenithan's cars are the only ones in the lot, and their offices are on the opposite side of the building. Finally, she remembers the combination and pulls the heavy door open and trudges down the long, back hallway. She stops in the kitchen to pour herself a cup of coffee, and then she hears it, faintly at first. But when she walks toward the sales department, the sound grows louder. She swings the door open to the small conference room across from her office, and there is Rose, playing his guitar, eyes closed and singing softly

185

to himself. He is leaning back in his chair, his slightly scuffed, brown cowboy boots propped casually on the table. A big smile spreads across White's face.

Rose stops strumming and says, "What's up, Maura?"

She tells him that she doesn't think sales have been going well and that she's felt tense about it. "When business gets muddled, it's time to get back to simple things, to the basics," Rose says. "I've got an idea."

Half an hour later, the sales staff and a few other people from the company are gathered in the conference room for the regular morning meeting. Rose, White, and Steve Lamm, a sales administrator and founder Jeff Lamm's son, are the last to enter the room. Rose and White are both carrying their guitars. The chatter stops, and all eyes are on the trio. "Maura and I want to play a few tunes for you this morning," announces Rose, who is wearing blue jeans and a light blue shirt. "The past few weeks have been kind of rough, and we want you guys to relax. If you don't feel good, you can't sell."

Rose starts off playing and singing an Eagles' song called "Peaceful Easy Feeling." Lamm joins in on the chorus with a strong tenor voice. The young man frequently accompanies Rose on salmon-fishing trips in Canada. They often while away the hours singing soft rock tunes together while on the French River. Next White sings a song she wrote entitled "Backpack." She accompanies herself on her guitar, and her mezzo-soprano voice fills the room. Rose plays an old song "Kansas City," and to everyone's surprise, Diane Katz breaks into a soaring solo on the second verse. She sings with joy and abandon. When the impromptu jam session comes to an end, everyone is smiling and laughing, and the jocular mood that typically marks these meetings has returned.

Alan Fendrick stands up and hands out a playing card to each of the seventeen people seated around the table for this morning's sales meeting. This exercise, a brainchild of Fendrick's, is yet another designed to make the people in the room stretch their communication skills. Shuffled among the cards are four aces.

Whoever draws the ace of clubs must take the position of the contrarian. ("That's the stance customers tend to take," Rose explains. "So we train in this room to deal with that type of person.") The ace of clubs presents a prickly challenge, since the tone of the morning meetings is already contentious, reflecting Rose's view that the meetings are a battleground for ideas.

The person who draws the ace of spades must remain silent, unless he or she is directly addressed. The purpose of that card is to enhance listening skills, which, Rose preaches, are crucial to being a good salesperson. The recipient of the ace of hearts strives to inject humor into the meeting. Quick wit is another quality that Rose prizes in a salesperson.

And the person who gets the ace of diamonds—the "What's your point?" card—is responsible for getting the meeting back on track if a speaker begins to ramble. ("Rambling is a killer when you're making a sales presentation," Rose notes.) No one reveals the card he or she is holding until the meeting's end.

Rose is leaning against one of the tables off to the side of the room. "The definition of *esemplastic.* Any ideas?" he asks, his eyes sweeping the room.

No one says anything. So he reads: " 'Shaping or having the power to shape disparate things into a unified whole. Skeptics wondered whether the director possessed the esemplastic power to join the elements of song, dance, special effects, and real human emotion into a seamless play.' Esemplastic is the ability to take what are normally unrelated things and put them into a unified whole. How could you use *esemplastic* to relate to our business?"

One salesman says, "One of the advantages of dealing with Data-flex is its esemplastic product offerings. You can incorporate many different manufacturers' product lines into one solution."

Rose sits down at the head of the table and pushes back in his chair, his hands cupping the back of his head in the position that body-language experts call "The Chairman of the Board."

"Good," he says. "Today I want to talk about a book that helped me tremendously early in my career. It's called *The 36 Biggest Mistakes Salespeople Make.* I think one that is most pertinent for all of us is fearing a prospect. Whether you are selling carpet tacks or Cadillacs, one of the first questions prospects ask themselves is, 'Do I have confidence in the salesperson and his or her company?' If you are radiating fear, your chances of making a sale dwindle considerably. How do you deal with the fear factor in selling?"

Banach-Walther says, "On the way to the appointment I concentrate on being positive."

Mosher replies, "I picture the customer as a friend."

Gerry Zagorski, one of the IBM representatives for Dataflex, comments, "Preparation is the key to overcoming fear."

Rose says, "I start to get the juices going on my way to the appointment. I shoot the breeze with everyone I encounter along the way. I talk to people in the elevator. I also think about the goal of the sales call. When I go on a call, I'm determined that I won't leave until one of two things happens: I accomplish the predetermined goal or they throw me out."

"You become afraid when things are out of your control," White remarks.

"Fear," observes Mannix, "is a function of the importance of the situation. Everybody feels fear. The question is how important the situation is to you."

"Another fear that ties in with number thirty-one on the list of mistakes is the fear of not being liked," says Rose. "That may even be the reason some of you got into sales in the first place, because people told you that you were a likable person."

"That's why I got into sales," interjects Constantino.

Rose says, "And I think your compulsive need to be liked has inhibited your abilities as a professional salesperson at times." Constantino presses his lips together tightly and nods in agreement.

Rose continues: "Salespeople battle the thought all the time that they are already starting from a negative image, that the customer sees them coming and is expecting to be bamboozled. That prejudice exists."

Corcodilos responds, "I don't think that way. Whenever a prospect gives me an appointment, I gain confidence from the knowledge that the prospect wants me to have exactly the product or service that he or she wants. It's a mistake to view the customer as an adversary, rooting for you to fail. I assume that the customer wants me to be the last salesperson that he or she is going to need to see."

"Good point," says Rose. "So what quality do you think is more important to a salesperson than likability? According to this book, being respected is more important than being liked. Respect, not friendship, makes the sale. What do you respect?"

Koedding replies, "Knowledge. People respect doctors because they have knowledge."

Rose groans. "That can be a case of respecting the uniform," he retorts. "The individual may not be worthy of your respect."

He drums his fingers on the table for a few seconds. "Any other thoughts on fear?" he asks. When no one speaks up immediately, he says, "I think people fear being measured, being judged. Look at the lengths some people will go to avoid it. We've had people quit because they didn't want to look at the numbers up on the board."

Schultz adds, "For me, fear of the unknown is a big one."

Corcodilos says quietly, "I don't think it's the unknown that's scary. I think it's what you do know."

The primary topic of the day is orchids and onions, which in Dataflex lingo means a potential account that is worth your time and trouble versus an account that saps your resources without producing any orders, much less profits. "When a big customer or a little customer says no, it still means the same thing: You lost the order," says Rose, jabbing a finger in the air for emphasis. "But if they both say yes, there's a big difference. And that difference is the one thing you can't teach most salespeople.

"If a salesperson doesn't know how to distinguish between an orchid account and an onion account, pretty soon there's trouble. Salespeople waste a tremendous amount of effort chasing down accounts that won't give the profit margin the company needs to thrive in the first place. We need to be able to distinguish between a good sales prospect and a bad one.

"Another common pitfall for salespeople is trying to please people completely. Salespeople waste time trying to sell customers 100 percent on an idea or a product. All they have to do is sell them 51 percent. Chasing that other 49 percent is utopia and wasted energy.

Rose turns on an overhead projector showing the orchid-and-onion grid. It looks like this:

In a previous class, the salespeople discussed "showstoppers"—things that arise during a sales cycle that dictate that one should cut bait. After a lot of debate on the subject, the following were determined to be onion identifiers.

1. If a potential customer does or says something that doesn't make sense two or more times.

Annual Potential	30 Days	60 Days	90 Days	180 Days	6 Months to 1 Year
100 K		X			
250 K			X		
500 K				X	
1 MILL+					X

IF THE FOLLOWING THINGS HAPPEN MORE THAN ONCE, FORGET IT!

- A Lack of Common Courtesy
- Not Doing What They Say They Will Do
- Getting Answers That Don't Make Any Sense

2. If a potential customer doesn't keep his or her word in two instances.
3. If a potential customer is rude even once.

"You have to have something to measure against, so you know where you are in the selling cycle, which is a time line. 'Orchids and Onions' is a time statement, which helps you determine whether a particular account is worth the effort. The main two factors we've plotted on your orchid-and-onion grid is the time spent and the potential of the account."

"The first step," says Glenn Koedding, who is renowned for his love of prospecting, "from the probable stage to the prospect stage is that you have to get appointments. That's it!" There is laughter all around the table.

"There are a lot of suspects out there," adds Rose, "and what you want to know is, are they prospects? Whether they can produce orders within a reasonable time is part of their being prospects. Is that time frame in which they're going to do something worth the investment? There are a lot of suspects. We're going to take them through the 'orchids-and-onions' filter, and if they pass, we'll take them through the rest of the stages, constantly reevaluating them.

"How do you progress from one stage to the next? Set up an appointment to discuss their needs. Moving from the probable to the prospect stage is more involved. You must qualify the account." Rose spends a few moments discussing the different qualifications a salesperson may look for.

Says Elaine Mosher, "Let's say it's been six months since you first had solid contact with an account. And they're right on target with that grid."

"But," Rose interjects, "they're going to be a million-dollar potential, right?"

"Right," Mosher answers.

Rose queries, "Then it's an orchid, right?"

Mosher looks befuddled and replies, "I'm saying that it could be an onion, even though it has. . . ."

Rose interrupts, "Wait a moment. What you're saying is that any account at any time could potentially be an onion. We knew that before we started."

Mosher questions how to determine if she's wasting her time.

One salesman suggests, "Look at the prospect's past performance. Has this man always done what he said he was going to do with you?"

Rose interjects, "I can give you accounts that will do everything they say, but they still reek of onions! You're saying if someone always does what he says, he must be an orchid. That's not right."

"I'm not saying that," the salesman retorts. "I'm saying it helps."

"We're going backward into the mystical thing that determines orchids from onions. You say that if they tell the truth consistently, they're orchids. What we've said is if they start not telling you the truth, they become onions. I did not say that if someone tells you the truth, he or she is an orchid.

"I would like to be able to say that if a prospect places an order within four months after you've talked with him or her and that person initially told you he or she was happy with the precious current vendor, you have an orchid. But it's not that simple, regrettably.

"What we're trying to do is improve our odds. People who understand horse racing know what split times mean, know all the different drugs horses can be doped up on, the equestrian lineage of these horses, the type of track on which the horses won't run well, and the trainers of individual horses. What that information allows those people to do eventually, after betting on thousands of races, is to pick more winners than you and I would by throwing darts at a board or by whether or not we like the jockeys' colors. They will improve their odds by awareness, understanding, research, and experience.

"That's what we're trying to do with 'orchids and onions.' We are not going to pick a winner every time, we are just going to improve our odds. Assuming we can work only on X accounts in a given period, we want to improve our odds by working on X potential orchids as opposed to a hit-or-miss approach.

"The whole reason for this discussion is that people who can't see the difference will charge as hard after an onion as they do after an orchid. At some point in time, you run out of hours in the day. If one can go after only ten accounts at any given time and half of those are orchids and half are onions, and someone else can improve to six and four, then that's a 20 percent increase in business. Isn't that what people who handicap horse races are looking for? That slight edge?

"Card counters aren't going to win at blackjack every time. There's the probability that the dealer can win every hand. But they know when the chances are in their favor to bet a lot of money. And so they do. Sometimes they lose, but over thousands of hands of blackjack they will improve their odds."

Mannix notes, "We're trying to give you the logic that shows you how you can take the prospects you are working on and apply them to an orchid-and-onion grid. Everything is a time line, right? The first thing you say is, 'I'm not going after the entire list of Fortune 1000 companies in the metropolitan area. They must be multi-million dollar, they must have IBM mainframes, they must. . . .' I whittle out a lot of the things that I think are onions. Now you've got a suspect, and you've got to find out something about this customer. Do I understand the customer's needs? Do I know the decision maker? Do I know the decision time frame? How does that look against my grid? If it fits into my grid, it looks more like an orchid than like an onion."

Rose says, "There are some guidelines that we can employ that will assist us. One is, have an orchid-and-onion grid. Whether you use mine as is, modify it, or use your own, have some rules, some absolute showstoppers that indicate: 'When the following things happen, there's no way I'm continuing.' If we agree that's the system that we are going to use, we can set some realistic time frames for when events should happen if an account is eventually going to blossom into an orchid.

"We have to become handicappers. Are we going to win every time? No. But over the course of having hundreds of accounts over a long period—five or ten years—we as a salesforce will bring in more business than if we say, 'I can't tell the difference. I'm going after all of them.' Eighty percent of your prospects, right now, are onions, and you don't know the difference. I gave you a test last week, and the majority of you were unable to distinguish an orchid from an onion.

"Most of us keep pursuing more and more information about an account. You are so far into it when you finally can smell the onion that you hate to give it up because of all the time you've invested."

Rose stops pacing around the table and looks at the salespeople. Suddenly he shouts: "I am looking for orchids, sports fans. I'm desperately looking for an excuse to call them orchids, not a reason to stop working on them. I'm in the most beautiful floral garden in the world, and all I have to do is pick the most beautiful orchids.

"If none of our showstoppers appears, I'm going after it."

White comments, "I store incidents in my memory that trigger something in me that says, 'Beware.' "

Rose looks disgruntled and says, "That is why you should never bet on a football game when you have an emotional tie with the team. You cannot be objective. I cannot bet on the Army-Navy game. I can't see the data in front of my face because I'm so prejudiced about the way the thing should be! I am much better off betting on Slippery Rock University versus the University of Pennsylvania. I can look at the spread and do my fact finding. You must eliminate your prejudices to become a great handicapper."

White disagrees: "I think that there is somewhat of an emotional element to picking orchids and onions."

Rose says, "That is the very reason I always made a lot of money. A lot of the salespeople I worked with made emotional decisions, but I went in and made logical decisions about the accounts that they cast aside and sold tens of thousands of dollars worth of equipment to them. Many salespeople give up on an account because some guy hung up the phone on them! Conversely, some of my peers thought that anybody who talked to them was an orchid. That's what making emotional decisions will get you."

Rose continues: "I don't understand the statement: 'Sometimes a little flag comes up.' If the answer is that there are emotional subtleties, let's move on to the next subject because there's nothing more to discuss here! Because I can't teach this." White is staring at him, her jaw tightening, but she doesn't say anything more.

Fendrick says, "If only 20 percent of the accounts you're going after are going to turn out to be orchids, regardless of how you do it, the more you go after, the more orchids you're going to hit."

Rose grins and asks, "What subject are we debating? I'll tell you what we are debating. It's the age-old question: Are salespeople born or made? If they are born, we're wasting a lot of time here. And if you want to stay and hang on with that, that they are born, then let's have Alan and Diane procreate!

"If you want to concentrate the discussion on little flags and emotions, then you are telling me that great salespeople are simply born with a built-in antenna that lets them know they are onto a hot prospect. You can't teach a basic instinct like that. You can talk to me all day about little flags going up, and it doesn't mean anything. If I could spend some time with a horse handicapper and all the handicapper said to me was, 'I gotta tell you. I get this feeling. And when this feeling comes over me. . . .' I would be wasting my time! But if he said, 'I checked out the last four races. In the last four races, if the horses finished a minimum average of third, I checked the purse, I did blah, blah, blah. . . . When that happens, that horse has a good shot at winning!' I can program that.

"We'll talk about this topic some more on Monday."

Koedding says, "Rick, please tell me you had the ace of clubs today."

Rose grins and flashes the card that shows Koedding is on the money. He comments, "Leading a meeting and being the contrarian at the same time is one of the tougher roles I've had of late."

RICK ROSE: Years ago, I was sitting in my office in California, thinking about ways to increase my sales. Because of the time zone I was in, I would come in at 5 A.M. to start making calls to the East Coast. I would prospect on the East Coast until around 9 A.M. my time, then I'd start making calls to the Midwest and to the West Coast from 9 A.M. until noon. Then I'd put some more calls out to the East Coast to catch people after lunch. And finally I'd wind up from 5 P.M. until 8 P.M. prospecting on the West Coast and in Hawaii. For almost a year I put in fifteen-hour days prospecting. But finally, I reached a point where I knew I'd done everything I could do in that area. If I was going to improve my sales, it had to come from somewhere else. It reminded me of when I played football: For several years, I got things done by sheer brute force, but when my body started to revolt against me, I started concentrating on playing smarter.

The time had come to learn to work smarter. I had run out of daylight. I started thinking about orchids and onions. I tried to understand what made some accounts better than others. If I could only come up with a formula in which time invested would equal the reward. There had to be a way to filter out the accounts that sap your energy, yet actually produce little in profits and commissions. Time passing is a salesperson's worst enemy. I had come to believe that all accounts can be sold eventually, assuming you have sufficient product knowledge and the other essential sales skills. But did I want to invest the time to sell everyone? No.

Over the years, I've decided that the difference between orchid accounts and onion accounts is the only thing you can't teach salespeople. What you can do is figure out who on your staff is good at knowing the difference and ask them to make themselves accessible to your other salespeople. When the others have accounts they are unsure about, they should ask one of the people who can sniff out onions. On our staff, the good orchid pickers are Diane, Alan, Jayne, and me. Do I miss some orchids? You bet. But my overall track record is excellent.

Ken Constantino already has several messages waiting for him when he gets to his cubicle. He listens to them, carefully making notations on the legal pad encased in a burgundy leather pouch that he is seldom without. He is one of the few salespeople who takes notes in the morning meetings. Almost all the others leave pads and pens behind at their desks in deference to Rose's assertion that taking notes inhibits your listening skills. In fact, note-taking seems to distract Rose when he's speaking. He doesn't use any prompters, but his need to absorb everything going on in the room drives him to try to read whatever is being written down.

One message on Constantino's voice mail provokes a victory yell: The manufacturer was able to shake loose 100 systems for the customer who was being unreasonable on Tuesday by insisting that Dataflex deliver upgraded systems. They are rushing the systems to Dataflex. That means the company won't be losing $40,000 after all and Constantino's gross profits won't be diminished. Constantino bounds the short distance to Rose's office to spread the good news.

Fridays take on a special life of their own at Dataflex. The atmosphere is even more relaxed than usual, although work is still in progress. The baby boom at Dataflex is evident on Fridays. Associates bring their toddlers and newborns to visit. When you walk around the building, you see heads pop up, peeking over the cubicles, as people exchange jokes and stories. You never know what to expect, although clients are forewarned not to expect people to be dressed in regular business attire. The work load remains the same, but there is an air of frivolity on Fridays that is unmatched during the rest of the week. Maybe it's the company meeting, maybe it's the barbecues, but you feel it as you make your way through the maze of cubicles.

Asked about the mood change, Kevin Denecour agrees that Fridays are different, but not because of the TGIF syndrome that afflicts so many companies. "People genuinely enjoy their work here," says the twenty-six year old whose phone is constantly ringing. "It's an attitude. You'll see people in here on the weekends. I prefer to work at home, but I'll easily put in eight hours on the weekend. I love it, and I come in on Monday and boom! I'm ready to fly again."

On this particular Friday, salespeople and the sales-administration staff are darting around in strange costumes. Sales is sponsoring an open house today in the main conference room, and the first group is coming at 10 A.M. Bethann Wapinski is wearing a silk robe over her regular clothes. Several men and women are wearing dark glasses like the Blues Brothers.

Steve Lamm, a sales assistant on Jayne Banach-Walther's team, struts into the room wearing a trench coat, sunglasses, and a baseball cap on backward. Lamm worked in the warehouse along side Scott Rose off and on during his teenage years. But as a twenty year old, he was, he says, "spending my time sitting in the sun in Florida, drinking beer." Rose called him late one Saturday afternoon and told him to be in Dataflex's office the following Monday morning at 10 A.M. for an interview.

"That was the kick in the tail I needed," says Lamm, who has wavy, strawberry blond hair and a light goatee. On his way out the door, he told his surprised father where he was going. "Rick called me because he's my friend. My father had no idea." Lamm got in his 1985 Honda Accord and drove seventeen hours straight until he reached New Jersey. He started at Dataflex in January 1991 as a sales administrator and has gotten four promotions since then.

Fresh juices, coffee, tea, a fruit tray, and bagels are arranged on a side table in the main conference room. The receptionist's announcement that the open house will start in five minutes sends all involved in the program scurrying to the conference room. Glen Koedding stays on the phone until the last possible moment, making it to the room just as the door is closing.

As Dataflex associates come through the door, they are handed desk-top published programs on light blue paper. The Dataflex wheel is emblazoned on the front with the line: "We're a hit because of you." Russ Schultz gives the welcome, and Maura White explains the sales strategy. First, they show a short film entitled *A Day in the Life of a Sales Rep*. It features Tom Beer making countless prospecting calls and the variety of responses that sales reps encounter. The theme of the open house revolves around an eight-round boxing match between Dataflex and its major competitor. Associates are handed bags of popcorn just before the fight starts. The staff has gone to the trouble of putting together a video of Beer, who once played semipro baseball on a farm team for the New York Mets, representing Dataflex in the bout. The referee alias Fendrick starts the match by shouting: "May the best value win."

Beer is duking it out on film with a masked monster, who represents the competitor. (It's actually Schultz in a hideous mask and wearing Day-Glo colored biking shorts.) The running gag is that the competitor's only punch—delivered below the belt—is a low price. The trainer in the competitor's corner hollers over and over again: "Keep the prices low. We'll make it up in volume!"

Between rounds, different salespeople explain the various advantages that Dataflex offers to the client, such as the functionality and quality of the product when it arrives, service and support, training and assistance. During this section Doug Feldner, a sales assistant, puts on a mustache and does a terrific imitation of tech support's Kevin Denecour, who is known for being abrupt at times, and Bethann Wapinski makes a cameo appearance as Prasad Srinivasan, the credit manager, nixing a $1 million deal because the customer has owed $3 for close to sixty days. Both get big laughs. Next, they explain investment protection (Constantino talks about Dataflex's trade-up program, which enables customers to trade in old machines for new ones; Dataflex processed 2,000 trades in 1991. Glen Koedding talks about Dataflex's sixteen years in business and its financial stability. Russ Schultz's topic is systems integration. He notes that Dataflex has nine LAN engineers on staff with combined experience of forty-five years. This portion of the program also allows the other departments a chance to get to know more about each of the salespeople because Constantino and Fendrick give some of their background.

During a commercial break, Lamm leaps onto the center of the long table, and three women in dark clothes and dark glasses join him in a rap song about team-order processing.

Constantino and Fendrick comment on the fight, freeze framing certain punches and scoring each round. Of course, Beer finally knocks out the competitor in the eighth round. Although the hour-long presentation is funny, it is also chockful of information on how the sales staff competes against other companies that claim to do the same thing as Dataflex, but often only have slashed prices to offer. At the end, White hands out paddleballs printed with the message: "We're a hit because of you."

Rose returns to his office after the sales open house and sorts through his mail quickly. It's already a few minutes past 11 A.M. This Friday is payday. Associates are paid every two weeks. Rose's check is lying on his desk in an envelope. He picks it up and flushes crimson. Each paycheck envelope is stamped with "Courtesy of Dataflex's customers." It's a nice reminder, but Rose's stamp is virtually illegible, a black smear on the crisp envelope. Two weeks earlier, the stamp had been slightly smeared, and Rose had complained about the irony of its quality not being up to snuff. And now this messy job. He dials Ann Marie Bernet's extension. Bernet picks up her phone.

"Ann Marie, this is Rick," sputters the president. "If Antoinette can't stamp these envelopes properly, find somebody who can. This looks so sloppy, and I'm apalled." Antoinette Ogno is an accounts-payable administrator who dates Rich Dressler.

He goes across the hall to show the offending smudge to Liz Massimo. "Can you believe we can't even get a stamp done properly around here?" he asks, shaking his head in disgust.

Massimo looks at it briefly and agrees it's sloppy work.

Then Rose peels open the envelope. Inside is a second envelope with the stamp perfect. On the envelope, Ogno has neatly penned the words, "Gotcha, Rick."

Rose doubles over with laughter.

At 11:30 A.M. the executive committee gathers in Rose's small conference room to take a survey on what news to present at the company meeting. The mood is light, and at times, it seems more like a competition to see who can come up with the best one-liners than a meeting of the head honchos of a company.

"Attention Dataflex, attention Dataflex, the company meeting will start in five minutes," Maria Infusino announces over the intercom. People come pouring into the conference room from all over the company. Most associates are wearing T-shirts, jeans, and athletic shoes. By 11:45 A.M. the room is packed with men and women. The group is loud and raucous. Rose stands in the front of the elongated room.

He has a few notes scribbled on the back of one of his business cards. He rarely uses any notes when he speaks. Rose says, "We have a few guests today. Wayne Isbitski's family is here."

Isbitski's three-year-old son Ian walks halfway down the conference room table as the associates cheer him on. Next he introduces new associate Wendy Pate, a training and software specialist. A flurry of hands motion her toward the table, and Pate, in stocking feet, pads down the table to the shouts, claps, and laughter of the associates. It is an initiation rite that all associates undergo.

"Congratulations to Charlie Milo and Tony Hunter for winning the top awards in their Dale Carnegie classes," Rose says. He hands out a $100 bill to each engineer who had the fastest response times for the week.

"This month the executive committee has selected Ceil Abramski, our senior dispatch administrator, as Performer of the Month. She also gets $100 and a reserved spot in the parking lot."

"Our five-year dinner is coming up," he continues. "Currently, we have eighteen members in the five-year club, and at the dinner we'll be inducting nineteen new members, which means 20 percent of this company has been here more than five years."

Everyone applauds.

Rose announces that the sales force has chosen two people to send on the Tour de France trip. Terry Pallosi gasps, clutches her throat, and collapses into a co-worker's arms giggling when her name is announced. Donna DeVito is en route to work from another doctor's visit when the announcement is made. The young woman is suffering from a rare blood disease and has spent endless weeks in the hospital of late. The room erupts in applause for the two women.

Rose tells the gathering about IBM's dealer-recognition event. "There are 2,000 dealers in the nation, and only the top 10 percent are invited to this event," says Rose. "This was the fifth year in a row that we've been selected."

More good news: "The marketing department just completed our first quality assurance survey. About 3 percent of the 6,000 we sent out to customers were filled out, and 70 percent of the 180 who responded said they were 'most satisfied' with our performance. I have personally called each one of the respondents to talk to them further about what we can do to improve. In the future the ten of us on the executive committee will be calling respondents to keep a pulse on what's happening with our customers."

He also announces that the company's stock was recommended on CNN's "Business News" yesterday. Four-month-old Megan Isbitski, content in her father's arms, coos at that moment. Rose laughs and says, "She knows it's exciting."

Next he announces a new contest called a "belly-off." Finance's Peggy Abromaitis and marketing's Joanne Lowy are both five months' pregnant, and Rose proposes a contest in which people will bet one dollar on the person whom they think will have the biggest belly by the pregnancy's end.

Rose says, "I want to congratulate Antoinette on nailing me this morning. She gave me my check with the stamp that says it's courtesy of our customers smeared all over the place. I'd complained before that it was blurry, so this time I went nuts. Then I opened it up, and there was another envelope with the stamp perfect. Anyway, that's the best one anyone's gotten me with in a while. Good job, Antoinette." Ogno flashes a wry smile, and her prank provokes laughter in the room.

Rose continues, "I want to wish Deana Behringer the best of luck. She is trying out for the show *American Gladiators* next week. Finally, I'd like to say good-bye and good luck to Deron Illarraza. It's his last day with us because he's gotten a job as a policeman, which is, as many of you know, his dream. I am grateful that we had the privilege of working with you here at Dataflex, Deron. You've always done an excellent job for us. Thanks all of you for coming today." The meeting lasts exactly fifteen minutes.

ACTIONS

☑ Keep business simple. When the atmosphere becomes too tense, catch people off guard by breaking the routine.

☑ Look for creative ways to hone communication skills. The playing cards have added a new dimension to our morning meetings, but it wasn't my idea. Alan Fendrick came up with it. Even after eighteen years of conducting sales meetings, there are always improvements to be made.

☑ Be willing to discuss topics even if you don't know the answers. Ultimately, I still think picking orchids and onions comes down to intuition. It's something a person is born with. I can give parameters, but I can't teach people how to do it. However, that didn't stop us from devoting not one, but several sales meetings to it.

☑ Give your staff a chance to tell you what exciting changes are taking place in the company before you try to conduct a company meeting. Otherwise, you'll miss out on several good storytelling opportunities.

☑ Company meetings should be positive and fun. If you wonder if yours are dull, they probably are. If you don't have them at all, that's even worse. You'll never build team spirit unless you get the team together in a huddle.

Take a look at this chart for specifics on this delicate art.

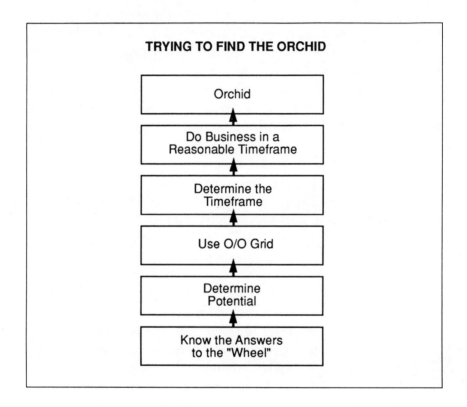

TRYING TO FIND THE ORCHID

Orchid

↑

Do Business in a
Reasonable Timeframe

↑

Determine the
Timeframe

↑

Use O/O Grid

↑

Determine
Potential

↑

Know the Answers
to the "Wheel"

10

Chances

At noon, Rose walks out the front door and to the far side of the building. He dons a chef's apron and hat—a gift from Rich Dressler—for his next duties. Every Friday, from Memorial Day until Labor Day for the past five years, Rose and Mike Rinaldi, a senior warehouseman nicknamed Rhino, have grilled hamburgers and hotdogs for associates during the afternoon. Occasionally, others volunteer for grill duty as well.

Immediately after the company meeting, associates begin lining up in the lunchroom to get plates and load them up with the potato salad, coleslaw, macaroni salad, chips, pretzels, grapes, watermelon, and cantaloupe that are heaped on two tables. Often customers are invited for the barbecues. "Some of our best business conversations are conducted while eating a burger on the lawn during the picnic," White notes. "Customers love coming to them, and everyone is more relaxed."

The freshly mowed lawn, partially shaded by pine trees, is swarming with people. Some are reclining in the shady spots on the lawn. Others are tossing Frisbees or playing Wiffle ball. McLenithan initiates a game of badminton. Ron Jones from marketing practices his golf shots on the front lawn. Cars slow down as they pass by and the drivers honk, and the associates wave.

A game of touch football is well under way. Some of the players try to talk Rose into playing, but he begs off, pointing to his cowboy boots. Rose still loves football, but he rarely joins the football games because of the knee surgery that kept him in a hospital bed for three months while at the U.S. Naval Academy. His knee bears a deep scar. Those were the days long before laser surgery lessened the trauma associated with such a severe knee injury.

Rose is content to trade jokes with everyone who comes by to get a burger. Dressler heaps his plate with two burgers and goes back in his office. He is wearing jeans and a T-shirt and has his feet up on his desk with his boom box blasting a tape of the last gig that he played with his band, The Minerals. Dressler provides the lead vocals, plays bass, and writes music for the band. He smiles, thinking about the evening that The Minerals last performed: Rose and McLenithan surprised him by showing up at the club, and more than 100 people from Dataflex boosted the show to sell-out status.

Dressler's phone rings. A headhunter is on the line. "Would you be interested in talking to a company in your industry about a similar position?" the person asks.

"Tell me who the company is," says Dressler, between bites, "or I'll hang up."

After a few minutes of waffling, the headhunter names a competitor at which several of Dressler's friends work. Dressler knows the culture and knows it's nothing like Dataflex. He also met the president a few times and took an immediate dislike to the man.

Dressler replies, "If I could come to work on Fridays in jeans and a T-shirt and the president of the company would flip a burger on a bun for me and I could play my music in my office as loud as I wanted, then maybe I'd talk to you."

It's 1:45 P.M., shortly before the weekly process meeting, when White finds Rose in the kitchen, getting a root beer from the vending machine. He pauses to weigh himself on the new scales that have been put next to the snack vending machine. When associates were giving their visions of greatness, several mentioned wanting to lose weight. Rose asked Dressler to order a scale for the kitchen. Several associates have listed their weight and their goal on a weekly chart someone has taped to the vending machine, which is stocked primarily with healthy snacks.

"We've got a problem," White says. "Ken's team pulled the order for the bank."

"But we told them, not once, but twice, to hold off for the updated software," says Rose in a mildly exasperated tone.

"I know, I know," says White, sighing.

She follows Rose back to his office, where he rustles through his drawer for something. Finally, he finds what he's looking for and pulls out a nametag like you would get at a trade show. Only the name Huckleberry is neatly penned on it. "Time for the award, huh?" says White, her arms crossed.

"Yep," says Rose. Constantino is on the phone when Rose and White appear behind him. When he hangs up, he whirls around in his chair. "Oh, no, not that thing," he says as Rose holds the infamous Huckleberry pin.

"I hereby decree that you wear the Huckleberry pin for the rest of the day because of the bone-headed move your team made by pulling that order after we'd specifically told them not to," says Rose.

Constantino rolls his eyes. Looking sheepish, he says, "Rick, I've got one request."

"What is it?" asks Rose.

"Let me wear the court jester's hat instead. Bethann will wear the pin."

Wapinski overhears him and pokes her head around the divider separating her cubicle from Constantino's. "Gee, thanks, Ken," she says.

Rose says, "Come on around, Bethann, so Maura can pin this thing on you. You guys just got in too big a hurry this time. I'll be back in a minute with your hat, Ken."

He is stretching to reach for the court jester's cap, which he has placed on the shelf with the other hats he's collected over the years, when Massimo comes to remind him that the process meeting is in five minutes. The meetings started a few years ago primarily as problem-solving sessions, but they evolved to a point where the participants found themselves setting company policy, so Rose decided to inject himself into the process.

The process committee meeting starts promptly at 2 P.M. in the main conference room. At the weekly meeting, the process owners—meaning the people who are responsible for the different components involved in processing customers' orders—convene to get input and feedback to help each other remove defects from the system. The meeting is an integral part of the quality program Mannix installed when he was a consultant with Connective Management, Inc. Seventeen people are at the meeting.

Greg Coccetti opens the meeting by reporting on a customized software program that he spent a day examining. He agrees to meet with Rich Dressler and Stacey Bernstein later to talk in depth about what the system has to offer. He also informs the committee that he has yet to receive a proposal for the inventory software program.

Joe Rizzo brings up the Malcolm Baldrige National Quality Awards. "We're already using the assessment checklist from the award program," he says. "Maybe we should talk about what it takes to win. Even if we decide not to enter, I believe going through the exercise would wind up making us a better company."

Heidi Gray, quality coordinator, adds, "Ken Cavanagh was a member of the submitting committee at Milliken when it won a Malcolm Baldrige in 1989. Why don't we have him come in and talk to us about it next week?" Everyone agrees.

Bernstein tells the group that she spoke to Maura White regarding an invoicing problem one of the salesmen was having with "Flexbucks," Dataflex's marketing program that allows customers to earn points called Flexbucks that can be redeemed for services and products. It's a popular program and a brainchild of Rizzo that has stimulated customers to try new services and products that they might not have otherwise considered.

Deana Behringer, the RGA (returned goods authorization) coordinator, suggests that the company develop a publication that explains the RGA program and put it into the box with every system it ships. Dataflex has had a money-back, thirty-day guarantee for sometime now, but some customers have gotten confused on exactly how the system works. "I think we should distribute an FYI internally, too," says Behringer, who just turned twenty-three years old and has worked at Dataflex for three years. RGAs are approved for a variety of reasons: sales errors, customer errors, technical-support errors, vendor errors, warehouse errors, and any number of other reasons.

"In three months, can you review all the statistics, so we can let

IBM know exactly what their program cost us?" asks Mannix, referring to a new thirty-day, money-back guarantee program that IBM has just instituted.

Behringer nods.

Rose is seated at the head of the table and leans forward. His voice has the conspiratorial tone that it takes on sometimes when he's enlisting somebody to take on a challenge. "Deana, how many RGAs do we get a month?"

"About seventy-five."

"How much does it cost us to process each one?"

"Approximately four hundred dollars."

Rose stands up and starts pacing. "So, Deana, do you think that if we do a better job and eliminate the mistakes that are within our control you could cut our RGAs down to thirty a month?"

"Well, I don't know," answers Behringer, cocking her head to one side. "I've gotten a lot of resistance from the sales staff. They just don't want to make any more calls."

"But if you explained to them that the two or three mistakes their teams are still making, multiplied by ten, are adding up to twenty or thirty RGAs a month that could be avoided—as well as a big cost to the company—do you think you could?" asks Rose. "How about if I give you $10,000 if you get them down to thirty a month or below and hold it to that level for four consecutive months. Then do you think you could do it?"

"I'm insulted. It's my job," Behringer replies.

"I know it's your job, but if you save the company $72,000 by slashing our RGAs, it would be my pleasure to give you $10,000," Rose insists. "We were having 140 RGAs a month when you took this job, and now I'm asking you to take it one step higher."

A grin slowly spreads across Behringer's tan face, and she says, "OK, Rick, you're on."

An announcement reverberates over the PA system at 3:30 P.M. summoning the sales staff to the kitchen. "C'mon guys, it's our week to clean," calls out Steve Lamm, who has changed out of the rapper's gear he had donned for the sales department's morning open house. Only seven people in the sales department answer the call. Soon, Lamm is busily swabbing down cabinet fronts with Formula

409. By the time the crew completes the task, the kitchen is spotless. Rose, fresh from the process meeting, comes in for a cup of coffee and stops Mosher from dumping the pot.

"It looks good in here," says Rose. "But where is everybody? I don't remember the sales staff being this small."

Lamm replies, "A lot of people are out on calls or on the line with customers." Rose acknowledges his explanation with a slight nod and then darts back to his office to check his voice mail.

McLenithan and Rose often spend a half hour or so late Friday afternoons wandering around, getting a pulse of the company. Rose walks back to technical support in search of Kevin Denecour. He waits until the young man finishes a support call with a client and then asks, "Hey Kevin. Am I getting an invite to your bachelor party?"

"Sure, Rick. You should have gotten it by now because I mailed them on Monday," replies the twenty-six year old who has a dip of snuff in his mouth, causing his lower lip to jut out and emphasizing his mustache. "Hey, Rick, you know that problem that customer was having with their displays? I've been working with IBM on it the past few weeks, and I found the solution to it today. I'm just about to call the customer and let them know."

As Rose starts to walk away, he says over his shoulder, "That's good, Kevin. I'm glad to hear it."

"Rick," Denecour shouts a few seconds later. Rose turns around just in time to see Denecour leaning over the top wall with a Nerf air gun in hand. He lets one fly and catches Rose right between the eyes. Denecour grins mischieviously.

"Your bachelor party is going to be one wild ride," says Rose, laughing, and turns on his heels.

The pond-scum meeting starts at 4:30 P.M. on Friday afternoons. Rose hit upon the name for the afternoon meetings with the first year sales reps when Dataflex was still in its old building. He wanted a nickname for rookies. He had decided plebe wouldn't work. It was a bright, sunny day, and he was gazing out his office window at a pond that the company had to build because of poor drainage on the property. It was a beautiful pond with a fountain and several ducks.

"The light was streaming through the water, and I could see the algae floating on top," Rose recalls. "I thought, 'That's the lowest form of life in that ecosystem. Why not have pond-scum meetings?' " When Rose announced the pond-scum meeting that Friday, Maurice Scaglione who had been with the company only a few weeks thought that he was supposed to stand by the pond in front of the building, waiting for everyone else to show up for the meeting to start. Then Rose paged him to report to the conference room.

Schultz, Mosher, Fendrick, White, Corcodilos, and Koedding are at the meeting this afternoon. The veterans attend essentially to support the new recruits, but they are likely to receive constructive criticism as well. The feel is more intimate than the morning meetings because the group is smaller. Yet the topics covered are just as serious and often more personal in nature. One salesman recently left the company after a pond-scum meeting in which his peers told him that he was unwilling to accept constructive criticism. White had asked the group to rank themselves on their current performance and potential, and this salesman ranked dead last on everyone's list except his own. "He had many chances, but he refused to admit any of his weaknesses," says White.

After that pond-scum meeting, the salesman requested a one-on-one with Rose and asked whether the president agreed with the perception of the sales staff. Rose told him that he needed an attitude adjustment because he always blamed others for his problems. Rose suggested that he think about what he'd done in the past and then ask his peers for a fresh start at the next morning meeting. The young man said, "I'm not willing to do that because I don't think I've done anything wrong. So does that mean I'm fired?"

Rose replied, "No, because I'm not the one who can make that decision. That's Maura's responsibility. But I'll call her in here." White answered her extension and came across the hall. The salesman repeated what he had said to Rose.

"OK," said White. "You're fired."

Today, though, Rose is relaxed and smiling. He likes to open meetings with good news. He says, "We are becoming more and more important to our vendors, and I'm excited about that. It's important to have a reputation."

Rose shares the news that his wife, Linda, is pregnant. He is thrilled, but trying not to get too excited because his wife has suffered several miscarriages. However, he feels comfortable talking about it with the sales team. His vulnerability makes it easier for other people to reveal their joys and concerns.

He spends some time talking about the upcoming sales-recognition event. As it stands, Banach-Walther, Mosher, and Corcodilos did not make the qualifiers that had been put in last year. However, Rose wants to waive the rule (there had never been a qualifier to attend before) because he believes all three have worked hard and made significant contributions to the company. He asks for feedback on whether they should be allowed to attend. "Of course, if the group thinks we should stand by the letter of the law, we will, but I want to open it up for discussion because these people are falling a little bit short of the requirements," says Rose.

One veteran comments, "I think everybody who has made it through a year here should go. Simply by virtue of surviving this intense environment, they have demonstrated an enormous commitment."

Constantino and Banach-Walther slip into the pond-scum meeting late. Unlike other meetings at Dataflex when knocking on a closed door is taboo, latecomers are welcome because sales reps are often out of the office on sales calls or on the phone late in the day on Fridays. Constantino quickly catches the drift of what is being discussed and disagrees. "When is a deal a deal?" he asks. "It's like the question of me becoming an account executive as opposed to a sales rep. I've been here five years. I've worked hard and contributed a lot. Being made an account executive would be great, but I haven't made the cut according to the qualifiers. And you could say it isn't fair because the qualifiers keep being changed, but I agreed to accept them. I'm disappointed, but I know a deal is a deal."

Rose says, "I don't think there's a lack of integrity in changing the rules. The criteria we came up with were experimental. We'd never tried setting a qualifier for the recognition event before. The only change would be to make it more fair."

Rose solicits the feelings of the three involved. All clearly want to go and believe they deserve to go; however, to the person they have accepted the fact that, according to the original deal, they don't qualify.

Someone else suggests that the problem lies in calling the event a sales-recognition event. Banach-Walther says, "The sales staff is small enough that I don't see the point of taking only half of us. An event like this one builds camaraderie and the very foundation that we say we are trying to accomplish."

Mosher fervently agrees.

"So you are saying we should just acknowledge the fact that it's a time for the sales staff to grow closer and dispense with the idea of its sole purpose being to recognize sales?" asks Rose. He looks thoughtful and declares that the discussion will continue the following Monday when the entire staff is present.

Then Rose asks, "Has any of you done anything lately that has made selling easier for you?"

Banach-Walther answers, "I constructed an agenda and faxed it to a client the other day before a meeting. They seemed so impressed by that. It immediately set in their minds that I'm organized and that I'm not going to waste their time."

Constantino nods and smiles, adding, "I do that, too. It shows customers that you know how to prioritize, and it also gives them a chance to let you know what's on their minds as well."

"Good point," says Rose. "I used to like to set appointments at odd times like 1:18. When the client would ask why that time, I'd tell them it was because I realized their time was valuable, and I didn't want to waste a moment of it.

"The words we choose in every situation are critical to making sure we don't get stuck in an onion field. Getting orders isn't the key. Building customers is."

Rose's attention turns to Elaine Mosher, who has shadows under her blue eyes. "Is there anything the company isn't doing for you, Elaine, that would make your job easier?" he asks, tapping a pencil on the table as he talks.

"Can't think of anything," she says. "Day by day my morale is improving, but some days are better than others. Since my experience, I've gone through a reevaluation." Like Banach-Walther, Mosher had a major setback a few months ago when a big account fell through.

"What chance do you give yourself of succeeding as a salesperson here?" Rose persists with a question he asks the salespeople almost weekly at these meetings.

"Seventy percent," she replies and bobs her head in affirmation.

Rose raises an eyebrow, and a slight smile plays on his lips: "That's very high. But if you can learn how to sell in this environment, you'll never have to worry. You can do anything. When the PC business was going like gangbusters, a dog with a note in its mouth could sell these products. Now it takes much more talent and real selling ability. I've been through four recessions in this industry—in 1974, 1979, 1985, and 1991—and I've never seen a market as tough as the one we're in now."

"Changing seats and being near Ken has helped," says Mosher, whose cubicle is now just a few steps away from Constantino's. "I learn a great deal listening to him talk to his customers, and I can turn around in my chair and ask him questions if something comes up."

Schultz asks her, "Who is helping you?" She names almost everyone on the sales force.

Fendrick, sitting Indian style on one of the side tables next to the board, looks glum and mumbles half under his breath, "Sounds like you get help from everybody but me."

Mosher ignores his comment.

"Our group is getting smaller," observes Koedding, who has traded in his customary double-breasted suit and corporate suspenders for a simple button-down shirt, blue jeans, and loafers.

Constantino, sitting with his knees propped up on the side table with Fendrick, says, "It's a tighter huddle."

Rose nods, "It's a better group." He asks Banuch-Walther if she will succeed.

She nods yes confidently and says, "I would not have stayed in the industry if it hadn't been for Dataflex."

Rose turns to Schultz. "How do you think things are going for you, Russ?"

Schultz replies, "I have one account where they run everything by the seat of their pants, and they beat us up in the process. I'm starting to wonder if it's worth our time and effort."

"An orchid is turning into an onion, eh?" asks Rose.

Isbitski says, "It was Russ's ability to manage their account that made them choose us in the first place."

Schultz asks Rose, "Would you keep jumping through hoops for them if you were me?"

Rose answers, "You are really emotional about this account, Russ." He then says to the group: "Russ comes into my office frequently and asks my advice on accounts. And lately what I would do and what he would do are two different things because his emotion is clouding his judgment."

"My question for you, Russ," Rose says, gazing intently at Schultz, "is why do you want to get out of sales?"

The question hangs in the air. Schultz appears discomfited. At length, he answers, "I don't want to get out of sales. I want to develop expertise, but I'm still going to do all the functions of sales, except prospecting. I want to do what Wayne does."

"That's not what I've understood from the conversations we've had," says Rose. "My understanding is that you want to go on salary and concentrate on becoming a LAN expert like Wayne. That's very different from being in sales. Are you seeking a career path, or are you afraid to be in sales?"

Rose continues: "I'm not going to make this switch easy for you, because I believe you are one of the best salespeople we've got. You'd be an excellent resource as a support engineer for the salespeople, but I don't think it's the best move for you or for Dataflex."

Schultz notes that his career has always been marked by periods when he stopped selling to gain product knowledge in one area or another. "I believe this is just another one of those education cycles," he says.

Rose says, "You are afraid of relying on your ability as a professional salesperson. I'm no different from you. I have a strong aversion to going out on sales calls to push services because it's unfamiliar territory to me. But I have the confidence that I can overcome anything."

Corcodilos has been sitting quietly observing and asks, "Are you doing it to avoid fear, or are you doing it because you want to become an expert?"

Schultz replies, "I'm not doing it out of fear, I don't think. I just want to become an expert."

"You are rationalizing," White says firmly. "Admit you're afraid."

Mosher, saddened and stunned, says, "Russ, I can't believe you're talking like this right now. There's a marked difference in your attitude from three months ago when you were ready to chew through walls and do whatever you needed to do to rekindle your sales career. I think you've had a few failures and gotten scared."

Katz, who came in a few minutes earlier from a meeting at a client's site and is dressed to the nines, says emphatically, "Russ, come on. If anybody should be scared, it should be me. Who is more of a bozo than I am when it comes to new technology. But I just drag somebody along with me like Wayne or Tim who knows all about the stuff. I don't worry about it. I believe I'll figure out what I need to know as I go along."

Schultz's blue eyes start to water, and his cheeks register a faint pink blush. After much discussion, Schultz finally admits that with a wife who isn't working and two young children to support, he is afraid to rely on commissions during a time when the emphasis is shifting to a new product—LAN services—that he is unfamiliar with. "I've worked hard and a long time to get what I've got now," says Schultz, his voice trailing off as he adds: "I've got a nice house and a nice life, and I don't want to lose it."

Rose asks, "I want you to answer one question for me. If I told you right now that I'd give you Alan or Diane's base of clients, would you stay in sales?"

Without hesitation, Schultz answers softly, "Yes."

"That," pronounces Rose, "is your acid test. If you'd switch places with Diane or Alan, don't cop out. Figure out what the difference is between you and them and work real hard to duplicate their success. If we do the right thing for you, it will be the right thing for Dataflex. Has there ever been a time when you weren't treated fairly here?"

"No," Schultz responds.

"Then think about these things some more. I am telling you as your friend, Russ, that I don't think you should get out of sales. Don't be afraid to take chances," Rose states.

"Thanks to all of you for your input," says Schultz. "It means a lot to me that you'd take the time to discuss it here."

"Ken," Rose asks, "what's going on with you?"

"I'm in a boondoggle with one of my accounts. We can't get the billing right," Constantino replies, looking distinctly uncomfortable. "I'm frustrated with all the bureaucracy."

Koedding suggests, "Get Ralph in there. He's great at sorting out those kind of problems."

Rose props his cowboy boots on the table. He asks a few questions, ferreting out the details, and then, shaking his head, says softly, "You are terrible administratively. I am begging you, Ken, seek some help from Maura or some of these other people around here who are good at it. Making great sales doesn't do us a bit of good if we can't get paid for it. You have to improve in this area.

"Let's have an empowerment-card check. Who has theirs?"

From their wallets, Corcodilos, Fendrick, Schultz, Rose, and Constantino all pull out the laminated cards that were put together to remind them of their mission. "No fair," protests Mosher and Banach-Walther simultaneously. "We don't carry wallets."

Rose's contact lenses are bothering him, and he is so intent on the conversation that he pops his left one out and dips it in the glass in front of him. Then he returns it to his eye, which immediately turns red and watery. He starts to speak, but Constantino interrupts, "Uh, Rick, did you realize you just dipped your contact in your root beer?" Everybody, Rose included, starts to laugh.

Turning to Ralph Hrovat, who holds a new position called sales specialist/maintenance, Rose asks if he's pleased with his own progress. Hrovat, aged forty, blonde, and balding, looks sort of like an aging surfer. He says, "I feel like I'm finally coming out of the fog here. I understand what I'm supposed to concentrate on and I'm not getting caught up in the less important tasks that I used to waste days on. People aren't coming to me with trivial problems now, and I've increased my ability to say no."

Mosher comments, "I respect your time more."

Fendrick adds, "Yeah, Ralph used to be like Mikey. Give it to Ralph, he'll do anything."

Rose says, "It even shows in the way you look Ralph. You look healthier and seem much happier."

Banach-Walther asks, "Are you still living with Ken?" Ralph nods yes.

Koedding teases, "You don't have to pay rent until Ken learns how to invoice you." Constantino flushes and smiles sheepishly as his peers laugh.

Rose draws the conversation back to Hrovat's appearance. "When someone looks good, you can count on how it's going. Without even talking to Ralph, I knew he was doing well. One look at Elaine's face, and I know right away what she's going through.

Jayne is tougher to read, but I think it's because I don't know her as well yet. Always be suspicious of sickness in yourself."

Isbitski is grinning like a Cheshire cat and says, "I think the next thirty days are going to be a milestone for me and the company." He takes a few moments to tell the group about some of his plans.

Banach-Walther, who has already sold several LAN accounts, turns to Isbitski and says, "I've learned so much from you. Customers are so wowed by what you have to say. I just hope you aren't lying about all this stuff." She cracks up laughing.

Isbitski asks, "Rick, are you listening? I think I hear a raise being offered."

Rose says in mock disgust, "Jayne, couldn't you have waited until after April to say all these nice things? Wayne's review is coming up."

Isbitski's mood suddenly turns serious as he says to Rose, "I will not negotiate my comp plan. I trust you to do the right thing for me and my family."

Rose explains to the group that each year he writes Isbitski's compensation on a piece of paper and seals it in an envelope that Isbitski is allowed to open on April 1. It is a deal that both men are comfortable with and that transpired two years ago after a particularly contentious negotiation. Rose told Isbitski that his review was one of the few things about his job that he actually dreaded. "These negotiations are always a killer," said Rose, looking drained. "You're too much like me." After thinking it over, Isbitski drew up an agreement that gave Rose the right to set Isbitski's compensation each year and presented it to Rose the next day.

The bright light turns on Fendrick. "So," Rose says, "what are you going to do if NYNEX goes away?" The phone company is Fendrick's biggest account by far.

"Have more time to sell services," Fendrick replies. "And I can honestly say I feel excited about that."

Koedding, who spent a year working on Fendrick's team, notes, "I'm impressed by the way you've turned around. The only thing you used to like to do was sell hardware over the phone. I remember the first time you were going out to see a customer. You were so nervous that you sent me out to buy candy for you because your throat was so dry. Now you're out of the office two or three times a week with customers."

"Thanks, Glenn," says Fendrick, whose vision of greatness is to become a partner and expand the three amigos to four. To do that, he knows he must expand his knowledge and skills on all fronts.

When all eyes turn on Koedding, almost before Rose can ask the question, the young man is assuring him that he will be successful without a doubt. "You sound pretty sure about that Vito," says Rose. You can see the competitiveness glinting in Koedding's black eyes as he returns Rose's gaze. He aches to see his name at the top of the board. Rose has ascertained that the way to get him to perform is to tease him with the thought that Koedding may not "be packing the goods." It makes Koedding crazy and drives him to prospect with a fury no one has achieved since Fendrick's days as a rookie. As a motivator, Rose knows that some people respond to sticks and others respond to carrots. And for each person the stick and the carrot are different.

Isbitski grins and says, "Glen's a prospecting machine."

Rose, cupping his hands behind his head and tilting back in his chair, says, "There's nothing like the thrill of bringing in a new account. Managing accounts is the tough part. It's a never-ending job like cleaning house."

Hrovat observes wryly, "Yeah, a house with kids in it."

When Rose calls on him to put a percentage on his chance for success at Dataflex, Corcodilos is characteristically cautious, giving himself even odds.

Finally, Rose casts his eye on White. "Are you happy here?" he asks.

"I'm excited about our new comp plan," says White. "I want to put my thumbprint on something, and I'm anxious to make a contribution. I've gone through a real tough time the past three months, but putting together my vision of greatness was a turning point in clarifying the trust I have in all of you." White had moved many of the sales staff to tears when she presented her vision. She opened up much more than she had when she presented it to the executive committee, and she divulged how growing up with very little had fueled her desire to have a comfortable life. When she talked about never wanting to have to shop at K-Mart again, there were more than a few nods of recognition in the room.

Constantino asks, "Maura, you said you want to put your thumbprint on something. Do you not feel like you've made a contribution here?"

White replies, "I think I've served as a sounding board for a lot of you."

"I know you've given me some creative ways to attack accounts," Constantino states.

"Well, logistically, there are some aspects of my job that need to be worked out," White says softly.

Nothing slips by Rose, and he pounces on that last comment: "Exactly what logistics do you mean?"

"For example, there have been some big meetings with clients lately that I haven't been in on and I think I should have been there," says White, carefully enunciating her words and looking Rose in the eyes.

Rose sighs and says, "I don't care whether you are there or not. I just don't want to go traipsing into a meeting with an entourage of people. That's overkill. Diane feels comfortable having me there because I helped her sell the account in the first place. And I don't think that's going to change. I want you to bring people onto the staff who will be as successful as Diane, Alan, and Tom Beer have been."

Fendrick asks, "Was that what you thought the job would be?"

"I came in," says White firmly, "to help direct the best sales force in the industry."

Rose says, "Look, you can try to do the whole thing at once. Or you can find, hire, and train successful salespeople. In my book, if you develop the latter skills, you're a successful sales manager."

Schultz speaks up. "I see something else in this room that no one else sees."

"Elvis?" Fendrick quips.

Schultz continues: "Having sat in your seat, Maura, what Rick is saying is exactly what you should do if you want to be a success here. You have to make your own place. Forget doing the administrative duties and get off all the committees. It killed me because I was trying to do it all."

Rose says, "Find your own business and manage it. I want to see a manager's mark, and you aren't going to make that mark by making Russ and Alan better. Get Nick Corcodilos to be a top producer. Then you will have made your mark.

"And don't worry about whether you are in on every meeting. I'm not sought out to go on appointments to sell services. I don't deserve to go. I don't know how to sell services yet. So Tim Mannix is the one people rely on, but that doesn't bother me. I look at it as a challenge."

Corcodilos adds, "That's such a different attitude than what you find at most companies."

Mosher turns toward White and asks, "Do you know what I do every day?"

"I think I have a pretty good idea," says White.

Mosher replies, "I wish once a month that you would sit in my seat for several hours, calling on my accounts, because I don't know if you know what we go through each day."

Rose winds up the discussion, "Maura, I'm never going to remove myself from sales, but it would make me very happy if the people I brought in here were the minority."

It's almost 5 P.M. when Kerry Mutz hears his name being paged. When he answers the call, one of Dataflex's biggest customers is on the phone. Mutz, who is the systems-integration manager, listens while the customer complains that their LAN, consisting of eighty-seven workstations, is giving them intermittent problems. "Look, it's our fiscal year end, and we've got a real crisis on our hands unless you can do something," says the voice on the other end. "We've got to be up and running by Monday morning."

Dataflex has had the account for only six months, and a previous vendor installed the workstations. Also, the manufacturer of the equipment that the company purchased put out an FYI stating that the problem the customer was describing did not occur in workstations. While the customer detailed the exact glitches, Mutz was looking at his empowerment card, tacked up on the bulletin board. He knew from previous experience that the problem was on the workstation. Is it right for the customer? "Yes," he thinks to himself.

Next question: Is it the right thing to do for Dataflex? That's a tough one. First, technically, it could be argued that it isn't Dataflex's problem, since Dataflex wasn't the vendor that installed the workstations. Second, the manufacturer may be at fault. Not to mention the cost to the company of sending out customer engineers on the weekend to replace the network interface cards that Mutz suspected was causing the problem. The cards themselves will cost Dataflex roughly $5,000, Mutz figures. But weighed against the possibility of losing a customer, he finally decides the answer is yes.

Is it ethical? A resounding yes.

Is it something for which you are willing to be accountable? Again, Mutz decides the answer is yes.

Is it consistent with Dataflex's basic beliefs? Yes.

The final admonishment on the card says, "If the answer is YES to all these questions . . . Don't ask, just do it!" In that instant, Mutz makes up his mind. "Don't worry about a thing," he says, "I'll get back to you in a few minutes with details."

Mutz hangs up the phone and immediately starts mustering the troops. First, he tries to call Rose. No answer. He leaves a message on Elaine Mosher's voice mail, letting her know that their date is going to get a late start. He calls the sales rep who was in charge of the account. Again, no answer.

Alan Maglaque, a network engineer in Mutz's department, sticks his head in, "What's going on, Kerry? Anything I can do to help?"

Mutz runs his hands through his hair and straightens his gold-rimmed glasses. "Nah, just stick around a little while for moral support," he replies.

Next Mutz calls customer engineering and Charlie Ruvolo, a manager, is still in his office.

"Charlie, this is Kerry," he says. "We've got a little problem at one of our mainsites. We're going to need some customer engineers over there in the morning. Who can you send? Can you also arrange to get eighty-seven network cards out of the warehouse?"

"Sure, Kerry, I'll take care of it," says Ruvolo.

Tim Mannix, who has caught wind that something is up, pokes his head in the doorway of Mutz's office. "What's up?" Mannix asks.

Mutz quickly explains what has happened and his decision and concludes by saying, "The empowerment card was the clincher for me."

Mannix leans against the door jam, arms folded, and then says, "Sounds fine."

Mutz calls the customer back. "Everything is under control," he says, tapping a pencil on his desk. "We're hand delivering the cards in the morning, and our engineers will install them."

There is silence on the other end of the phone for a moment.

Then the customer says, "First thing Monday will be fine. Thanks. I never imagined that you could get it together this fast. I wasn't even sure I'd get someone in the office after 5 o'clock on a Friday, but I thought I'd give it a shot."

On Fridays at Dataflex, you learn to expect the unexpected. Rose's biggest surprise took place one Friday a year ago. Two months in advance, Maurice Scaglione had requested that Liz Massimo block off time on Rose's calendar on a Friday evening from 4 P.M. until midnight. Rose, who can't stand being kept in suspense, bugged Massimo every day for those two months trying to find out what Scaglione had planned. At the appointed hour, Scaglione pulled up in his Saab 9000 at the side entrance of Dataflex to act as a limo driver for Rick and Linda Rose.

An hour later, the trio was deposited at Lattanzi, an Italian restaurant in Manhattan. Scaglione had prepaid for the meal and had arranged for the waiters to bring a sampling of several dishes to the table. At the end of the meal, Rose reached for a cigar in the breast pocket of his coat. Scaglione touched his hand and stopped him. Knowing that Rose loves cigars, Scaglione had contacted Jeff Lamm in Florida to find out what brand to buy him. Since Tueros were not available, he bought Dunhill of London. "I believe you might prefer this one," said Scaglione, pulling it from his own pocket. "You have just enough time to smoke it. Then we're off to see O. G."

"Who's O. G.? Some stand-up comic?" asked Rose, inwardly groaning because one of his least favorite things to do is go to comedy clubs.

"You'll see," replied Scaglione mysteriously.

Scaglione hustled the couple out the door and walked a few blocks to the Majestic Theatre on West Forty-Fourth Street. He led the Roses to three seats in the fourth row from the stage. By this time Rose realized he wasn't going to a comedy club. He was there to see Andrew Lloyd Webber's hit Broadway musical *Phantom of the Opera*. O. G. stood for the opera ghost. Rose started getting excited.

"Rick," said Scaglione, grinning, "I planned this evening using the skills I've learned from you during my four years at Dataflex. Tonight marks my fourth year with the company. I wanted to give you a gift that would express my gratitude, and Linda suggested that an evening out would be appreciated."

Rose was overcome: "Tonight is the nicest thing anyone has ever done for me. Thank you. In fact, I've had so much fun that I want you to help me put the exact same evening together for my mom the next time she's in town. And I want you to come with us because what made this evening so special was spending time with you, Maurice."

This was a typical work week at Dataflex, and an average Friday. But one Friday, a month later, is anything but average: Two buses, each filled to their capacity of fifty with Dataflex associates, pull out of the parking lot at 2:30 P.M. headed for Atlantic City. During the 2 ½-hour trip, the associates sing Motown songs, play cards, and mingle. Sodas, beer, wine, and chips are provided.

On the lead bus, Rose stands and announces that traditionally Fendrick gives him $25 upon their arrival at the casino with the instructions to bet it on red on the roulette table. Then if it hits, doubling the money, he traditionally places a $50 bet on the pass line in craps. Within the first few minutes of four of the past five trips to Atlantic City, Rose has turned $25 into $100 with that formula. Says Rose, "It's total luck, but if anyone wants to do it with us, let's place one big bet." A flurry of hands pass up $25, and when Rose counts the money, he's surprised to see that sixteen people have kicked in money for a total of $400.

The buses arrive in Atlantic City at 5 P.M. and unload in front of Trump's Castle. Tight clusters of people scatter in different directions. Twelve casinos—three owned, in part, by Donald Trump—glitter along the boardwalk. In the twilight the ocean is dark and roiling. Inside, the casinos—bedecked as Roman temples, Indian palaces, and Mississippi riverboats—are largely populated by elderly people who are bussed in from New York City and points beyond. There are few swank couples in sight. Overall the city, silhouetted by a brilliant red sunset, seems somewhat frayed around the edges. The recession has exacted a heavy toll on this gambling mecca.

But that doesn't dampen the spirits of the crew from Dataflex on its annual pilgrimage. Rose, Massimo, Dressler, Fendrick, Stacey

Bernstein, and the others who chipped in twenty-five dollars with Rose make a beeline for the roulette table. Another twenty people come along for the ride.

The Dataflex group crowds around the table and erupts with a yelp of joy when red hits. Security, already slightly panicked by this mass of bodies around a single roulette table, arrives to inquire about all the noise. Fendrick and Rose briefly explain that this group is harmless, just $400 dollars richer. "We're just a company here to have fun," Rose says. Rose takes the $800 and places it on the pass line on the craps table. It hits on the first roll. The noise that issues from the Dataflex crew sounds like a bomb has gone off. Trump Castle security comes rushing over. In the midst of the throng, Rose divvies up the winnings. Some people continue gambling, while others stroll on the boardwalk. Rose and several others splurge on a sit-down dinner at the Scheherazade in the Trump Taj Mahal, where lobster and duck breast are served with a flourish from under a dome. The restaurant is dizzyingly gaudy with gold and white everywhere and a gold mirrored ceiling. Purple tablecloths are set with gold flatware. Gold brocade wallpaper sets off the glinting effect.

After dinner, everyone scatters. But eventually Ken Constantino, Stacey Bernstein, Rose, Fendrick, and Kerry Mutz end up at the craps table. It's twenty-five minutes until the bus leaves at 10 P.M. Elaine Mosher, a novice at craps, is throwing the dice. Fendrick is down to thirty-seven dollars. But Mosher gets on a hot streak. Everything she throws hits. She keeps handing her winnings to Mutz. A crowd has gathered. Smiling faces, flushed with excitement, press in all around Mosher, and her friends from Dataflex begin chanting, "E-Machine, E-Machine, E-Machine." The Dataflex crew that is betting on Mosher quickly rakes in $1,500.

She flings the dice. And it hits.

ACTIONS

- ☑ End the week on a positive note. Have a picnic or do something to build unity. You want associates to leave work on Fridays eager to come back the next week and see what else will happen.
- ☑ Serve associates. Don't expect everything always to be done

for you. If you think you are above certain jobs, that attitude will quickly filter down through your troops.

☑ Dare to open yourself up to criticism.

☑ Give people a forum where they can give and receive constructive criticism. Keep the group small and immediately remove the weapon from any ax grinders.

☑ Above all, have fun.

STEPPING OUT ON THE WING

When I was seven years old, we belonged to a country club that had a swimming pool. My dad, who was a diver in college, was trying to teach me how to dive. He asked me if I knew how, so I awkwardly plunged head first off the board. "Not bad, Son," he said. "Now get up there and let me give you some pointers." My dad was six feet two inches tall, and as I looked at him, I felt myself blush.

"Dad, I don't want to do this again in front of all these people because I'm no good at it," I said.

My dad looked down at me, and I'll never forget what he said, "Do you honestly think all these people are sitting around looking at you and worrying about how good you dive?" I'm forty-five years old and I can still close my eyes and see that scene. One, I learned that there really aren't many people paying attention to what you're doing. Two, I learned that if I was going to get anywhere, I couldn't be afraid to try things or be too embarrassed to take a risk.

I always asked the best-looking girls out. Most of them told me they appreciated being asked out because no one else would. Other guys were too intimidated.

When I was a quarterback in high school, I learned a new lesson. My coach sent a play in that I believed was wrong, so I called another one. My play failed miserably. I never got to play quarterback again. I discovered that there are some people who care what you do: They're called coaches. I decided I wanted to be a coach.

I've bet this company more than once. When I came here, Gordon and I terminated 50 percent of the staff in the first sixty days. Some of those people caused such a commotion that others who we needed started threatening to quit. I said, "Fine, just don't let the door hit you on your way out."

Our industry was changing. It was making a shift from selling dumb terminals to selling personal computers. I called IBM to find out what it would take to get a medallion, which is what we needed to sell to large corporate accounts. They told me that there were no medallions left, and the only way to get into the program was to have a proprietary software program. So I hired a company to write a program on generating organizational charts, and I spent the next four months making myself an expert in the human resources field. In the end we had a value-added human resources product, and IBM made us a dealer. However, we still needed to get a retail medallion to get the best pricing on their products, and there was still a freeze on them. Finally, I heard about a company in the next town that had a medallion and was going bankrupt. They had already promised to sell it to another company, but the deal fell through, and we paid $220,000 for the medallion, which was pretty significant since our revenues were only $9 million at that time.

We were also selling only 1,200 computer systems a year at that time, but to qualify for the special pricing, we had to quadruple that number to 5,000. Once we made that commitment, it meant we could never go back. We sold 5,200 systems that year. If we hadn't sold enough, we would have been bankrupt.

Bringing Tim Mannix on board was a big risk. Tim's style is very different from mine and Gordon's, and had it not worked out, his presence could have seriously hurt the company. Gordon and I didn't want the company to have to foot the bill for his compensation, so we decided to divide the pot we were taking between us three ways, which has meant less money for me and Gordon in the past two years.

Our loyalty to IBM products has been a gamble. Our stockholders tell us we are insane, but I believe IBM ultimately will win, and if you chase products, you are like the car salesman who goes from dealer to dealer each year. I believe loyalty is ultimately rewarded.

Opening our Connecticut office is perhaps our riskiest move yet. I don't know how that decision will turn out, but we believed the time was right. And time will tell. It always does.

Epilogue

The Connecticut office opened in Wethersfield, Connecticut, on January 1, 1992. Rose expects it to bring in about $5 million in revenues in its first fiscal year. Maurice Scaglione is one of two salesmen in that six-person office.

After an extended battle with her illness, Donna DeVito died on September 30, 1991, at the age of twenty-seven. She was too ill to take the trip to the Tour de France. She is missed a great deal by her friends at Dataflex.

Rose's fourth son is scheduled to arrive October 28, 1992, by caesarean. Rick and Linda plan to name their new addition Richard Channon Rose, Jr. "I know you're supposed to name your first born after you, but I like to do things differently," Rose laughs, noting that his father named him after his two roommates at the U.S. Naval Academy. "My youngest son wants to name the new baby 'Buckethead,' which is the nickname of one of my good friends, because he says we always nickname everybody anyway."

Two associates chose to quit Dataflex rather than present their visions of greatness.

Veronica Cassiba says, "I have had my ups and downs. I'm an emotional eater, but everyone has been incredibly supportive. When I go off track, this time I have people around me to help put me back on the straight and narrow." As of June 1992, Rick Rose had shed ten pounds.

Alan Fendrick won Salesperson of the Year for the second year in a row. He sold more than $30.5 million worth of hardware and services worth $1.3 million in fiscal 1992. He made 132.52 percent of his balanced-performance quota (BPQ). Fendrick's team brought Dataflex $6.2 million in gross profits. Glen Koedding took Rookie of the Year honors. He topped $3.2 million in hardware sales and sold $446,472 worth of services. Koedding made 83.92 percent of his BPQ, selling more than $4 million worth of equipment and services. His team's sales yielded $606,835 in gross profits.

Russ Schultz has decided to stay in sales for now.

Ken Constantino was promoted to account executive.

Kerry Mutz spent the next two weeks on the phone talking to the manufacturers' development team because what he did fixed a problem that they were still claiming didn't exist. Mutz supplied the manufacturer with information on the network interface cards and a detailed outline of all the problems that were occuring on the customer's local area network. After taking a week to analyze all that information, the manufacturer admitted there was a problem and ultimately reimbursed Dataflex for the $5,000 it spent to solve the customer's problem.

As a direct result of visions of greatness, Charlie Ruvolo, who has been with Dataflex five years, achieved a promotion to manager of customer engineering. His dream is to teach younger people coming into the computer industry the importance of customer satisfaction, and this shift in responsibilities provides a step in that direction. Tony Vastola, the mainsite manager at Prudential, asked his girlfriend of three years to marry him. (She said, "Yes.") Jack Neary moved from the marketing department to services support where he is the business development specialist. Don Lorenzetti, a senior customer engineer, is training to compete in the archery event in the 1996 Olympics, and Dataflex has offered to sponsor him if he shows world-class talent in upcoming competitions. Says Lorenzetti, "Having the support of Dataflex has meant the world to me." Mindy Wood, a senior sales administrator, left the company to open her own hair salon. Says Rose, "Visions of greatness is working. For the most part, I work with people who seek greatness for themselves."

Dataflex is competing in one of the toughest industries around. A business writer in *Newsweek* recently referred to the computer industry as the "Middle East" of business battles.

Indeed, for the first year since Rose and McLenithan joined Dataflex, revenues and profits were down slightly from the previous year. Revenue for the Fiscal 1992 ending March 31 was $89,613,939 with net profits of $4,020,850, compared to Fiscal 1991's record

$92,586,885 with with net profits of $4,571,155. As of June 1992, the stock price was hovering around $7 a share.

However, McLenithan says, the company's balance sheet is stronger than ever. "We've always prided ourselves on our balance sheet. Both Rick and I have always hated debt. During the past year, work capital debt got as high as $9 million," he says. "As of March 31, it was at $5 million. Today it's been totally paid off, and we have no long-term debt. Our return on equity is twenty-four percent versus the industry average of six percent." McLenithan is concentrating on seeking a company with a concentration in the service side of the business to acquire.

"Dataflex is certainly not immune to the pressures of our business," says Rose. "Our company is in the midst of remaking the model that will bring us another eight years of success.

"In the last few months, the margins in the computer hardware portion of our business have eroded even further to the point where selling hardware is impractical. The profit margins on services are three times the profits on hardware. We are completely committed to switching to services, because services is the equity that Dataflex owns at our customers.

"The challenge for us now is how to get people to try Dataflex. I have never sold a product that I didn't believe in, and we have a quality product that I believe in 100 percent. Dataflex offers quality services, and if people try us, they become customers for life.

"The problem is, as in most industries, many people claim to do the same thing. Service is intangible, and it's hard to sell intangibles. Selling something to someone that they'll use and appreciate in the future is tough. But service has become increasingly important to our customers in the last two years, because they have these local area networks and more complex systems that must operate smoothly. They can purchase hardware fairly easily. The difference in vendors is the level of service that they receive.

"We are in a difficult sales situation, because many competitors have been unreliable. So customers feel they have to manage the vendor by dictating the number of staff available and other items, which may not in actuality be the most effective allocation of people power or assets. The whole reason to outsource is so that you don't have to manage and to relieve the support departments. But the failure of many competitors to live up to their promises has created a climate where some customers expect a gopher rather than a capable steward. Our job is to work with our customers as an extension of their staff.

"We are in the process of reorganizing the company for the shift to services. Tim Mannix has taken over responsibility for the technical operations department, and we have merged the customer engineering department with them. This move will enable us to provide better service and will yield cost savings of ten to twenty percent.

"We never intended this book to be a tutorial for growing your business at a rate of fifty percent annually—although that's what happened here—but our intention was to show a different way of managing a company and making decisions. The fact that our industry is being whipsawed by change makes what we do within our realm of control all the more important.

"In the last five years, our industry has seen almost fifty percent of its manufacturers and dealers consolidate or go out of business. But with our strong balance sheet and the commitment of our people, we will once again figure out the formula for our next successful run."

As much as things change, some things never do. Take a look at this letter.

BEAVER COUNTRY DAY CAMPS
791 HAMMOND STREET
CHESTNUT HILL 67, MASSACHUSETTS
TELEPHONE: LOngwood 6-4715

JOSEPH DePASQUA, DIRECTOR
145 WASHINGTON AVENUE
NEEDHAM 92, MASSACHUSETTS
TELEPHONE: NEedham 3-0926-R

August 29, 1952

Mr. and Mrs. Elliot R. Rose
194 Gerry Road
Chestnut Hill 67, Massachusetts

Dear Mr. and Mrs. Rose:

After having Ricky with us for six weeks at
Beaver we found him to be a very well-adjusted child.

In his physical development we noted that his
ability in using his large and small muscles was very
good. He also was very active and skilled in the outdoor
sports, such as swimming, riding the ponies, sliding,
climbing, etc., but as far as rhythms or artwork, Ricky
showed very little interest.

Ricky tends to get very excited and at times this
made it very hard for him to share or wait his turn;
however, he enjoyed playing in an organized group and was
always a popular member in his group.

He got along very well with both counselors, but when
excited, he often found it difficult to do what was asked
of him.

Ricky was a very good eater, but a very restless
napper.

We felt Ricky enjoyed his six weeks here, and we
found that he had made a very good camper. We are looking
forward to working with him again next year.

Sincerely yours,
Joseph DePasqua
Director

by _____
Director of Kindergarten Unit

Acknowledgments

Managing me was not easy. I am sure that the additional gray hairs my managers acquired while I was around were not coincidental. My thanks to Travis Young for teaching me to be myself, to Jim Brennan for giving me a chance in the computer business, to John Sasso who first let me try my own ideas, to Dennis Cagen who provided me with insight into being a decent human being, to Jeff Lamm who made me a believer that honest people still existed, and to my dad who taught me to sell and to tell the truth all the time.

Working for me is not easy. Over the years I have had my share of making a contribution to others. It was my pleasure. I always got something in return for my efforts. Thanks to Alan Fendrick, Diane Katz, and Ken Constantino for allowing me to be their friend; thanks to Liz Massimo who keeps me organized; thanks to Wayne Isbitski who lets me know what it must have been like for my managers; thanks to Joe Rizzo who reminds me that intensity is worth something; and thanks to Kim Kenderes who keeps me looking good.

Working with me isn't easy. I've always wanted things my way. My thanks to my partner Gordon McLenithan for regularly indulging my impatience.

Living with me isn't easy. Thanks to my mother, Phyllis, for taking me to the Boys' Club for my football games, for all the roast beef dinners, for picking out my clothes, and for her unconditional love. Thanks to my sons Scott, John, and Charles for motivating my shorts off; and most of all, thanks to my wife Linda, who has encouraged me every step of the way.

—Richard C. Rose

Additional thanks go to:

DATAFLEX CORPORATION DIRECTORY

Liz Massimo, Assistant to Rick Rose; Gordon McLenithan, Executive Vice President, COO, CFO; Mary Sheehan, Executive Secretary; Timothy E. Mannix, Senior Vice President; Mary Ann LaSala, Executive Secretary.

Office of the President

Cindy Styron, Administrative Assistant; Maria Nicola, Office Coordinator; Maria Infusino, Receptionist.

Sales

Wayne Isbitski, Director of Systems Integration; Maura White, Director of Sales; Beth Franchina, Administrative Assistant; Tom Beer, Account Executive; Alan Fendrick, Account Executive; Diane Katz, Account Executive; Russ Schultz, Account Executive; Jayne Banach-Walther, Sales Representative; Ken Constantino, Account Executive; Nick Corocodilos, Sales Representative; Glen Koedding, Sales Representative; Elaine Mosher, Sales Representative; Maurice Scaglione, Account Executive; Ralph Hrovat, Sales Specialist/Services.

Marketing

Joe Rizzo, Vice President, Corporate Marketing; Joanne Lowy, Senior Marketing Support Specialist; Ron Jones, Marketing Support Specialist.

Finance

Ann Marie Bernet, Director of Finance; Diane Hunt, Accounting Manager; Prasad Srinivasan, Credit Manager; Mary Storms, Accounting Operations Manager; Peggy Abromaitis, Senior Accountant; Josephine Cassella, Contracts Administrator; Veronica Cassiba, Credit & Collection Specialist; Colette Durkin, Financial Analyst; Melissa Kuc, Inventory Administrator; Michelle Nevin, Senior A/P Administrator; Antoinette Ogno, A/P Administrator; Terry Pallosi, A/P Administrator; Phil Lear, Facilities Manager.

Sales Administration

Stacey Bernstein, Sales Operations Manager; Deana Behringer, RGA Coordinator; Stacie Bender, Sales Assistant; Christine Colligan, Sales Administrator; Gail Dizengoff, Sales Assistant; Christine Estok, Senior Inside Sales Representative; Leslie Feinson, Sales Administrator; Nancey Lynch, Senior Sales Administrator; Bethann Wapinski, Senior Inside Sales Representative; Chrissy Zielinski, Sales Assistant.

Human Resources

Nancy Ebery, Human Resources Manager; Diana Lombardo, Placement Coordinator; Kim Van Vliet, Human Resources Administrator.

Materials Management

Rich Dressler, Vice President, Materials Management; Brenda Arroyo, Purchasing Agent; Lysette Perez, Purchasing Administrator; Linda Robie, Senior Purchasing Agent.

Distribution

Bob Wallace, Warehouse Manager; George Douglass, Assistant Warehouse Manager; Wayne Alexander, Warehouseperson; George Fizer, Senior Warehouseperson; Dexter Jasper, Receiving Administrator; Cameron Pitt, Warehouseperson; Mike Rinaldi, Senior Warehouseperson; Norman Sefton, Receiving Administrator; Sean Styron, Warehouseperson.

Services Support

Matt Ainge, Services Support Manager; Heidi Gray, Quality Coordinator; Jack Neary, Business Development Specialist; Alan Maglague, Hot Line Support Specialist.

Dispatch

Ceil Abramski, Senior Dispatch Administrator; Roseanne Holzheimer, Dispatch Administrator.

Customer Engineering

Peter Galati, Vice President, Customer Engineering; Craig Wider, New Jersey Customer Engineering Manager; Mike Desiderio, New Jersey Mainsite Manager; Carl Neff, Manager of New Jersey Mainsites; Charlie Ruvolo, Customer Engineering Manager; Norman Greig, Customer Engineer; Don Lorenzetti, Senior Customer Engineer; Marco Merizalde, Associate Customer Engineer; Dan Schulte, Associate Customer Engineer; Dave Williams, Associate Customer Engineer.

Logistics

Fred Ford, Logistics Manager; Chris Eastman, Logistics Analyst; Larry Neal, Logistics Clerk; Gilbert Guzman, Logistics Coordinator; Artie MacFadyen, Logistics Coordinator; Kim Mazzeo, Logistics Administrator; Tracy Newsome, Senior Logistics Administrator.

Product Repair

Scott Comerford, Product Repair Manager; Mike Carlino, Associate Bench Technician; Kyriakos Georgallis, Senior Bench Technician; Lisa Scott, Senior Bench Technician; Rudy Waldinger, Senior Bench Technician.

Systems Preparation

Rich Burke, Systems Preparation Manager; Sophia Cathcart, Preparation Technician; Mike Marks, Senior Preparation Technician.

Information Systems

Greg Cocetti, Director of Information Systems; Greg Linde, Systems Analyst; Rob Ready, Information Systems Operations Analyst.

Product Training & Support

Ken Cavanagh, Product Training & Support Manager; Arlene Schaper, Training Coordinator; Kevin Denecour, Senior Product Specialist; Pam Meyers, Product Specialist; Gary McHugh, Senior Product Specialist; Joe Novak, Product Specialist; Wendy Pate, Product Specialist; Debbie Mleczko, Product Specialist.

Systems Integration

Kerry Mutz, Systems Integration Manager; Scott Srager, Consulting Systems Engineer; John Connolly, Network Engineer; Ben Lamboy, Network Engineer; Percy McNab, Network Engineer; Charlie Milo, Systems Engineer; Brian Sullivan, Systems Engineer; Bob Castles, Network Engineer; Scott German, Network Technician.

Remote Sites

C. Winston Taylor, Customer Engineer; John Brancella, Customer Engineer; Carlos Gomez, Customer Engineer; David Moore, Senior Customer Engineer; Charlie McNamee, Customer Engineer; Jay Hindle, Senior Customer Engineer; Jim Quarry, Customer Engineer; Barry Wise, Senior Customer Engineer; Anthony Chin, New York Customer Engineering Manager; Tony Hunter, New York Site Manager; Jonathan Hemingway, Customer Engineer; Steve Flynn, Customer Engineer; Jim Nash, Senior Customer Engineer; Greg Stampfl, Senior Customer Engineer; Joe Lensen, Senior Customer Engineer; Richard Ware, Senior Customer Engineer; Tony Vastola, Prudential Mainsite Manager; Anil Gandhi, Customer Engineer; Eric Schweikert, Senior Customer Engineer; Manny Ochoa, Site Manager; Allan Pashkevich, Senior Customer Engineer; George Daubert, Customer Engineer; Mike Stieglitz, Senior Customer Engineer; Shawn Cummings, Customer Engineering; Jerry Janny, Squibb Mainsite Manager; Colan Cassell, Customer Engineer; Myron Garnel, Senior Customer Engineer; Micheal Henry, Senior Customer Engineer; Hung Nguyen, Customer Engineer; Terry Potalivo, Administrative Assistant; Ken Skinner, Customer Engineer; Rory White, Senior Customer Engineer; Manny Alves, Customer Engineer.

Everyone told me that writing a book isn't easy. They were right, but there are scores of people who made my first experience a pleasurable one. Thanks to Jeremy Weithas, who proposed the story idea to me in the first place. Thanks to Rick Rose for saying yes when I proposed writing this book. Thanks to Paul Brown for explaining the ins and outs of book publishing to me. Thanks to Mona Simpson for encouraging me to get an agent. Thanks to my literary agent Denise Marcil for her vision and encouragement. Thanks to Virginia Smith, our editor, for her keen interest in the project and her willingness to get up at 4:30 A.M. to trek to New Jersey for sales meetings, as well as her editorial wit and wisdom. And thanks to the gang at HarperBusiness for their tremendous support and vision for the book.

Thanks to the entire Dataflex family for opening your lives to me. Liz

Massimo, Cindy Styron, Kevin Denecour, Mary Ann LaSala, and Ken Cavanagh deserve special mention for their patience and help. Joan Perryman, Carolyn Kitch, Nancy Joyce, Mary May, Jo Beth McDaniel, Suzy Vanarsdel, and Greg Matusky read all or parts of the manuscript and contributed much-needed feedback. Most of all, thanks to my husband Kevin Garrett, who took photographs for the book and who spent many late nights reading the chapters aloud and offering suggestions; to our son Caleb for being a terrific two year old who helps me be a decent human being; and to Elorne Jean, who made sure the Garrett household ran smoothly. And finally, thanks to God, who does more than we can ask or imagine.

—Echo Montgomery Garrett

Index

Visions *(cont.)*
  and new hires, 155
  and potential, 139–40
  public announcement of, 141–42, 155
  purpose of stating, 141
  and reality, 60, 155–58, 228
  and recognition, 142, 146, 148
  and respect, 145
  and risk, 151
  and self-actualization, 142, 155–56
  and self-esteem, 150
  and self-evaluation, 138–39
  and support, 142, 150–51, 157

  and teams, 145
  and trust, 157, 217
Vulnerability, 108, 157, 210

Wandering around management, 29–31, 51,
    208
Wednesday sales meetings, 114–26
Whack on the Side of the Head, A (book),
    181
Word for the day, 3–4, 63–64, 114, 187
Work ethic, 29
Work schedules, 29, 56–57
Work-with attitudes, 20–21